PORT OF CALL

OTHER BOOKS BY MOLLEE KRUGER

Unholy Writ

More Unholy Writ

Yankee Shoes

Daughters of Chutzpah

Admiral of the Mosquitoes

Ladies First

A Purse of Humorous Verse for the Jewish Woman

The Cobbler's Last

The Swift Seasons

Kosher Salt

PORT OF CALL

Memories of an Ancient Mariner

Mollee Kruger

A MARYBEN BOOK

Kruger, Mollee
Port of Call

1. Memoir 2. Travel 3. Humor 4. Marriage 5. Science 6. Judaica

ISBN: 978-0-9912289-2-8 (paperback)
ISBN: 978-0-9912289-3-5 (e-book)
Library of Congress Control Number: 2017910525
LCCN Imprint: Rockville, MD

Design: Carolyn K. Lewis, www.cklewis.com
Cover image: John Caleb Steele

Printed in the United States of America

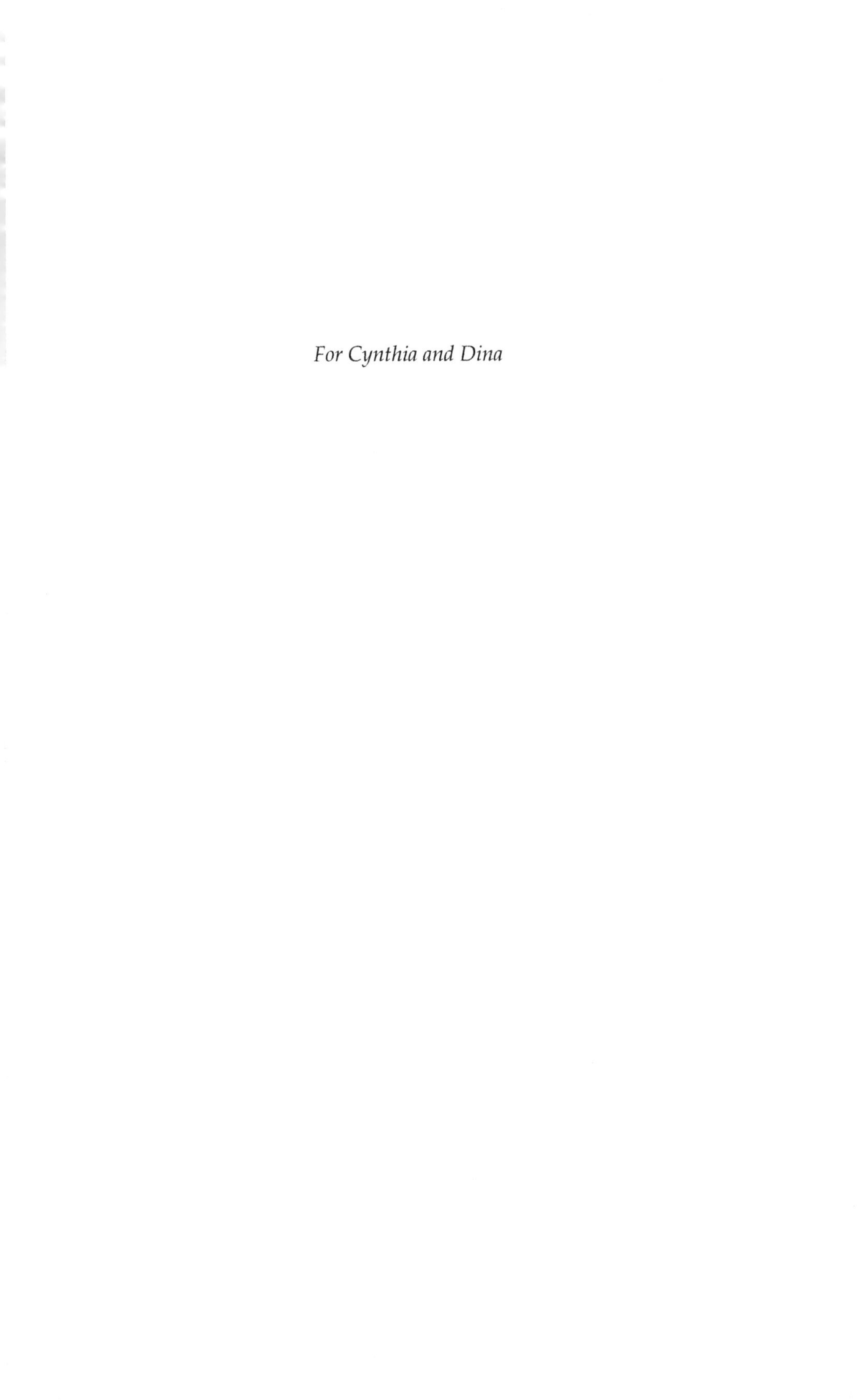

For Cynthia and Dina

ACKNOWLEDGMENTS

Washington Post, *Pen Woman* magazine, Electrochemical Society, *Baltimore Evening Sun* (now defunct), *Gazette* newspapers (now defunct), University of Maryland, Fernando Passoa's *The Book of Disquiet*, *Collected Sonnets of Edna St. Vincent Millay*, Walt Whitman's *Leaves of Grass*, Benjamin Disraeli's *Sybil*, Samuel Coleridge, and Herman Melville. A salute also to the editing of Kathleen Mills, the design by Carolyn K. Lewis, and the vital technical assistance and loving support of Len, Joe, Dina, Cynthia, Mira, Isaac, and my good friend Ray.

Words to Launch By

"Are you one of those mad scientists?" the petite young brunette asked.

"No," he said, grinning at her, "but I do get irritable sometimes."

He reached for the crystal decanter on a nearby card table converted into a bar. Above it hung a classic photo of a relaxed Adlai Stevenson during his recent failed presidential campaign. The picture highlighted a folksy hole in the bottom of his shoe displayed for all the world to see.

"More May wine?" her host asked. She nodded and examined the bachelor's apartment for clues about this man she had just met.

He noticed the way she studied his colorful walls. "Let me take you on a tour," he said. Passing his other guests, the two strolled through the sparsely furnished living room to the bedroom. She noted the modernist prints of Picasso and Utrillo; the black wrought-iron bookshelves filled with the poetry of Robert Frost and Stephen Spender; the racks of recorded Ambrosian and Gregorian chants of the medieval period, along with recordings of Bartók and Villa-Lobos, composers she had never heard of.

"What kind of scientist did you say you are?" she asked.

"I'm a physical chemist."

"Oh," she said after a sensible pause. She moved back toward the open door. At the time, she didn't wish to find out how physical he was.

He took her hand. "Well," he said, "I think we should get back to my other guests."

She looked into his sensitive gray eyes and realized he was already smitten with her.

So much for what is known as a narrative hook, savory details to follow in chapters yet unborn. Who are these two shadowy figures from out of the past? Read on. Meanwhile, we'll be awash in a nautical motif because I've always envied Herman Melville, who went to sea and left us with a tolerably good fish story. In truth, I am not and have never been a sailor, and it makes no difference that I was born in Maryland, home of the Chesapeake Bay and the United States Naval Academy. Even so, the reader may find in our epic memoir a ripple of clichés involving ports, bays, harbors, oceans, lakes, rivers, creeks, and other diverse waterways encountered in my nine decades of treading water. This well-worn traveler hereby pipes all passengers aboard. Like the Old Salt in that Samuel Coleridge poem, I, too, am an ancient mariner with a cargo of words to unload.

PART ONE

Ports of Entry

A Slack Tide

At mid-century our country had spent five years switching to a postwar economy, and the danger of dropping back into another depression bothered President Harry Truman. The Korean War had begun, the public feared Communists lurking behind every fire hydrant, and as always, writing jobs were hard to come by. Classified pages of newspapers listed vacancies for "Chocolate Dippers" but not one single ad read "Young Female Writers Urgently Needed."

My best chances of gainful employment were laid out before me: nurse, secretary, or schoolmarm. I did not care to be any kind of marm, although at the state university I had switched to the College of Education, the academic factory that ground out masses of young teachers after boring them silly with deadening courses in Educational Sociology and Educational Statistics. In a moment of filial weakness during the end of sophomore year, I promised my immigrant mother that I would make her dream come true and spend my life writing lesson plans and taking attendance.

In my book *The Cobbler's Last* I described how my aging parents rented out their village shoe store on Main Street in rural Bel Air and moved to Baltimore. They purchased a semi-detached brick house in a new neighborhood just inside the city line. Three older children and their offspring lived in the same northwest part of town.

Because I helped my parents relocate, I missed taking the qualifying exams that would certify me to teach in the Baltimore city school system. My mother insisted that I try the next time tests were scheduled. Teaching is a noble profession, but wasn't there something more exciting than that? I was too much of a homebody to consider moving to New York City. I had never romanticized the place. Growing up in a hamlet where one could reach all places by foot, I valued proximity. Distance meant losing control. Our transfer to Baltimore was more than enough travel excitement for one lifetime.

"New York will have to come to me," I said with bravado. It was the era of powerful scribes like Walter Lippmann, Dorothy Kilgallen, and Walter Winchell. Journalism beckoned. The role of newspaper columnist would suit me fine. My plan was to storm no less a mighty fortress than the *Baltimore Evening Sun*. Another paper existed, the *Baltimore News-Post*, but having seen Orson Welles' *Citizen Kane*, I meant to avoid all Hearst newspapers. No, the *Sun* was the only game in town—even though it was whispered they didn't hire Jews, but that had changed somewhat since the war, hadn't it? Surely, the *Sun* editorial page could use someone like me with a half-civilized, half-kooky outlook on life. I would write for the *Baltimore Evening Sun* and become a celebrated member of the Fourth Estate. It is here our sea chantey begins with all its barnacles.

Rudderless

"Mr. Hardwick will see you now," said the heavy-set, middle-aged woman in a navy blue suit with a badly wrinkled peplum. Her nasal Baltimore accent played in my ears with all the subtlety of a musical saw, a popular instrument favored by radio contestants on the *Major Bowes Amateur Hour.*

I couldn't believe my hard work had paid off. All summer long since graduation I secretly planned a devilish strategy for nailing down this interview. Earlier I read somewhere that William Saroyan, the popular author of *The Human Comedy*, achieved a breakthrough with editors by bombarding them with a new short story every day for a month. His audacity appealed to me. I had no connections with anyone on the staff and didn't know whom to contact. There was no Internet, no Google. To become a columnist, should I borrow Saroyan's brash technique and swamp the *Baltimore Sun* with unpublished gems? Possibly, but only as a final act of desperation.

Earlier, I had mustered enough nerve to call the newspaper and chat with the switchboard operator. At the time I thought it was a brilliant ploy, a sure way to accomplish the impossible. Obviously, she would brush me off if I introduced myself as an adrift writer looking for a job. I knew this faceless telephone person wasn't an important star in the journalistic universe. She couldn't hire or fire me. Still, it might lead to great things.

"The *Evening Sun*," she said in a mechanical tone.

"I am a schoolteacher," I said, lying in my teeth. "I'm preparing a unit for my students on local newspapers, and I'd like a list of all your editors." That way, I was certain, she could give me a whole roster of names I could reach.

"What?" she answered. "Who do you want to talk to?"

I didn't know for sure and stammered, "I know you have a lot of editors there and I'd like to have their names because I'm a schoolteacher."

"What?"

I broke into a cold sweat. "I mean, on your masthead there aren't any names of editors. But I see that your publisher is A. S. Abel. Should I talk to Mr. Abel?"

At that point, she disconnected me. I felt shamed and belittled. I did have credentials if she only had let me tell her. Even as a high school student, I had written a column, "Teen Topics," for a Harford County weekly. In college I contributed a column, "The Mocking Molecule," to the university newspaper and articles for our humor magazine. In the grand style of James Thurber my sassy essays cast an evil eye on freshman mixers and snooty sorority girls. Readers, especially veterans on the G.I. Bill, liked my sardonic approach to childish campus activities. Frivolous pom-poms and freshman beanies were for children just out of twelfth grade, I complained.

Now it was time to remove my genteel white gloves and play hardball, unleashing the William Saroyan blitzkrieg. I searched the *Sun* for names of journalists whose bylines appeared each day. After making an all-inclusive list, I battered these reporters with endless mail, praising their work, and sending a barrage of outrageous letters that ended with, "By the way, do you have anybody there who can tell me what bigshot is in charge of hiring a future columnist?"

Somehow that worked. A kind soul must have passed one of my letters on to the managing editor, and now it was he who was about to interview me for a job that would launch a dazzling career in the world of newsprint.

"How many minutes do I have?" I asked him before even sitting down. That was to show him how aware I was of newspaper people working on deadlines. "Five," said Mr. Hardwick (not his real name), "if you're lucky."

I don't remember what I babbled during the interview. I talked fast. The more I spoke, the higher pitched my voice became, which made me sound more like Minnie Mouse than a savvy, sophisticated journalist who one day might possibly win a Pulitzer. The editor, whom I had pegged as a well-educated aristocrat from ritzy Roland Park, seemed interested in what I was pitching.

"It would be a lighthearted column based on campus activities at local colleges," I said. He barely scanned samples I brought along from my column in the University of Maryland *Diamondback*, and muttered, "Okay, let's see what you can do with this idea of yours." If they decided to buy it, he said, they would pay $15 a column, and if readers liked it, the paper might run my work as often as three times a week. That would come to $45 each payday, not a bad beginning.

At last everything was clicking into place. Off I trotted to my alma mater at College Park, where I discovered a University Theater rehearsal of *Macbeth*. Since I was no longer a student, a friend let me sleep that night on a raffia mat in her dormitory room. My article about innocent-looking student actors committing bloody murder took little effort, and I mailed it off to the man who, I thought, had just hired me for the job of my dreams. When I called him two days later, he said he liked it. I told friends and family to watch the paper for my byline. A week passed, then two.

JOURNAL ENTRY: OCTOBER 1950

> No response on the column. I'm not schlepping to any other colleges until I hear something. Despite numerous phone messages for the editor, nobody has called me back.

That same week two sample chapters and the synopsis of my first novel, *She Waded in the Water*, returned from Random House, bearing only a standard rejection slip. What was happening? Hadn't my idol, F. Scott Fitzgerald, scored immediately with *This Side of Paradise*, written when he was my age? By December I succumbed to registering with a commercial employment agency. In return for finding me a job, I promised to pay them a heavy chunk of salary each week for three months. The places where the agency sent me had little to do with the literary world. It was clear that my advisor, Miss Wood, didn't know what to do with me.

"Honey, the next time they give that teacher's exam downtown," my mother said, "take it and get yourself a decent job."

The Gulf of Glick

Two months later Miss Wood received a request for a Girl Friday from the producer of a children's television show. "Sometimes these things lead to something better," she said in a wheedling voice.

Television was a whole new game in the early 1950s. The best place to be was New York, but Baltimore would have to do for someone like me. If I could get a toe in the door of a local TV station, my future was assured. A versatile writer would find it easy to turn out TV scripts on demand—comedies, dramas, musicals for which I'd supply the book and lyrics. Nothing could stop me now.

Mr. Glick, the producer/director, worked out of an office in a first-run movie house, which still featured live stage shows. I was hired on the spot. My job would be to answer the telephone, type scripts, and file letters from any fans who knew how to write. His program, *The Kandy Klub,* televised on the local NBC channel, featured Baltimore's most overweight children. They didn't have to do anything except sit quietly at bridge tables covered with white tablecloths. Gussied up in their Sunday School finest, the plump little darlings, ages five to ten, listened placidly to the jovial comments of a master of ceremonies named Mel, who occasionally posed the question, "Are you ready for Popeye, gang?" The children would stop eating, answer in a robot-like monotone, "Yay," and then resume stuffing themselves.

Although more sophisticated kiddie shows in New York and Philadelphia featured talented small fry who could sing, dance, or toot a horn, the only action required of the Baltimore cast was to ingest bottle after bottle of orange soda, grape soda, cola, and ginger ale. They devoured chocolate marshmallow cookies, miniature fruit pies, cupcakes, vanilla wafers, mounds of teeth-rotting candy corn, coconut bars, licorice sticks, saltwater taffy, jelly beans, and chewy caramel nuggets. The script consisted of commercials about how delicious everything tasted. At the beginning and end of each program, the pudgy ensemble was asked one question: "Where do we have the most fun, boys and girls?" Their apathetic reply was always the same: "At the Kandy Klub, Mr. Mel."

"Does anybody ever throw up on camera?" I asked Mr. Glick.

He waved away the question. "What do you mean? The parents are beside themselves to see their kids on television. They can't wait to tell all their relatives and friends to watch the show. Sponsors are crazy about it!"

A job is a job. Maybe I'd be discovered by a New York producer and find myself writing for one of those live drama shows like *Westinghouse Playhouse* or *Philco Playhouse*. I'd start at the ground floor and rise to the top in this new entertainment medium that was beginning to rival Hollywood movies. Or maybe if Mr. Mel ever made it to network TV, he would take me with him. I could end up writing comedy sketches for *Your Show of Shows* with Sid Caesar and Imogene Coca.

My employer was a balding Jewish man of about forty whom I am calling Mr. Glick, not his real name because even now, after almost seventy years, I don't wish to embarrass his great-great-grandchildren. The initial interview with him went much better than the *Sun* debacle with Mr. Hardwick. I had not played it needy and casually spoke to Mr. Glick about my love of Victorian literature, especially the poetry of Coventry Patmore, a bard most Americans have never heard of.

Mr. Glick seemed delighted that I considered him worthy of hiring me to work in his magic kingdom, which wasn't vast and consisted of just him. I began the following week with joy in my heart. Friends and family were told simply, "I'm now in television." Each day I entered the Hippodrome Theatre, not as a customer with ticket in hand, but as a hardened show biz insider.

Typing was easy, a skill I had acquired at the age of ten. Mr. Glick's scripts offered a chance to learn camera jargon like dolly, pan, and fade. My speed increased to sixty words a minute on the Remington typewriter, and after two days on the job I handled carbon paper with panache.

A more difficult task was answering the phone. I had little aptitude for this. In the small town of Bel Air, my immigrant parents ran a humble shoe store. The shop as well as our upstairs apartment had no telephone for twenty years until World War II when my brothers joined the U.S. Army. Only then did my mother insist it was necessary to install a phone. For that reason, I never became intimately acquainted with the instrument. Rarely did I make or receive casual calls. Later in college, each floor of the dormitory had just one hall phone in constant use by garrulous coeds but avoided by me.

The upstairs Glick office was somehow connected to the downstairs switchboard of the movie house. On my desk, a well-choreographed line of tiny red lights danced whenever the phone rang. I was expected to relay incoming calls to the theater as well as those directed to us. Even though Mr. Glick showed me how to work the complicated apparatus the very first day, and the second, and the third, it didn't sink in. I was the kind of student who did poorly in physics and chemistry and have always been technologically challenged. Whenever the right phone rang at the right time, I became flustered, picked up the receiver, and mumbled a fearful "Hello?"

"You have to say, 'Raymond Glick Productions,'" my boss explained. That sounded pretentious to me. We handled only one show.

Mr. Glick forgave everything. He was a kind, easygoing man, but his wife, Sylvia, who called every day from home to see how things were going with the new girl in the office, was not pleased. I could tell we would never be best friends. For some clumsy reason, I kept connecting her calls to the theater box office. They must have complained.

By the end of the first week, Mr. Glick said, "This isn't the job for a quality person like you."

He saw my shocked reaction and spoke in a softer voice. "What I need is an ordinary high school graduate who can type and answer the phone, that's all."

A nerve twitched in my left eye. He continued, "Maybe after I get things rolling here, I can rehire you to do something creative, but for now I have to let you go."

Then came the final indignity. Apologetically, he asked me to give back his extra key to the office.

I blinked away tears and handed it to him. What does a person say when she's fired? Thanks? Have a nice day? For lack of anything better, tears running down my cheeks, I said, "Great moments in history." Mr. Glick's face took on a stricken look, but he didn't change his mind. I was sacked.

Panic on the Patuxent

To make matters worse, I was marginally in love with a former Navy Seabee whom we'll call Zachary. A New Yorker with dark, inscrutable eyes, my college sweetheart had attached himself to me while we attended the raucous parties held by classmates who worked on campus publications. We first met at the beginning of our junior year while toiling together in the office of the university newspaper, I the columnist, and he the production manager in charge of printing.

The two things Zach and I had most in common were (1) we were both Jewish and (2) we were both short. At five feet one, I measured four inches less than he. Although he was six years older and not a *luftmensch* like me, we found each other in a close-knit crowd of agnostic non-Jews recently returned from the war. Zach, a future bacteriologist, delighted in looking through microscopes. I could never see a damned thing while using those gizmos but pretended I did. My germicidal swain inspired me to write a poem for our humor magazine that began: *"Won't you come into my bac lab?" said the coccus to the bacillus / "We shall split a bit of agar; we will meet some aspergillus."*

We planned to be married far off in the distant future but not until Zach finished graduate school and found a well-paying research job. In the fall of 1950, he was accepted at the Harvard School of Public Health. I felt proud that Zach had docked in a prestigious port like Harvard, but a latent jealousy lurked beneath my cheerful exterior. Surrounding him at every turn lay historic Boston and its glorious literary ghosts: Emerson, Whittier, Longfellow,

Thoreau, Alcott, Oliver Wendell Holmes. Breathing that rarefied academic air would have done me a world of good. Instead, I remained behind to wander through the gray industrial morass of Baltimore.

My adopted city in those days bustled with commerce fed by Bethlehem Steel, Glenn L. Martin aviation, McCormick tea, clothing factories, and the coming and going of merchant ships hailing from all parts of the world. Ethnic neighborhoods included the streets of Little Italy, the enclaves of Polish, Lithuanian, and Irish residents, and row houses filled with poor-white Southerners drawn by the magnet of industrial jobs.

Added to the mix was the burgeoning, poverty-stricken black population. Jews had already moved from East Baltimore to the northwest part of town: Liberty Heights, Forest Park, Park Heights Avenue, and Reisterstown Road. Carefully restricted neighborhoods existed in the upper northeast of Baltimore. Homeowners trembled in constant fear of "blockbusters," who would sell houses in all-white neighborhoods to people of color. Here was the proud but segregated city of Baltimore, where I beat the bushes looking for a job.

It was not helpful to be in love with Zach during this time. We wrote to each other once a week. He began his letters with the unromantic greeting, "Beloved Nut." I never thought to complain. Whenever we were together, he seemed to be watching me as if he expected top-notch entertainment and wasn't getting it. He did not impress my mother. "He's so little," she said.

In December Zach joined me for a rash of Christmas parties with our former college newspaper crowd. I took a holiday from job hunting to spend every minute with him. We even caught the train to New York, where I met his Gotham relatives, who couldn't hide their disappointment.

"You're the writer?" his aunt said in an authentic Brooklyn accent. "I expected you to walk in here wrapped in sables and leading two greyhounds on a leash." And then a ten-year-old niece pointed at me and whispered in a shocked voice, "She's not even wearing nail polish!"

On the train back, Zach rebuked me. "Why did you stay so quiet with my people when you always say all kinds of nutty things to me?"

I didn't want to criticize his lower-middle-class family without sounding like a snob. "Guess I was just homesick," I said.

"Homesick?" he snapped. "You were there only for a weekend."

In the new year he returned to his studies in Boston, and I bought a copy of *Letters of Emily Dickinson*. The recluse New England virgin and I wallowed in our isolation together. Throughout January, I wrote letters to the world of classified ads that never answered me.

By then it no longer mattered what kind of job it was. Anything an employment agency would inflict upon me would do. My mother, unhappy that I had not fulfilled her dream, urged me once more to join the Baltimore city school system. I couldn't see myself struggling with belligerent high school students who were taller than I. I didn't know exactly what I wanted, but the list was long on what to dodge.

During those bleak winter months, Miss Wood at the employment agency told me about a position that had opened up at a place we shall call the Jacob Kamenetz Company, not its real name, but I'm protecting the innocent, most of whom would be well over a hundred years old by now.

"It's the largest advertising agency in town," Miss Wood said with her usual faux enthusiasm.

"I've heard of it," I said, and decided that if there were any spot in the city where it wouldn't be a total embarrassment to work, this was it.

Miss Wood didn't describe what kind of work was involved. She merely said, "You'll love this one. It's an entry-level job, lots of fun. Mr. Harrington will tell you more about it when you get there."

Advertising? I had read Frederic Wakeman's novel *The Hucksters* and even saw Clark Gable in the film version. A nasty occupation, but maybe this was my destiny. Address in hand, I found the street and stood facing an unassuming three-story brick townhouse, which, according to Hollywood's lavish standards, wasn't how a 1950s ad agency should look. Inside, however, the place was all business, completely renovated. A switchboard operator sat in an alcove near the front door. A polished wood foyer led me to a hallway lined with ordinary offices, the first of which bore the sign "Media" next door to "Accounting."

A grim man in his sixties, Mr. Bertram Harrington, identified himself as head of the Accounting Department and manager in charge of hiring the firm's clerical staff, a job he took seriously. Around him sat a quartet of young women pounding typewriters and poking buttons on adding machines.

"If I take you on," Mr. H said, "you'll be a clerk assigned to the Media Department." My face must have registered puzzlement because I didn't know what a Media Department was. "You'll be typing insertion orders and outdoor billing," he explained. "You'll file newspapers and magazines, especially those in which our clients' ads appear. You'll collect tear sheets and keep them in their proper folders. Think you can handle all that?"

All that? I nodded but added, "Will I be doing any writing?"

"Writing?" He rubbed a badly wrinkled forehead. It was obvious he hadn't been asked this question before. "What kind of writing?"

I hesitated and whispered, "Maybe ads?"

"Oh no, no, nothing like that. This job involves typing and filing work. Writing? No, copywriters take care of that upstairs in our Retail and National Departments. I have nothing to do with that bunch, thank the good Lord."

I must have looked crushed because he added, "You may be writing an occasional letter, of course," he said, "to remind a client of a delinquent bill."

So I was to become a miserable wretch on a tall stool like Bob Cratchit or Melville's pitiful Bartleby? I recalled that F. Scott Fitzgerald, my hero, had started out in advertising, but at least he worked as a copywriter and even came up with the immortal slogan "We keep you clean in Muscatine."

The typing test proved to be no obstacle. Mr. Harrington gave me a frugal smile. "Welcome to the firm," he said. Just before I left, he added another dollop of merriment to the whole bleak transaction.

"As for salary," he said, "in the newspaper classified ad we offered $35 a week. However, since you have no previous experience in office work, we're taking a chance on you, and your pay will be $32.50." He seemed livelier now, relishing the chance to speak in numbers. "We'll expect to see you promptly at nine o'clock Monday morning."

I left triumphant in a minor league sort of way. At least this time there was something positive to show for taking two sluggish buses and a streetcar to reach that distant part of Baltimore, many miles away from the street where I lived. At home my mother did not seem enthralled by this latest success. "Such a big business like that must make plenty of money," she said, "so why did they chop off a lousy $2.50 from your salary?"

She would raise that question frequently in the days ahead.

Harrowing Headwinds

The Media Department at the Jacob Kamenetz agency was a repository for newspapers, magazines, catalogues, pamphlets, flyers, and all other manner of printed pages, including copies of bills for space orders and time orders and brief letters pertaining to radio and television spots. The floor-to-ceiling file cabinets held carbon copies of billing for outdoor signs and billboards, and wooden shelves were weighted down with monstrous notebooks jammed with tear sheets from newspapers.

The desks surrounding mine belonged to young unmarried women from ethnic neighborhoods citywide. The roster included vivacious Jewish girls from northwest Baltimore, devout Catholics from the Polish neighborhoods, and an Appalachian mail clerk representing a poor-white slum of East Baltimore. Also stationed on board was a fiftyish man, Mr. Weisenhaulter, whom the crew affectionately called "The Weasel." I never did find out what he did except snarl, "Stop the jabbering, girls, and get back to work."

In a separate vestibule sat a woman in her mid-thirties, who sang operatic arias to herself as she transcribed the dictated letters of Mr. Macdonald, a company vice president and titular Media Department director. Shut away in an office all to himself, he was a reticent gentleman who had as little to do with the staff as possible and spent most of his time at the agency's New York office. His assistant was a harried career woman of about thirty, who took seriously the buying and selling of print space, radio spots, and commercial time for television. It was she who assigned daily tasks to the clerk/typists.

The latter did all they could to liven up things by discussing in graphic detail their shopping trips, their do-it-yourself home permanent waves, their periods, their bunions, their dental work, their bad manicures, and scandalous gossip about anyone who had just left the room. I learned that my position had been vacated by a young unmarried woman who, pregnant, vanished to have an abortion, illegal at the time. Every woman in the building except me knew all the details of her "operation" as well as the name and location of the female doctor who performed the procedure.

The most preferred topic under discussion was, of course, men: recent dates, thoughtful dates, rotten dates, muscular dates, handsome dates, creepy dates, alcoholic dates, generous dates, cheap dates. Other popular subjects: weight restrictions to observe while out on dates, clandestine out-of-town trips with dates, money-borrowing dates, deadbeat dates, and above all, the marriage eligibility of dates, past, present, and future. More fascinating were ongoing debates on whether to become involved with married men or, if the speaker happened to be Catholic, handsome parish priests. The Jewish girls in the office did not have this problem. They seemed more concerned about avoiding dates with anyone not a direct descendant of Abraham, Isaac, and Jacob.

Lilace, our mountaineer mail deliverer, personified the worry and angst of every country-western song ever written. Each morning, unasked, she gave a detailed report on her longshoreman boyfriend, who, she claimed, liked to extract her chin whiskers with his teeth.

"He says he does it because he loves me so," she explained. The office staff appreciated Lilace's stories, especially when she described her drinking partners at the neighborhood saloon.

"Last night," she related, "this sailor comes up to me and he don't sound like no American. So I say, 'Hey Buddy, you from England or what?' And he's as drunk as a skunk and he says to me, 'I'm from the House of Lords.' And I say to him, 'Well, that's nothin'. I'm from the House of Correction.'" Everyone knew she was referring to one of the minor prisons in our state, but we doubted she had a record. Mr. Harrington wouldn't have hired her.

Lilace liked to play the role of raw hillbilly, but in reality she was a high school graduate like the other girls. She also filled the role of office file clerk, a job she found entertaining. Our agency received stacks of newspapers every day. Whenever the papers arrived from the town of Intercourse, Pennsylvania, Lilace couldn't resist firing the inevitable question aimed at anyone who entered the office: "Do you take *Intercourse Daily*?"

Although somewhat rough around the edges, Lilace never used filthy language. None of us did. Unfortunately, she enjoyed "lifting a few," as she put it. She took pills she called uppers to battle depression and an equal number of downers to counteract them. This eventually took its toll. I even wrote a short story about her, a Shakespearean tragedy about a West Virginian doomed to a tragic end from which no one could save her. My starkly realistic tale reaped standard rejection slips from women's magazines, which preferred to run stories about housewives losing their shopping lists at the supermarket.

I was always late for work. My casual lack of punctuality was destined to make a difference in my life. A haphazard commuter, I found it tiresome each day to chase buses, obtain transfers, and catch a meandering streetcar, which unloaded me six blocks away from the agency. I hated the anxiety, the breathless walk, the slinking late into the office. Most of all, I dreaded bumping into the big boss himself, Mr. Kamenetz, whose chauffeur dropped him off at the front door promptly at 9:30 a.m.

Lilace, my closest rival in tardiness, at least had a valid excuse. She was out on the town almost every night. When other laggards discovered that nothing horrible happened to chronic offenders like us, they followed suit. The situation worsened until finally Mr. Macdonald assembled the office staff to lecture us. A well-weathered man of few words, he also served as account executive for our largest national client. Mr. Macdonald rarely dealt face to face with mere clerical workers. For him to address us on this ominous occasion underscored the crisis.

"Mr. Kamenetz will not tolerate this behavior any longer," said Mr. Macdonald. "In the future, if you're late, you'll have your pay docked or be discharged without a reference." He took a deep breath. "Always remember, girls, life is a two-way street." Then he strode majestically to the doorway of his office and faced us. "Yes indeed," he intoned, "life is a two-way street!"

Returning to my desk, I weighed the situation. Here was a person who wielded real power at the agency, the right-hand man of the big boss himself. I dared not approach the emperor, Mr. Kamenetz, but I could make myself visible to his prime minister. I would appeal to his sense of humor. Although Mr. Macdonald did not look like a jolly person, it was worth the risk.

That night I jotted down sixteen lines of light verse full of sensible reasons why I came to work late every day. I dealt specifically with the long ride from home on a smelly bus that stopped at almost every corner, hit every red light, and navigated around poky school buses and a policeman on horseback. "My Book of Job," written in rhymed couplets, deplored everything from surly drivers to the Express bus, which was even slower than the non-Express bus. I ended by quoting Mr. Macdonald's immortal line, "Life is a two-way street," and suggested that if the Baltimore Transit Company would only measure up,

"Life could be a whole Harrisburg Pike, and it wouldn't bother me much."

Early the next morning I arrived before anyone else in the office. Holding my breath, I slipped into Mr. Macdonald's office and dropped the masterpiece on his desk. His watchdog secretary, Joyce, was absent with the flu, and no human eyes, other than mine, would see this business envelope addressed "To Mr. James Macdonald—Personal."

When I returned to my insertion orders, remorse set in. What a rash thing to do, an outright stupid, idiotic, reckless thing. I would pay dearly for it. Why did I think this dour Scotsman had a sense of humor? Never had I seen him smile as he passed my desk. How would such a person receive a poem written in classic college humor magazine style about a deadly serious topic like being late for work, a sin he warned us to avoid at all costs? Worst of all, I had made fun of him and his favorite expression.

He would crumple the paper and toss it into a wastepaper basket. He would not bother to fire me in person. I wasn't that important. Most likely, he would phone Mr. Harrington and say, "Get rid of that labor agitator you hired."

The day passed uneventfully, as did the next. Mr. Macdonald's secretary returned. During her lunch hour I peeked into the office to see if the poem was still on the desk of her boss. It was gone! Meanwhile, Mr. Macdonald would be away in New York for three days. Had he even seen my poem? Had he seen it but then forgotten about it? Had he read the first line and torn it up?

The following Monday morning Mr. Macdonald passed my desk without a glance in my direction. Nothing to worry about. He had never looked at me in the eight weeks I had been at the agency. Better this way, I told myself. He had either forgotten the entire incident or overlooked it. Or he had read the verse, took offense, and deliberately ignored it, the worst punishment of all.

I put the disaster out of mind and tackled a pile of outdoor billing until I was aware of the giant frame of Mr. Macdonald looming overhead. He waved a sheet of paper in my direction and said in a booming voice, "I, too, have been trying my hand." Then he placed the paper on my desk and vanished back into his office. Dumbfounded, I realized what had happened.

This bigwig vice president of the Jacob Kamenetz Company had written me a poem! In the same iambic pentameter I had used, Mr. Macdonald offered some masterful advice. He wrote: *So get up earlier, avoid the mob / That's what you'd have to do in any job.* The next morning when he passed my way, he nodded in my direction with the hint of a smile. Days later, no other sign of recognition flickered across his ruddy face.

My struggle for corporate visibility continued. I looked for subtle approaches, nothing too pushy. It was crucial to remain everyone's friend. I learned that no female copywriter had ever worked at the agency. To become part of the creative staff, I would have to break down seawalls never breached before, not an easy task for an Emily Dickinson masquerading as Tugboat Annie.

Co-workers in the Media Department didn't know about my poem to Mr. Macdonald nor his response. It wasn't wise to tell them because such aggressive behavior could diminish me in their eyes. Although they knew I was a college graduate, they didn't hold it against me as long as I typed a respectable sixty words a minute and joined them at lunch every day, laughing at the jokes, commiserating over failed romances, exchanging the latest scuttlebutt, and always walking on eggs. Jews like me, who grew up in small rural towns, acquired those skills early.

In contrast to my girlish contemporaries on the first floor, the copywriters on the second floor were men in their late thirties or forties (except for one grandfatherly account executive who took us girls out for whiskey sours every Friday and asked nothing in return). Most of the men were married or divorced, held college degrees, dressed in expensive suits, and owned houses in Baltimore's better neighborhoods. To a twenty-one-year-old like me, they dwelled on an elevated creative plane. In my eyes all copywriters were a madcap tribe of lunatics spouting wisecracks and wacky ideas, and I wanted to join them!

Periodically they dropped by our office to make sure their print ads had appeared in specific publications or to study the format and content of successful ads run by competing agencies. They considered us an informal library. Any employee could browse through our publications, which ranged from *Esquire* to *Better Homes and Gardens,* from *Harper's Bazaar* to the *Baltimore Afro-American.*

Lilace, our eye on the world, revealed personal secrets about all personnel, male and female. She learned from a pal on the cleaning crew that the copywriters often walked off with her magazines before she could file them. "Know what they do?" she asked us. "They read them magazines on the john in the restroom, and then just leave them there in the stalls." She thought this was hilarious, but when she told Joyce, Mr. Macdonald's no-nonsense secretary, the word reverberated to her boss. Ultimately, Mr. Kamenetz himself issued an edict that all publications arriving in Media must remain there, available for research only.

Lilace's tale inspired me to record this deplorable crime in a piece of light verse entitled "The Ghost Who Walks Media." In my epic poem an invisible phantom is spiriting away magazines and leaving them in the men's lavatory. Joyce made a copy of the original for her boss. He, in turn, sent it to the front office. Three days later the icy Miss Gluschfield, longtime secretary to Mr. Kamenetz, honored me with a phone call.

"Mr. Kamenetz liked your poem so much," she said, "he had me mail it to *Tide*. They want to publish it with your byline. Okay?"

I didn't hear her correctly. "You mean *Time* wants it?" Henry Luce's world-famous magazine accepted such a vulgar little poem?

"Not *Time*," Miss Gluschfield said. "It's not that good." She further explained that *Tide* was the bible of American advertising. In the back pages of the trade magazine, the editor ran a column of office miscellany submitted by agency people. My work would appear there.

Although it was hardly the caliber of Fitzgerald's *This Side of Paradise*, I considered the publication of the poem a career milestone. Surely, I thought, something momentous would result from all this national exposure. Nothing came of it except one response from a former college classmate, who had dashed to New York after graduation. Still unemployed, he wrote, "Can you get me a copywriting job at the Kamenetz agency?"

Weeks and months wore on as drearily as ever. Lilace quit her job for undisclosed reasons, and I became the official mail clerk in addition to my regular duties. Pushing a heavy wire cart from office to office, I discovered on the second floor a soul mate, a troubled Southern gentleman of fifty or so with a master's degree in English from the University of Virginia. As a student there, he had once lived on the Range in the same quarters as hard-drinking Edgar Allan Poe, a dropout from Mr. Jefferson's temple of learning. Montgomery Willowby (not his real name) was a besotted creature who loathed every minute of his work. When I showed him an ironic sonnet of mine about feeling buried alive under piles of ominous space orders and outdoor billing, he urged me to preserve my poetic sensibility as well as my virginity.

"Oh, hasten! oh, let us not linger," he said, quoting Poe's "Ulalume." *"Oh fly—let us fly!—for we must."* Wild-eyed, he waved his hands in the air. "Vanish, girl! Depart! Begone before it's too late or you'll be damned to hell like me!" I could smell bourbon wafting across the cluttered cubicle that served as his office. A few weeks later, Darlene, his occasional secretary, informed everyone in Media that Montgomery had invited the Kamenetz copywriters, artists, and production staff to a Saturday-night debauchery.

"No women from this agency are allowed," she said. "Mr. Willowby asked me to collect $10 from all the guys who are coming." In return, he promised his guests a saturnalia, an evening of delights, a bewitching Walpurgisnacht at the Belvedere Hotel. It would rival even the company's annual Christmas party. Darlene spoke with authority about the upcoming event because she had arranged the logistics and distributed mimeographed RSVP invitations.

Willowby attracted a full house. Afterward, according to Darlene, the guests complained bitterly. "They were crowded into a room filled only with rows of chairs like for a prayer meeting," she said. "They never saw a trace of the whiskey or the wild women that Mr. Willowby promised them in the flyer. Instead they sat for an hour and a half while he read them his dumb poems, and that was all they ever got for their money."

Had I found my mentor at last? No, Willowby's final moments at the agency came too soon. One morning as I dumped a pile of First Class mail onto Darlene's desk, he chose that moment to lurch out of his office. He had inserted unlit cigarettes into each of his nostrils, his mouth, and both ears. Darlene looked away, slightly annoyed. He didn't come to work the next day. In fact, we never saw him again. His disappearance saddened me. Gone was a refreshing break from my humdrum workaday world. A week before, Willowby had sent me an inspired couplet that combined T. S. Eliot's "J. Alfred Prufrock" with an author closer to the inebriated copywriter's heart. It read, quite touchingly: *People come and people go / Speaking of Edgar Allan Poe.*

Not every male at the agency was an alcoholic or deranged. A few happened to be what we young women tolerantly called "jokers." Today in the twenty-first century they could be indicted for sexual harassment. Their desks were so arranged that we had to pass through their territory to reach the Ladies' Restroom on the second floor. It became upsetting when the more vocal creative types bellowed at us, "Immediate seating in the balcony, girls!" At those times I longed for the soused, but gentlemanly Mr. Willowby.

Winter turned to spring and spring to summer. Meanwhile, at home I pounded out reams of bitter poems, pointless stories, and nasty essays accompanied by self-addressed, stamped envelopes. My favorite was an article titled "Don't Be Afraid to Break Your Engagement." I erred in sending it to a bridal magazine. Every one of these literary extravaganzas returned home, where my mother commented, "Honey, you wouldn't have to put up with all this foolishness if you were teaching school." She meant well.

Making rounds with the U.S. mail one morning, I overheard a conversation in the Retail Department between Mr. Bamburger, the major account executive in Retail, and Mr. Mankowitz, another savvy copywriter. Snatches of their comments led me to believe changes were afoot in that office. The next day I asked Joyce, Mr. Macdonald's secretary, for an appointment to see her boss. She gave me an incredulous look because clerk/typists did not make appointments to see vice presidents of the company. I confessed to her my career goals although I suspected the news would spread through the agency like the

Baltimore fire of 1904. Startled by my unexpected chutzpah, she promised to add my name to his schedule.

Face to face with Mr. Macdonald, I reminded him of the poems we wrote to each other, and finished with, "I could be of more value to the company as a copywriter than a mail clerk."

"I agree," he said in a solemn voice, "but all I can do is put in a good word for you with the big guy. Better talk it over with Miss Gluschfield first. Maybe she can work you in to see him."

The sudden reality of it all terrified me. I hadn't expected to engage Miss Gluschfield in the front office. Each morning when I brought mail to the domain of the formidable Miss Gluschfield, we rarely made eye contact. Once she gave me a tight smile. We never spoke.

Everything that mattered at the agency passed through this powerful woman whom the Media girls called The Glusch. For thirty years, she had protected Mr. Kamenetz from all evil. Still, of the two giants, I was less afraid of The Glusch. We brushed elbows in the Ladies' Restroom, where she could be heard admonishing the youthful clerical staff for their lack of hygienic protocol.

"You girls should take care not to flush sanitary napkins," she said. "I'm always on the phone with the plumber."

Miss Gluschfield's radar could detect fawning with miraculous precision. I had to proceed with caution. Still, she seemed more approachable than our employer. In the hallway, whenever Mr. Kamenetz appeared menacingly in his trademark black fedora and camel-colored overcoat, I fled down the nearest staircase. His furious voice boomed through the walls as he reprimanded his account executives. I would see them stumbling out of his office in tears.

My Media cohorts spent untold hours discussing the ego of our boss. A typist named Cookie once borrowed my copy of *Shakespeare: Major Plays and Sonnets* to impress her boyfriend, a student at the University of Baltimore. On her way home, she bumped into Mr. Kamenetz in the elevator. According to Cookie, he glanced at the book title and said, "A guy who hires girls that read Shakespeare can consider himself a big success." That told me all I wanted to know about the big boss. He was a stereotype, the quintessential crusty employer in movies and comic strips, a combination of Lionel Barrymore at his meanest and Mr. Dithers, nemesis of Dagwood Bumstead. Yet the glacial Miss Gluschfield, probably goaded by Mr. Macdonald, worked an amazing miracle.

"Mr. K will see you tomorrow morning at 9:30," she told me.

Sink or Swim

I didn't sleep that night. The following day the big boss never arrived at the office. His enormous black Buick had been rammed by another car.

"Mr. Kamenetz wasn't injured," his secretary said, "but the car is in the shop for repairs."

Each day I expected him back. Every morning I arrived with a polished new pitch for the interview. No approach seemed good enough. I had no strong women to emulate except Rosalind Russell and Bette Davis, and even they folded by the end of the movie. If Mr. Kamenetz could make grown men weep, what trauma lay ahead for me? Would he scream at me and order me out of his sight? Where was he, anyway? Return he did after two weeks away, but no call came from The Glusch.

When Mr. Macdonald asked about the interview, I told him it had not been rescheduled. He took care of it immediately, and that's how I found myself, jittery and unprepared, entering the hallowed ground that was the office of Jacob Kamenetz, self-made man, ill-tempered autocrat. What do I still remember about that day? A monstrous black umbrella hung on a hat rack not far from his desk, where, seated in his shirt sleeves rolled up to the elbows, he commanded me to sit in an enormous leather chair opposite him.

It couldn't have come at a worse time. That June afternoon in 1952 an oppressive heat wave blanketed the city. Our agency's windows sported no air-conditioning units; they would be installed the following year. To top it off, Zachary, my husband-to-be, was finishing his master's degree at the Harvard

School of Public Health. He phoned the night before my appointment with destiny.

"I've applied for a research position with the New York State Board of Health," Zach said. "I'll probably get it. If so, here's what we'll do. I want you to leave that stupid job and move to Albany with me."

When I suggested that we mustn't be hasty and that he ought to look for work in Baltimore or Washington, Zach issued an ultimatum: either follow him wherever his career took us or . . . or else. With this on my mind and his graduation only a few days away, I now faced Mr. Kamenetz, who gave me permission to speak. My pitch contained no frills. "I learned you may soon be needing another copywriter in Retail," I began, weak as a kitten.

"Let me tell you this before you go any further," the great man answered. "There's no opening for you here."

"Everybody told me that Mr. Mankowitz was leaving Retail," I said. My voice, now strained and thin, rose even higher than usual.

"Mankowitz was helping with a special campaign. Now he's back to handling national accounts, which was what I hired him for in the first place. There's no vacancy in Retail."

This was not going well. I felt feverish. It could have been over ninety degrees in the room. I fidgeted, lost in that gigantic chair. My short legs dangled, unable to reach the floor. Across the back of my new brown-and-white-striped seersucker suit, the material clung to my skin, wet with what comedians called flop sweat.

"Besides," he said, "my golf buddy, Morty Shastock, just asked me to give his daughter a job writing copy here, and I hired her last week. I can't take on anybody else now."

I nodded helplessly, thinking of all the damnable insertion orders and outdoor billing I had typed for a year and a half, all the mail sorted and delivered, all that time wasted. But wasn't Zach in the wings waiting with outstretched arms? Perhaps now was the right time to cut and run. My eyes fell on a formal oil portrait of Mr. Kamenetz that hung on an adjacent wall. It made him look like that blustering old movie actor, Wallace Beery, minus the jowls.

Mr. Kamenetz took notice of my interest in the painting. "Recently, I found this young guy, an artist, who was doing a lot of that crazy modern painting, all those smears and dots. But the kid had talent. And so I asked him if he could do a picture of me, and that's it. My wife says it doesn't look like me. What do you think?"

"It's nice," I lied.

"Tell you what," he said. "I worked ten years as advertising director at the Holst Company. They're the biggest bargain department store in this town because of all I did for them. So look, I can easily get you in at Holst's," he continued, "writing fashion copy. You girls like that sort of thing, don't you?"

Did I want to slave away, promoting Dacron blouses for some second-rate department store? Zach had asked me to join him in Albany. Would it really be a better life to spend the rest of my days with him and his microbes? I could see myself, alone, digging through five-foot-high piles of snow to make a path to the bus stop, where I would head for yet another employment agency, another Miss Wood, only to be told there were no writing jobs in Albany, nothing for me, but maybe I should take a course in shorthand.

Mr. K leaned forward. "Well, what do you say? All I have to do is phone." He paused and glanced at the gold watch on his wrist. It was growing late in the afternoon. The day had not cooled down. I thought about running in the heat to catch two buses and a streetcar. At home, my mother would be upset about having to warm dinner for me in our sweltering house. "Honey, the whole meal gets all dried out when you come home so late," she'd say. "If you were a teacher, you'd finish work early."

Mr. Kamenetz rustled papers on his desk. He seemed surprised by my silence. "Well?"

"No," I said in a tone that sounded like a toddler about to burst out crying. "I don't want to work at Holst's. I want to work here. I want to work here." My voice broke. "I love this place." Which was probably true.

He stared at me for ten seconds and then reached for his phone. "Get Bamburger in here," he said to Miss Gluschfield. The Retail office was across the hall. Sy Bamburger, director of Retail and one of the agency's best copywriters, appeared at once.

"Find this little girl something to do," Mr. Kamenetz ordered. Bamburger was a congenial forty-year-old with a ready smile and a clever quip for everyone.

"Yes, sir," he said. He glanced at me and then at the ceiling as if to plead with an unjust Providence.

Mr. Kamenetz rose, shook my hand, and welcomed me to the firm. "Remember," he said, "you have to crawl before you can walk." Then he dismissed us with a royal wave of his hand.

An entry that night in my five-year diary read as follows: *Today at last, I'm joining the heavenly choir on the second floor.*

Walking the Plank

Word spread fast the next day. The Production Department director blocked my way in the hall to say, "You are the only person who ever came in here and got what you wanted." A graphic artist who had never acknowledged my presence on earth before, rested his ink-stained hand on my shoulder and said, "You are the luckiest girl in the agency." Fellow Media laborers were dumbstruck at first but then took me out to lunch, where we celebrated, dutch treat, with gin and tonic. Was there a thread of green envy subtly woven throughout the remarks of clerks and typists who toasted me? It didn't matter. I had reached celebrity status.

Mr. Macdonald's reaction brought me back to the real world. "What sort of financial arrangement did you make?" he asked. Whoops! Money was one thing that hadn't entered my fantasy world. Trying to save face, I told him the time hadn't seemed right to bring up that subject. Like most women of my generation, I knew nothing of salary negotiation. It would have been the height of female chutzpah for me to have responded to Mr. Kamenetz, "Okay, out of the goodness of your heart, you hired me. Now make it worth my while." Besides, just a month before, Mr. Harrington increased my clerical salary from $32.50 a week to $35. My cup had already run over. If those two frugal businessmen were to discover *two* pay raises for me in one month, I thought, they would boot me out the door.

Mr. Macdonald's dry response to my lack of initiative was, "Where were you?"

I didn't answer. It wouldn't have been professional to tell him about my love life and the conflict raging inside my head. When Zach called long distance to remind me of his graduation in Boston, I relayed the good news about my career advancement. He didn't sound elated.

"What are you doing?" he said. "I told them today that I'm taking that public health job in Albany." His voice took on a frosty quality. "I expect you to join me there."

"I'll have to get back to you on that," I said in a tone just as cold as the one he had used with me. Replacing the receiver, I remembered an incident from the previous summer when we lay side by side on the beach at Sandy Point. The noon sun was directly overhead, and my skin reddened in the August heat.

"Zach," I said, "I'm starting to get a sunburn. Would you please smear some of that Noxema on my shoulders and back?"

He lay on his back motionless, his dark hair still wet from our swim in the Chesapeake Bay. "No," he said.

I thought he was teasing. "Don't you care if I get burnt to a crisp?"

He turned over on his stomach and turned away from me, facing the opposite direction. "No," he said, "I really don't care."

I imagined he was joking, laughed it off, and forgot about it, but now it resonated. He didn't care, and he meant it. He had always seemed distant, removed. I was his run-of-the-mill bacterial specimen on a slide, his compliant white mouse in a lab experiment. I could see him as a husband, refusing to pick up after himself, refusing to grocery shop when asked, refusing to diaper a baby. I could see him not taking a toddler to the playground. His work always would come first.

Zach often spoke with disdain about being anchored to one spot. His words came back to me in a rush. He rejected owning a house or being tied down to the same job for the rest of his life. He hoped to see the world, he said, and I answered, "You saw it during the war. Wasn't that enough?"

"That didn't count," he said. Zach didn't mean all those unreasonable things, an inside voice told me. Even if he did, he would change his attitude after we married, wouldn't he? When I listed pros and cons on paper, the cons outnumbered the pros. How could I gaze into that handsome face and tell him our love affair was kaput? I had just been rereading *Letters of Emily Dickinson.* I wanted to unload my ambivalent feelings, laden with gossamer metaphors and golden similes, but pretty words were hard to come by.

JUNE 1950

> Dear Zach,
> Clearly, you think we haven't room for two careers in our marriage. It's Albany now, but in your line of work, you could eventually pack up and head for any laboratory anywhere in the world, and you'll assume I'll change my life on your orders without your even consulting me first. Pulling up stakes may be your *modus vivendi*, but it's not mine. Mr. Kamenetz has given me a rare chance. Do you realize how long and hard it took to reach this point? And yet you expect me to sacrifice all that now. It's not fair. I can't and won't drop everything to play Follow the Leader with you.

Zach phoned immediately. "You'll adjust," he said. "Other girls do it all the time."

"But I'm not like other girls."

"I'm beginning to think you're not," he said. As his big day drew near, I sent a telegram: "Congratulations on your graduate degree. Sorry can't go to Boston. What's the point?"

"Are you or are you not coming to Albany with me?" he asked on another expensive long-distance call.

"I don't think so."

"And exactly what does this mean as far as the two of us are concerned?"

My mother hovered nearby. "I can't go into it on the phone," I said. "Let me spell it all out in a letter."

"Always the writer," he said with a touch of bitterness and slammed down the receiver.

I composed my last letter, a barren one that settled the matter for good. I was not moving to Albany; I would not marry Zach. The next day as a U.S. Postal Service carrier emptied the neighborhood mailbox, I considered running outside and pleading, "Please, Mr. Mailman, I made a mistake and sent the wrong letter. Can you find it and give it back?"

That didn't happen. On the weekend of Zach's graduation, I cried a bit and filled the void by gorging on Edna St. Vincent Millay, who once wrote, *I shall forget you presently, my dear / So make the most of this, your little day, / Your little month, your little half a year. . . .* Zach and I had been engaged for two years, probably longer than most of Edna's love affairs, and even so, we hardly knew each other. After an hour I put the book on a shelf in my bedroom and went downstairs to join my parents in watching a brainless new television comedy called *I Love Lucy.* How soothing to focus on nothing except this obvious, trivial TV show that would probably last only one season. I proved wrong about Lucy, but was I right about Zach?

Cape of Good Hokum

It was a broad leap from the anonymity of the female typing pool to the masculine theater of the absurd on the second floor. Our Retail Department cast included Sy Bamburger plus Larry, a devil-may-care commercial artist closer to my age, and Clayton, a former merchant marine seaman, who had published a handful of dry articles on maritime topics. He somehow morphed into a copywriter, probably hired because of his posh British accent. Clayton had never worked as a clerk/typist at $32.50 a week. He could barely type with two fingers and a hangnail.

At twenty-two, I didn't want to jump ship and sever ties completely with my contemporaries, the Media girls. Now I was footloose and free to pursue any eligible Jewish man on the East Coast. Through the efforts of former co-workers, I blind-dated a parade of bookkeepers, accountants, shoe salesmen, hotel managers, tailors, fledgling entrepreneurs, restaurateurs, bartenders, and office managers, including one adventurous soul who enjoyed taking me to Friendship Airport where we watched planes land and take off.

Staying afloat, I learned to count the number of picas per inch and per line, absorbed the lingo of layout artists, studied how double trucks (centerfold ads) were designed, wrestled with the difference between institutional and product advertising, created a hundred variations of Christmas and Easter pitches to the public, and chopped my most poetic expressions into the fewest possible number of words to fit into tiny spaces determined by artists more interested in showing than in telling. For a local jewelry store I touted the ultimate wisdom of having diamond jewelry cleaned (heading: *When They Grow Too Old to Gleam*). Sy Bamburger added a new client to our department, a pretentious women's apparel shop for Maryland's horsey set. From the store owner, I gleaned information that enabled me to peddle riding habits, Scottish tartan wool skirts, Dupioni silk blouses, and shapeless houndstooth suits, designed exclusively for the upper crust. Not to my taste, they were the most unflattering clothes ever sold in the city of Baltimore, but it was my job to make them irresistible to those who rode to the hounds and pretended they were British.

Paddling into Politics

To replace Zach during that wickedly hot summer of 1952, I fell in love with Adlai Stevenson, the Illinois governor running against Dwight Eisenhower in the presidential election. According to my diary, Eisenhower had a hard time deciding whether he wanted to represent the Democrats or the Republicans. Either way he would have won. My parents, however, survivors of the Great Depression and defenders of the New Deal, marveled at the televised speeches delivered by Governor Stevenson. The man was eloquent, knowledgeable, and sincere, worthy of becoming the next president of the United States. That he was cultivated, well informed, and capable proved to be his downfall. Being pitted against the hero who led us to victory in Europe didn't help. Everyone liked Ike.

I rooted for the party of Roosevelt and Truman. Discovering a political group in my precinct inspired me to fire off a worshipful letter. I confessed to be madly for Adlai, as the popular slogan went, and asked what adoring citizens like me could do to get him elected. An oily-voiced gentleman named Mr. Murdoch immediately phoned back to agree with my remarks about Stevenson. I had second thoughts when the man referred to the candidate as "good ole Ad Stevison." After he invited me to join the Shaftsbury Political Club and help re-elect our local representative to Congress, I felt my earlier enthusiasm had been too hasty. Frankly, I didn't care a fig for the incumbent, a person unknown to me. Having lived in Baltimore only a year and a half, I knew nothing about the political terrain, but the name of the organization,

Shaftsbury, sounded classy. Perhaps erudite Adlai Stevenson himself would appear at a Shaftsbury meeting in person, and I'd have a chance to sneak him one of my own repressed love poems. Even though Zach had departed, it seemed a good idea to save copies of the poetry he inspired. Note: Writers like to recycle; waste not, want not.

Mr. Murdoch was a longtime ward heeler who immediately introduced me to his shop-worn buddies, folks two or three times my age, including our unimpressive incumbent Congressman. Mr. Murdoch informed me that his sleazy flock often mingled with political celebrities, and about this he did not lie. At that meeting he introduced me to the mayor of Baltimore, Thomas D'Alesandro, whose daughter Nancy much later rose to become the first woman to serve as Speaker of the U.S. House of Representatives. She must have been about eleven years old when I met her father, a jocund man of the people and everyone's dearest friend.

Otherwise, Shaftsbury membership consisted mainly of grubby men who seemed amazed that I, a female of the younger generation, was interested in politics. After the first meeting I wrote in my diary: "Went to Shaftsbury Political Club and got voted in before I even sat down. They strike me as a bunch of scalawags." After they welcomed me to their band of angels, they asked for a generous donation to their upcoming Monster Oyster Roast and loaded me down with a stack of posters to distribute door-to-door in the precinct.

"Make sure everybody puts one of these in their front windows," Mr. Murdoch said.

I am a shy person; I have always been a shy person, an introvert, inner-directed at all costs. I cringed at having to ring strangers' doorbells or begging them to display posters, which bore an ancient photo taken of the incumbent when he still had a viable head of hair. Even my parents refused me. "I didn't buy this new house to stick that sourpuss in my window," my mother said.

I continued to attend the Shaftsbury Club meetings in hopes that Adlai Stevenson would soon visit Baltimore and head out our way to mingle with the Common Man. My journal entry indicates that I sat at club gatherings with Mae, an ample woman, built like singer Kate Smith. Mae was a compassionate soul who always wanted to take up a collection for "The Sick."

"We ought to help out our neighbor Bertha," Mae said. "She's in bed with three doctors."

After the guffaws subsided, Mr. Murdoch suggested we send a trustworthy member to the opposition's next rally at the Emerson Hotel. "We gotta find out what they're up to," he said. Because she had demonstrated her integrity in raising money for unhealthy citizens, he nominated Mae. "We need somebody what looks good-hearted and don't attract no attention," he said, gesturing in the direction of hefty Mae.

"I doubt General Eisenhower will be there," Mae said with a hearty chuckle, "but if Nixon shows up, I'd like to choke him." Everyone applauded, and then to my chagrin, Mr. Murdoch handed me a list of registered voters to phone as soon as possible.

"You can talk a little about Stevison," he said, but the main thing was to cajole people into voting for our incumbent Congressman. I did summon enough nerve to call a couple of distant relatives. They agreed to do me a personal favor and vote for the man, although one cousin commented, "Why are you working for such a blockhead?"

On one of the final days of October Mr. Murdoch took me aside. Our Congressional representative had personally complained to him about the lack of visual support in my precinct. "Where are the goddam signs?" he wanted to know. Election Day, I went to the wrong polling place, couldn't find the right one, and was unable to vote for Adlai Stevenson. My sole comfort in this fiasco was that I hadn't cast a vote for our Congressman. He won anyway, despite the victorious Eisenhower-Nixon ticket. The Jacob Kamenetz agency, that advertising jewel of Baltimore, had been hired to help get Stevenson elected. The employees were crushed. We had done badly for Adlai. We had backed a loser.

JOURNAL ENTRY: NOVEMBER 5, 1952

> Gloom ran rampant today at work. Sy Bamburger, who wants to buy a one-way ticket to Canada, said, "This place today is so quiet you can hear a Democrat drop."

Why the Sea Is Salt

Picture the aged author of this memoir as a matchstick of a girl, laboring long days and weekend overtime to create a fresh, slightly humorous way of looking at the universe through advertising. By the end of that year I was still earning $35 a week and weighed eighty-nine pounds. My mother still wanted me to go into teaching. My former fiancé was battling the snowdrifts of Albany. And I had no date for New Year's Eve.

That year yielded the heaviest wave of weddings ever to hit the fragrant shores of Baltimore Harbor. Young women of the Kamenetz agency floated from office to office to flash their diamond rings in all directions like Halley's Comet. I attended their weddings and those of my nubile cousins with whom I never had the slightest thing in common. The nuptials are a blur now, but I do recall that receptions always included a band that played "True Love" for the bride and groom's first dance and a master of ceremonies who encouraged everyone to jitterbug to a rotten song called "Ragmop." Highlight of the evening arrived when the groom's uncle or grandfather would read aloud congratulatory telegrams from absent guests of which I wished I were one. At family weddings, members of the immigrant generation, kinfolks my parents' age, would grab my arm and point-blank confront me in Yiddish or English with "Nu? So?" Or, considering me the last leaf on the tree, they would give me a sympathetic smile, pat my head, and say, "Next by you."

At the agency, Sy Bamburger liked my work. I was assigned to write daily ads for another local jewelry store, R. & S. Unterstein (not its real name).

Their trademark was a lopsided diamond accompanied by the memorable slogan, "Marriages are made in heaven but engagements are made at R. & S. Unterstein." Sy even arranged for my salary to increase to a phenomenal $45 a week. When R. & S. Unterstein became the proud sponsors of *Stumping Shadows*, a weekly television program, Sy asked me to write the sixty-second spots. A local station had come up with the brilliant idea of casting shadows on a screen and asking two teams of contestants to compete in identifying what they saw. It was rather like a Rorschach test with cash prizes.

In those days all television was live, even commercials. For me, dreaming up TV spots came easily. The real danger lay in dodging potential thieves. Each week I caught a city bus that ran directly from the agency to the jewelry store. There the store manager would assemble for me tiny boxes of diamond rings to display during the commercials. He always placed the rings in a proletarian brown paper bag, handed it to me with words of caution, and then I boarded the Charles Street bus to take the swag to the TV studio.

On those occasions I dressed to look poverty stricken. With a paisley kerchief covering my head, I donned an oversized brown topcoat in a nubby woolen material called poodle cloth. On my feet, ungainly black galoshes added to the picture of a downtrodden woman carrying her humble lunch on her way to mopping floors at City Hall. No one dreamed that the brown paper bag held diamonds. I loved the drama of it. At the studio, I set the rings on a purple velvet cloth spread over a card table. Off camera, I stood guard until the end of the program when the store manager dropped by to collect his precious cargo and take it back to the store. For this perilous nighttime assignment, the agency paid my cab fare home.

Sy Bamburger was reassigned to handle only national accounts. A Philadelphia man took his place as head of the Retail Department. Al Chraine, a paranoid gentleman, rejected everything I wrote. Soon after his arrival, we landed a Baltimore department store account, and it was his job to handle all their print media, including double-truck ads hawking storewide sales on all kinds of sleazy merchandise.

These relentless schlock ads required little imagination. The dreary columns, unbroken by illustrations, listed in bold letters miscellaneous items on sale. We dealt with sullen buyers and salesclerks who never returned calls. Items and prices kept changing; it was meaningless hack work. I hated the piddling little rectangles of uninspired numbers and sparse copy that spread across the entire width of the newspaper's centerfold. Although Mr. Chraine had been hired to launch this campaign of mammoth sale ads, which ran week after week, he found the work beneath him. He proceeded to load me down with the entire mess, every column inch, every dollar sign. It was an unwelcome addition to five other retail accounts that I nurtured. My pay remained the same.

While complaining about this blatant exploitation at lunch, I touched the heart of a sympathetic companion. Sylvia, a bookkeeper in Accounting, invited me to join her at a Saturday-night dance held by a Jewish singles group at a Reform temple in her neighborhood.

"Screw the job," she advised me. "You're turning into a hermit."

"I do go out to the movies sometimes by myself," I told her, but Sylvia convinced me that I should avoid breaking one of the social rules of young unmarried women in Baltimore. "You should never be seen riding the city's streetcars alone on a Saturday night," Sylvia warned. "It tells everybody you're unpopular." Reluctantly, I agreed to go.

The dance at the temple social hall began with a dismal Paul Jones in which males and females paraded self-consciously to recorded music that featured Eddie Fisher singing "Oh, My Papa." There appeared to be more women than men, a situation I expected. Whenever the music stopped and I looked for a nearby partner, only other lonely females remained. Later in the evening, although Sylvia directed me to join the unhappy wallflowers at stage right, I managed to drift away to stage left where an unattached young woman would have less competition.

The following paragraphs are of the utmost importance. At this stultifying dance, a supernatural phenomenon occurred. Call it magical realism. It was here that a miracle took place. How else can one describe that heavenly creature, the Angel Herman? I saw him akin to the celestial fixer played by Claude Rains in the film *Here Comes Mr. Jordan*. Or Henry Travers as Clarence, the ethereal deliverer of James Stewart in *It's a Wonderful Life*. Like them, Herman arrived, sent down to earth with a noble purpose: to bind together the worlds of Science and Literature. In this case, I am referring broadly to advertising as Literature, even though at our agency Mr. Willowby often lamented, "Advertising is to literature what syphilis is to sex."

But back to that mating ritual in northwest Baltimore, circa 1954, when the Angel Herman appeared out of the Lucky Strike cigarette smoke and spoke his cherubic words in a distinctly Southern drawl, "Would you like to dance?" It's not that the young man was an Adonis with his sallow coloring complicated by five o'clock shadow. It wasn't even that he danced divinely; he knew only a monotonous two-step. And it certainly wasn't the meager conversation describing his technical prowess as an electrical engineer at the Glenn L. Martin aircraft plant.

Still, some Power beyond anything I could explain compelled me to stay with him all evening. I can remember babbling nonstop to prevent him from escorting me back to the despondent wallflower brigade. At our parting, he asked for my phone number and wondered if I'd be interested in going to a party the next weekend.

"A fellow I knew back at Georgia Tech is having a get-together at his place in Langley Park," Herman said. "That's in the Washington suburbs." I nodded yes, but during the week I changed my mind.

"If he calls, tell him I've moved and left no forwarding address," I said.

"Don't be like that," said my mother. "Go! Go! Maybe you'll meet somebody."

We skip now to the bachelor apartment and the party host, not an engineer but a chemist at the Naval Research Laboratory in southeast Washington, D.C. From the moment Herman introduced us, the seaworthy host, whose name was Jerry, insisted on plying me with imported wine. He had assembled a buffet table worthy of Perle Mesta, the official Washington hostess during the Truman administration. I was amazed that this young man could manage the intricate details of entertaining without a woman to guide him. Although he circulated to make sure his guests had plenty of corned beef, kosher pickles, seeded rye bread, coleslaw, and potato salad, he kept returning to chat with me.

Jerry insisted on taking me on a tour of his one-bedroom apartment, decorated with modernist prints and shelves of poetry by Stephen Spender and Robert Frost, racks of recorded Ambrosian and Gregorian chants, and albums of Bartók and Villa-Lobos. Before Herman and I left, our host scribbled my phone number on a napkin and offered me an apple pie to take home. Except for the wordless ride back to Baltimore, I had not spent more than ten minutes with Herman the entire party.

My mother discovered a mysterious item on her kitchen table the next morning. "Where did this pie come from?" she asked.

"Last night I met the kind of man I would like to marry," I dreamily said. As if on cue, the phone rang. It was Jerry calling with tickets for T. S. Eliot's *Murder in the Cathedral*. Was I free to join him next Saturday night?

Eight months later, in a simple ceremony at my parents' house, we were married. And the Angel Herman? Mission accomplished, he ascended into the heavens from whence he came.

Or so we thought!

Connubial Confluences

As a married lady, I could now pursue plans to become a full-time freelance scribe. My years as a professional advertising copywriter meant nothing. I was rejected by a full spectrum of publications, including a temperance pamphlet. In a women's magazine, I found a compelling ad that featured the blurry headshot of a haggard female author whom I didn't know. She enticed me with her startling endorsement, "I have spent half my life in hospital waiting rooms but still found time to write." That was good enough for me. I enrolled in a correspondence course that promised a sure-fire career in commercial writing without having to leave the comforts of home. For a nominal fee, I received reams of material on how to produce formulaic articles and short stories slanted toward all magazines in search of mediocrity.

From the company's New York office, an unknown mentor, who claimed he was also a literary agent, sent assignments based on instruction manuals. I studied narrative hooks and learned to avoid topics that were the kiss of death for any freelance writer who wished to invade prim magazines like *Ladies' Home Journal* and *Good Housekeeping.* Verboten subjects of the 1950s included miscegenation, abortion, criticism of Wall Street, tirades against organized religion, and above all, graphic sex. The latter could be implied but no details. Even back then, I hooted at one suggestive sentence in a *Woman's Home Companion* short story: "Mildred, a superb housewife, loved her husband thoroughly."

The best thing about this correspondence course was discovering *Trial and Error: A Key to the Secret of Writing and Selling* by Jack Woodford, a caustic writer who delivered bitter advice on how to find a publisher. The only thing I now remember about the book was him warning female authors in the hinterlands not to go to New York and try to sell stories by seducing editors. "Nothing annoys them more," Woodford wrote, "than to have some not very pretty female from Nebraska blow in filled with the notion that editors will instantly want her carcass." At the time, the word "misogynist" was unknown to me.

Matrimony helped me swallow a fear of the great unknown. At the age of twenty-six, I learned to drive a car despite several botched attempts at parallel parking. The first failure horrified the state police trooper who sat next to me supervising my test. I could tell he was upset because he yelled, quite emotionally, "You're losing control of the car!" The second time, my parallel parking took too long because the teacher at the driving school had taught me to line up certain rearview window screws with the barriers that defined the space or something like that. The Department of Motor Vehicles awarded me permission to drive after a third try. Even so, a few days later my feelings were damaged when a male driver bellowed out his window, "Hey lady, where did you get your license? Sears Roebuck?"

Marriage introduced me to the challenges of long-range travel, including my first trip on an airplane. I experienced the trauma of turbulent air pockets topped by a nighttime landing in Washington. When I dared to look down, there stood the Capitol building, the Washington Monument, the Jefferson and Lincoln Memorials, and all of D.C.'s skyline ablaze in lights. Country girl that I was, my jaw dropped a couple of inches.

"Your eyes are popping out of your head," Jerry commented.

As we started our descent into National Airport, I said, "I never dreamed the city would look this way from far up high. It reminds me of a floating barge of diamond rings from R. & S. Unterstein."

"Stick with me, kid," Jerry said, taking my hand in his. "We're going places."

A long car trip that summer took us to New England and the Gordon Research Conference, a five-day professional gathering for scientists. On the road, I learned even more about the man who had stood beside me under the marriage canopy. We were amazingly alike in a goofy sort of way. We sang together, just the two of us, all the way to the Granite State. Jerry taught me Yiddish and Hebrew melodies he had learned as a child. He came from a musical family in which his father, uncles, great-uncle, and brother, a graduate student at the New England Conservatory of Music, could burst into reasonable harmony at any moment and at any place. That could be terribly embarrassing.

With plenty of time on our hands, as Jerry drove from Maryland through Delaware, Pennsylvania, New Jersey, New York, Connecticut, and Vermont, we branched into composing original ditties with nonsensical lyrics that kept us laughing all the way north on Route 1. I remember a masterpiece about unrequited love titled "I Thought You Loved Me But You Really Didn't Love Me." We considered especially hilarious the lines: *I thought you'd lead my group / I thought you'd join my troupe. / But then you caught the croup / That night in Paris.*

My favorite was our version of "Polly Wolly Doodle," a dusty old American tune that begins with *Oh, I went down South for to see my Sal / Sing Polly Wolly Doodle all the day.* Jerry had been working at the Naval Research Laboratory on a project that involved a paint-thinning, corrosion-resistant substance called polyvinyl butyral. He ingeniously came up with *Oh, I took a cab to the Naval lab / Sing Poly-Vinyl-Butyral the Day.* Only Jerry could work a term like that into a song.

My husband brought to our marriage books by authors I had never read, including inexpensive paperbacks like *The Pocket Book of Modern Verse, 100 Modern Poems,* and *New American Poets.* In the mid-1950s we also belonged to a forum that sponsored contemporary writers who came to do readings in Washington. It was a rare privilege to see in person such literary lights as T. S. Eliot, Edith and Osbert Sitwell, Stephen Spender, Louise Bogan, Carl Sandburg, and Robert Frost. Imagine sitting in that audience and hearing them read from their works! The eccentric Sitwell brother-and-sister team caused a stir among adoring Anglophiles gathered in the audience. Edith arrived decked out in full flowing robes as if she were starring in a medieval morality play. "She always dresses like that," whispered an Englishwoman seated next to me.

No cultural wasteland, Washington offered many more opportunities than Baltimore. We attended operas at the Carter Barron Amphitheatre and treated ourselves to the musical innovations of composer John Cage. Book by book, I read my way through Jerry's library. There were other subtle literary influences on me during those years. On a trip to the Boston wedding of Jerry's brother, I met John Holmes, a New England poet and professor of English at Tufts. In the world of letters, John Ciardi, one of his former students, had received national recognition for his poetry. Holmes, a congenial faculty colleague of my sister-in-law's parents, offered to take me for a stroll around campus.

It was the first time I had ever met a writer of his stature. Holmes talked about Ciardi's work, which I knew about but hadn't read. My contribution to our chat was limited. In that pristine academic atmosphere, I dared not mention a word about advertising. When we passed a line of impressive-looking fraternity houses, Holmes said, "That's where the Greeks live," and I mentioned that at the University of Maryland, we had similar grand structures. "I call it Cannery Row," I said. He seemed amused by the reference to John Steinbeck's novel about migrant workers. When I questioned Holmes about his poetry, he gave me a booklet containing a long commemorative poem he had written recently for Tufts. Here was institutional advertising at its most sublime, but I didn't have the nerve to tell him that.

Sixty-five years later, while leafing through a disintegrating paperback, I discovered his verse in *The Concise Treasury of Great Poems*, 1953 edition. Now long dead, the poet seemed to be saying, "Hello! Remember me?" Holmes was in good company. The yellowed pages included such masters as Babette Deutsch, Richard Eberhart, Josephine Jacobsen, Theodore Roethke, May Sarton, Padraic Colum, Wallace Stevens, and William Carlos Williams. When new, this kingly literary treasure sold for only 35 cents.

Baltimore Clipper

In those early years of marriage, my desire to become a newspaper columnist lingered. Surely, I thought, there were enough credentials in my résumé to propel me in the right direction. In addition to a college writing prize from *Mademoiselle* magazine and experience as an editor on student publications, I had written columns for the *Diamondback* newspaper and earlier had been paid by the *Harford Gazette* for a weekly column, "Teen Topics." Now an adult woman, what did I have to offer as a feature that would entice a big-time newspaper? Inspiration struck one morning at 3:00 a.m. Unapologetic domesticity was in flower at mid-century. I was a full-time housewife. Why not produce light verse on the rituals of homemaking in the suburbs? What would be the best market for something like this? The *Washington Post* with all its emphasis on ritzy embassy balls and state visits by foreign leaders was too sophisticated.

I would produce poems on homey topics, pitch them to the *Baltimore Evening Sun*, and pray the envelope wouldn't be delivered to the same fickle managing editor who, six years before, had rejected my youthful college column. This time around, a more perceptive journalist would call, rave over the sample poems, offer a generous compensation, and beg for more. At least, that's the way it worked in the movies of the 1930s and '40s.

Instead, a listless woman phoned back. "This is Mary Louise at the *Baltimore Sun*," she said. "We'd like to run an article about you." *About* me? Not *by* me? She explained the piece would appear in her own column, "Ladies' Leisure" (not its real name, although I doubt that the real Mary Louise is still kicking after these sixty-odd years). My heart sank. I knew her column. Rendered in lavender prose, it was a fawning sop to our marginalized gender. And yet, still wet behind the ears and tempted by the exposure, I could think of no other answer than a weak "How kind of you."

When her article ran on the women's page, I realized my original pitch to the newspaper had fallen into the wrong hands. The column's subhead read: "The Satisfaction from Being Just 'A Housewife with a Typewriter.'" Mary Louise shamelessly usurped my words and clipped my sails. She used generous quotes from my proposal letter. Word for word, she pirated all the best phrases. In my zeal, I had undercut any possibility of selling the *Sun* a light-verse column or anything else. The newspaper presented me as an amateur at home with an odd hobby, composing "breezy verse." Feminists are cautioned to avert their eyes from the following excerpt from the pen of Mary Louise:

> When the monotony of household chores gets their morale down, some women resort to buying a new hat. . . . But . . . one Maryland housewife channels her pent-up energies and common, everyday annoyances from the "perversity of inanimate objects" . . . which (1) helps to blow off steam and (2) gives her the chance to enjoy the best of all jokes: one on yourself. [She] is convinced there's "a wealth of material in housewifery" . . . and turns out jingles and limericks about the multiplicity of trials . . . that formulate a housewife's day.

The society page reporter continues with:

> The much touted do-it-yourself clan of new household experts does not include Mrs. Kruger among its most enthusiastic members, however. In "What Man Hath Wrought" she opines:
>
> *"Do it yourself!" all the papers do cry*
> *Build you a mansion, or weave you a tie.*
> *Sew up a wardrobe, or paint your own rooms*
> *Carve your own clothespins, and grow your own brooms.*
> *Directions are plentiful, pamphlets galore*
> *Materials cheap at your favorite store.*
> *I'll do it myself and not tarry a day,*
> *But old butterfingers will get in my way.*
> *I'll do it, of course, but I have to rely*

On myself, and I'm not a reliable guy.
So pardon my rudeness if sudden I shout,
"You do it yourself and this time count me out!"

Mary Louise ends with a mealy-mouthed apology:

> While we cannot help but agree, to a degree, with [the] complaint about the do-it-yourself fad, we suspect she is talking a bit with tongue in cheek. . . . But there's the unique satisfaction of being able to view oneself with detachment and amusement—and on this score, we suspect the Maryland wife is herself a "household expert."

I should have sued for libel.

Bibs and Ballast

One thing know-it-all Mary Louise did not suspect at the time: I was pregnant. The following year I gave birth to a strapping eight-pound boy. He was followed in two years by his brother of the same gargantuan size. We had already moved from a garden apartment to a modest ranch-style house nestled in Silver Spring, Maryland.

To ward off suburban monotony and the numb feeling of forever diapering infants, I auditioned for the role of a gossipy society lady in John Patrick's *The Reluctant Debutante*, presented by a community theater company. These would-be thespians included a mélange of misfits, including a school principal who later appeared in court for stealing his pupils' milk money. For a later production they cast me as Olivia, the female lead in Emlyn Williams' *Night Must Fall*, in which I shamelessly faked one of the worst British accents of all times. Finally, at the age of twenty-eight, I starred in *The Curious Savage* as an eighty-year-old lady wearing a purple wig. On our best night, there may have been sixteen people in the audience, mostly blood relatives.

At his National Bureau of Standards job, Jerry advanced to chief of the Corrosion and Electrodeposition Section. During this period of transition, he abandoned his volunteer efforts as leader of a youth group involving spirited ten-year-old boys. He had performed this thankless task ever since obtaining a PhD at the University of Virginia and finding a job in the nation's capital. In his spare time, Jerry took seriously the challenge of working with youngsters. During our courtship days, his innate goodness enamored him to me, especially his patience with these pint-sized demons who tormented him every Sunday afternoon. Surely, I thought, if a bachelor in his mid-twenties could endure that kind of torture from children not his own, maybe he would be able to tolerate me for the rest of his life. And his future offspring as well.

In fact, I tried to share his torment. Before our sons were born, I led a troop of pre-puberty Jewish girls whose mothers wanted them out of the house on Sunday afternoons. In preparation, I spent evenings studying Solomon Grayzel's *A History of the Jews* as well as *Collected Stories of Sholem Aleichem* and Israel Zangwill's *Children of the Ghetto.* Jerry, as a child, attended an after-school Yiddish school where he learned to speak and read the language of our parents and grandparents. His copy of *A Treasury of Yiddish Stories* inspired me to transform a few of these tales into dramatic monologues. Dressed in a shawl, long skirt, and floral babushka tied under my chin, I remember delivering a one-person presentation of Aleichem's "On Account of a Hat" in a friend's living room. She invited me to perform at a synagogue Sisterhood meeting. Their rabbi booked me to give a repeat performance for his entire congregation. And that's how my writing career took off.

The early 1960s found me pushing a baby stroller by day and writing television scripts by night. They were public service programs, supervised by local rabbis and a Jewish community organization. Twice a month, the thirty-minute programs dealt with religious holidays, literature, history, and social problems, all beamed in glorious black and white. Our Radio-TV Committee included spiritual leaders representing Orthodox, Conservative, and Reform Judaism, aided by the director of the community council, who served as executive producer. I was supervised by his female assistant producer, who kept a close eye on me to make sure that all things were kosher from every angle. "If not," she said, "there will be hell to pay."

"No more talking heads," I told her. Until my arrival on the scene, most of their shows dealt with articulate leaders discussing civic problems or members of the rabbinate lecturing on proper observance of religious holidays. The committee assigned me to supply fresh ideas for programs and then write scripts based on approved material. My dream was to replace the humdrum with theatrical versions of biblical and historical events in the grand tradition of Hollywood's Cecil B. DeMille.

To create free time for designing these spectacles, I called the state employment office to hire a dayworker one day a week. She cleaned house and watched our little boys while I headed off to the library to do research on topics about which I had hitherto known absolutely nothing.

"There are two minor drawbacks," I told Jerry. "We have no money to hire professional actors, and the shows are scheduled for Sundays at 9:00 a.m."

"Not exactly prime time," Jerry said.

If federal government regulations hadn't mandated that television allot time for public service programs, our shows wouldn't have existed. Washington-area channels did not welcome frills or my complex instructions distributed to the floor directors, cameramen, and sound and lighting technicians. The poorly paid crew, all of them undernourished young men in faded T-shirts, showed little tolerance for charity programming.

As I explained to Jerry, "Their goal is to finish fast in time for a coffee break with goodies left over from the cooking show."

"Sounds tempting," Jerry said. "Can I hang around for the cooking show?"

I informed him that they didn't look like the kind of guys who would share. "And one thing more," I said. "Our programs are live on tape. That means kinescope."

"No retakes?" he said. "You're already in trouble."

Writing for these shows was not hard; casting them was fraught with danger. As talent scout, I attended auditions, rehearsals, and rocky opening nights in search of amateur actors. "How about some of your jailbird friends in community theater?" Jerry suggested.

I ensnared a few, but it was necessary to play the field. When I approached outright strangers and spoke the magic words, "How would you like to be on television?," they jumped at the chance. I didn't dampen their joy by telling them that hardly anyone would be watching by dawn's early light.

"All this gives me a sense of power," I told Jerry, who replied, "I married an impresario."

An even greater obstacle was finding amateurs who could memorize lines. In those bygone days, some network shows used off-camera boards hand-printed with dialogue for actors with unreliable memories. Electronic teleprompters, as we know them today, weren't available then, only the makeshift signs, which our local stations didn't provide for us.

For a Hanukkah script covering the battle of devout Maccabees in 166 BCE against pagan Greek influences, we were both blessed and cursed. A fine amateur actress joined us to portray a Hellenistic Jewish woman who had succumbed to the surrounding culture spread by Alexander the Great. In our low-budget show, she wore a linen tablecloth draped over one shoulder and a wreath of spinach leaves encircling her head. All went well until halfway through a chunk of valuable exposition when she forgot her lines. It wasn't dialogue that could be improvised unless you were a specialist in the Hasmonean period.

To emphasize the character's decadent lifestyle, I had directed the actress to recline on a couch next to a bowl of grapes. Stuck in that position, she filled the awkward silence by popping grapes into her mouth, ever so slowly, chewing and swallowing one by one. An eon or two passed until she finally heard me prompting loudly off-camera.

In another ill-fated script of mine, we located a fast-talking second-rate comic, Morty, who performed at small saloons in Virginia. I cast him as an itinerant Jewish peddler from Germany. The setting was Virginia in the 1850s. Morty played a character smuggling an enslaved woman to freedom in my one-act play, *Mr. Lincoln and the Peddler.* I chose Morty because he could fake a German accent, although sometimes it bordered on Yiddish Borscht Belt. He assured me he was a quick study.

As his television debut drew closer, Morty, never a good sport about working without pay, seemed less than eager to perform. He often made disparaging remarks about our show, *The Jewish Community Hour.* He called it *The Jewish Comedy Hour.* "One must take risks in show business," I commented to Jerry. "With a professional performer on board, this could be the script to make waves."

"Who knows?" Jerry said. "Maybe you'll be discovered by a visiting New York network producer who just happened to be wide awake at that godforsaken hour of the morning."

It might have happened, who knows, except that during the show, our peddler became confused in the middle of his longest speech. After a brief pause, he resumed with lines that belonged later in the script. In doing this, he eliminated a page and a half of dialogue. Too soon, we were headed at a fast clip toward the end of the show. Fortunately, I played opposite him as the spinster who had hidden the fugitive in her barn. Sometimes it helps to cast the playwright in her own play. I managed to ad-lib parts of the script he had mangled. We still finished the program five minutes too early; the closing theme music played a long, long, long time.

Not all our programs flopped. Based on considerable research, we launched an ambitious literature series on poetry of the Bible, including psalms, verses from the Apocrypha, and the magnificent work of Judah Halevi during the Golden Age of eleventh- and twelfth-century Spain. These shows were among our better ones during the six years of my tenure as scriptwriter. We never knew who admired us from afar. Our audience may have consisted only of our families, long-suffering friends, supportive clergy, Jerry's co-workers at his laboratory, and red-eyed insomniacs. We did, however, receive gratifying fan mail from Catholics left over from watching *Mass for Shut-Ins.*

Mom Overboard!

A stay-at-home mother, I continued to do sporadic writing during the evenings after the boys had been bedded down. At that time, as the parents of two small children, Jerry and I belonged to a cooperative babysitting club in which couples meticulously recorded how many hours we sat and how many we owed. Everyone took turns as bookkeeper, dutifully entering credits and debits into an official ledger. I enjoyed the long evenings away from home when I could settle down with pen and notebook and write uninterrupted for three or four hours. At one house where I had never sat before, everything appeared to be peaceful enough for me to make headway on a new play, *The Ballad of High Entropy*. It was based on the competition among scientists to publish their findings. For some odd reason, I thought it would make a good musical.

The parents for whom I was sitting appeared to be responsible folks. Before leaving for dinner and a movie, the couple showed me their baby asleep in a nearby nursery and pointed out the location of the bathroom and kitchen.

"No steps to climb, everything on the same floor," the young wife said.

During this orientation tour, we stepped over a chocolate-colored basset hound enjoying a nap next to the fireplace. "That's Cleo," her owner said before leaving. "She and the baby will probably sleep the entire time we're gone."

Seated in a cozy chair across the room from the snoring Cleo, I settled down to write. Fifteen minutes later, the dog woke up. We had never met before. My guess is she resented finding a total stranger in her domain. When she approached, growling, I tried to ignore her and concentrate on entropy, but she continued to make threatening sounds. It forced me to do what any normal coward would do when faced with such grim reality. I retreated to the bathroom, closed the door, and *locked it.*

Cleo, a sad-eyed pooch with droopy ears and very short legs, could not have opened that door even if she tried to butt it open with her head, which she was not inclined to do. She issued a few more tentative growls and remained on guard duty just outside the bathroom. When I summoned enough nerve to crack open the door, Cleo had disappeared. From the kitchen, I heard an ominous rattling sound and then some object crashing to the floor. I ventured forth.

Spread throughout the living room's yellow wall-to-wall carpet was a trail of eggshells, banana peels, empty milk cartons, onion skins, apple cores, peach pits, the works. The path of garbage continued into the kitchen where Cleo was happily munching on a drumstick bone from a tipped-over garbage can. Seeing me, she reminded herself that she was supposed to growl, and I headed back to the bathroom for most of the evening. This time I didn't lock the door. The baby slept through it all.

Upon their return, the couple blanched at what they saw. The husband became furious. "You get out of here!" he yelled at Cleo. He lifted her and tossed her out the front door.

Afraid I would be next, I said, "Your dog growled at me."

"Cleo? She wouldn't hurt a fly," the wife snapped. "She even lets the baby pull her ears."

I never sat for them again, but all wasn't lost. From time to time in the 1960s, the *Washington Post* purchased material submitted by freelance writers. The editor bought from me a 650-word essay about our sitters' club and Cleo. Later they published my true story of a secondhand bargain piano we bought at a Washington's Birthday Sale. After delivery, a piano tuner discovered a mouse nest inside. Removing it, he gave us a complete, professional diagnosis of the interior. "It's too dry inside there," he said. He suggested we water the piano every day, which I did. It didn't help. Although the *Washington Post* editor ran the article about this fiasco, he advised me to wait before sending any more.

"My office goes nuts when I run too much stuff written by outsiders," he said.

Those years of the 1960s brought dramatic change not only to the country but also to our families and the people we loved. Jerry's seventy-year-old father died; mine passed away at ninety. Two years later I lost my mother. During that arduous decade, we witnessed the birth of Lyndon Johnson's Great Society, tragic political assassinations, Cold War tensions, civil rights legislation, flower children, sit-ins, race riots, burning cities, Vietnam, and all varieties of social upheaval. But amid the chaos, our two young sons proceeded to grow and thrive with a little help from their full-time parents.

Totally at Sea

Family distractions constantly bombarded me. From my childhood, I remembered an old song that began, *Shut the doors, they're comin' through the windows / Shut the windows, they're comin' through the doors.* We lived in the Washington, D.C. suburbs, a port of entry for a multitude of visitors, and there was no place to hide.

It started during the sunrise years of our marriage. Jerry's brother Harry and his wife, both struggling professional musicians and recent graduates of the New England Conservatory of Music, first began to pass through town each summer. They were headed north on a long trek from their home in Georgia to Tanglewood in the Berkshires, where courses were taught each summer by outstanding European and American musicians. Founded by famed conductor Serge Koussevitzky, this was the home of the renowned Music Center, the Berkshire festivals, and the Boston Symphony Orchestra. Jerry and I provided the halfway sleepover site. Weeks later our wayfaring relatives, homeward bound, would also drop in to stay with us for several days. They were childless then and so were we. We enjoyed roughing it with them in our cramped one-bedroom, one-bath apartment.

Our musical relatives were grateful when we moved to the house in Silver Spring. We could better accommodate them along with their growing family, three lively children who, when added to our own two boys, brought the total to five kids under the age of six. They always arrived without much advance notice. As soon as they phoned us from the road, I would collect all the sheets and pillows and blankets we owned and set up barracks in the downstairs family room. They hit us like a thunderbolt, often very late at night, three or four hours after they were expected.

Professional musicians keep the same hours as bats and owls. They can drive hundreds of miles at a clip without going to the bathroom. They stay up late telling viola jokes. Their little ones never sleep much, accustomed to dozing off at other musicians' houses and then being awakened and taken home to bed by mommy and daddy when their gigs are over.

Each visit found me feeding the usual early breakfast to my own children and an hour or two later cereal for the other three tots. I'd leave food out for the parents, who had the habit of sleeping late, and then it was lunchtime for my kids, who were punctual noontime eaters. Sixty minutes later the little cousins would be hungry for their lunch, and further down the line, their folks as well. In the afternoon when the adults returned from sightseeing in D.C., they would welcome tea and cake. By then, Jerry would also have laid in a goodly supply of six-packs.

Before dinner, the relatives enjoyed a leisurely cocktail or two, delaying the meal. A chain smoker, smoke forever trailing behind him, Harry always brought along his own hard liquor. It is important to understand that his brood grew up eating late dinners at home after their parents finished rehearsals or performances. But we were a government worker's family, and, unless they were visiting, we played by the rules and ate dinner every evening at six.

Harry, who stayed up till all hours watching late, late-night television, frequently raided our refrigerator for a midnight snack and left dishes in the sink. Although these visits were an added strain to our lives, my brother-in-law, a brilliant symphony orchestra conductor, was an engaging raconteur, full of hilarious insider tales about Leonard Bernstein and violinist Mischa Elman, having worked with both of them. "I hate conducting for opera singers," he said. "They're a pain in the ass." But when Harry's deep baritone voice lapsed into a funny Russian accent as he imitated musical colleagues from the Soviet Union, he held us spellbound and could be forgiven almost anything.

During one visit, we hired a Finnish student nurse from a nearby hospital to babysit with the five children while the adults went out for dinner and a concert. Although the young nurse hailed from a land of the midnight sun, she claimed that evening was the longest she ever spent. Another year when The Call came from the highway, Harry said, "Hey, we have friends from the orchestra who got burned out in a fire, and we're bringing their daughter with us, okay?" Before I could answer, my kinsman-in-law added, "We also have their cat. It's slightly singed, but it's in a box."

The visits continued over a period of fifteen years, tapering off when their children and ours went away to college. In the meantime, it was open season for other family tourists, embarking and disembarking. Jerry's kissing cousins from Georgia would pass through town. His mother stayed with us a couple of times a year. And numerous colleagues from the scientific brigade came to dinner in return for the homey hospitality their wives offered my husband on his visits to laboratories foreign and domestic.

Indeed, at our dining room table we broke bread with many a wandering corrosionist from France, Great Britain, Belgium, Germany, Argentina, Brazil, Australia, New Zealand, Israel, Spain, Egypt, Japan, or the Soviet Union. To prevent one world-famous Russian from defecting to the United States during the Cold War, he was accompanied by an affable KGB agent, who knew less about science than I did. He spent the visit complimenting me on my roast turkey dinner and claiming to be a devotee of klezmer music. On another enchanted evening, a renowned chemist from Brussels sat down to perform Chopin on our dinky little piano and, much to our horror, the bench collapsed under him, bruising his European dignity. American colleagues from industry and academia also dropped anchor with the Krugers and bunked with us. Those were harried days of scuttling around to accommodate houseguests, weeks and months of grocery shopping, cooking, and cleaning up. I wasn't writing much, and who would dream that rewards for our labor would lie ahead in the years to come?

Was I a serious writer? So far, I had dabbled in advertising, dabbled in television, dabbled in journalism. Was freelancing the best I could do? It lacked ballast, not much weight there for stability. I loved the theater, but my life didn't leave enough time or energy to write a full-length play and find a professional outlet for it. Perhaps a graduate degree in drama at Catholic University in Washington could help me make some headway. The school enjoyed an impressive reputation for producing successful playwrights.

"If that's what you want to do," Jerry said, "go for it." But I wanted to be home when our children returned from school each day, and I couldn't schedule a part-time curriculum at the university.

On frequent nights, insomnia prevailed. I took inventory: two healthy, fascinating sons and a loving, supportive husband in a home of our own. What more should a woman want out of her life? Staring into the darkness made me wonder whatever happened to that unfulfilled vision of mine to write a newspaper column.

"I'm thirty-seven," I said to Jerry, "still marking time, still afloat but not swimmingly."

"Something will turn up," Jerry said.

"But what?"

A Freshwater Cove

The answer arrived in the shape of a modern miracle that occurred in a land halfway around the world. Although attacked and outnumbered, the army of that tiny country had won a war in just six days. To mark the occasion, I wrote a poem celebrating the removal of the Jerusalem wall in a hitherto divided city. The local Washington Jewish community newspaper, recently purchased by a retired Newhouse publications editor and his journalist son, liked my poem, "The Wall-Eyed World." They ran it and decided to launch a new feature on their editorial page, a column of light topical verse called "Unholy Writ." Each week the paper received from me a topical poem of twelve or sixteen lines on a Judaic theme. Every couple of months they sent me a paycheck from their National Press Building office in Washington. Soon I was driving into the city to write feature stories and conduct interviews for them.

The arrangement was perfect. I could be at home each afternoon when the boys came back from school, send them off to a piano teacher in the neighborhood, take them to the doctor when they suffered ear infections, and drive them to Hebrew classes. A rushing current of poems poured forth from my electric typewriter. Family, friends, and neighbors would pose the eternal query, "Where do you get your ideas?" It's a well-meant conversation topic that makes writers grit their teeth. Still, it provided the following grist for the "Unholy Writ" mill:

From Moses, osmosis, from hippie, from queen
From Alfred Lord Tennyson, Yitzhak Rabin
From synagogue foibles and clan veneration
From Nasser and Kafka and cross-pollination
From Agnon and Sugar Pops, Vitamin C
From mailman and Mafia, sometimes from me
From Cepacol, Proloid, Excedrin, and booze
From some of my very best friends, who are Jews
From mazel and chutzpah, insomnia, cunning
I get my ideas (when my meter is running).

In the column I mass-produced lighthearted verse about contemporary writers like Philip Roth, Saul Bellow, and Norman Mailer. I. B. Singer and Herman Wouk also received their critical lashes. Then thick and fast, vignettes of family members came bubbling to the surface: immigrant Cousin Jake and his love life among the widows of Florida, a dancing mother at her granddaughter's wedding, my aged father's weakened eyes forcing him to abandon his favorite Yiddish newspaper after reading it for sixty years, spilled kosher wine on Sabbath table cloths, familial strife over who would host the annual Passover Seder, the friendships of Christian and Jewish children, the United Nations as a Tower of Babel, and more seriously, reflections on a merchant whose grocery was burned in the riots that followed Reverend King's assassination. When inspiration evaporated, I would open my copy of *A Book of Jewish Concepts* by Philip Birnbaum, read a random page, and address traditional topics in a contemporary way. There was no end of material to write about.

Readers identified with the poems and wondered why they weren't available in bookstores. Editors and friends tried to interest Jewish book publishers in the idea. They learned there was no market for poetry although the column was popular, syndicated in New York, Pittsburgh, Chicago, Minneapolis, Kansas City, and Dayton. Reprints appeared in the national *Young Judaea* magazine, Hillel campus newspapers, and Conservative and Reform synagogue bulletins from California to North Carolina to Texas.

Most surprising, a note arrived from Christian theologian and writer Michael Novak, who suggested that editors of Catholic magazines might be interested in some of the biblical-themed poems. In another note urging me to continue writing verse based on current events, NBC foreign correspondent Robert St. John said he liked the way I pared down complicated news items into sixteen-line poems. He graciously commented that it would take him a whole book chapter to make the same point.

But newspaper poems are transitory and, with luck, may be posted on refrigerator doors. How could I share my work with the wider world when no established book publisher wanted to gamble on me? While mourning my mother's death in 1969, I battled an increasing sense of inadequacy. Had I failed her and myself as a writer? And then I remembered her final day in the hospital when she slipped into a semi-conscious state. Sitting at her bedside, I heard her whisper with an undeniable sense of conviction, "I made it myself!" As a little girl of ten, an immigrant child who crossed the Atlantic without her mother, she made the arduous journey in the company of strangers. Throughout her entire life she had endured hard times and survived.

"I made it myself," she said. The words haunted me. Perhaps this was her way of sending her daughter a final message. I was forty years old, still rudderless. In what direction should I steer? Writing poems and feature articles for newspapers kept me busy, but it wasn't taking me anywhere. A month after Mom died, I reached a decision.

"I want to establish a small press," I told Jerry, "in memory of my parents."

"Good idea," Jerry said. "People will be able to read your work in book form. Let me know what I can do to help."

With artistic and technical help from Jerry, I plunged into unexplored territory. The first book would bear the same title as my weekly column: *Unholy Writ*, with the subtitle *Jewish Poems for the Non-Neurotic*.

Setting Sail

Selecting the contents, typing and proofreading the manuscript, writing copy for the back cover, all these tasks fell into my area of editorial and advertising expertise. There would be no illustrations, but what to do for a front cover? How could I design a book without spending money to hire professional help, someone skilled in the graphic arts? The roughest of rough layouts had been the extent of my artistic talent at the Kamenetz agency, but I could depend on staff artists to save me. With disciplined design and imaginative color, they knew how to create commercial order out of chaos. Unlike me, they were painstaking, precise with measurements. They could manipulate tiny pieces of paper for paste-ups without sneezing and blowing them away.

Fortunately, I had married a scientist who could print legibly. He was meticulous and *metriculous*, always using the metric system. He even had the foresight to look ahead so that his hand-printed labels on charts and graphs didn't run off the page like mine.

"Will you be a sweetheart and design a cover for me?" I asked, convinced he would turn me down. He was busy preparing an upcoming paper to be delivered at an international conference on the passivity of metals.

"Of course," he said. My husband always took time out to rescue me from disasters, mostly of my own making.

On his lunch hour the next day, Jerry created the cover, thick black cursive script lettering against a white background. At my suggestion he added the subtitle printed in a circular design for which he used a compass, a metal gadget I remembered employing unsuccessfully in high school geometry class.

"The finished product seems a little austere," I said when he showed it to me.

"That," Jerry said smiling, "is its charm."

Where could we find an inexpensive printer adept at bookbinding? In a copy of the *Saturday Review*, I found a one-inch ad for a New Jersey company that promised, "We do book publishing at affordable prices! Send for our brochure!" Perhaps this printing plant was as down-to-earth as its advertising. We needed an ordinary print shop, not a vanity press. Doing business with a small place made good sense; I would feel freer to ask stupid questions. A big-city outfit might humiliate me for not using the required professional jargon.

Mr. Ritter, owner and sole employee, got in touch with me right away. He mailed a simple little booklet to explain the difference between hot type and cold type. I had never thought much about either one. Cold type, the method he used, involved some sort of electric photographic process I didn't exactly understand. His brochure included fonts, and he suggested that I could save money with a substantial order of three thousand copies, which happened to be the most his press could handle at one time. The fewer the copies, he noted, the higher the bill.

"How many books do you think we need?" I asked.

"Lots," Jerry said. "People tell me they read your 'Unholy Writ' column in the paper before anything else."

"I want to believe them," I said, "but did you ever think they're lying in their teeth?"

Even so, flattery always went to my head. I had received fan mail from elderly folks in Pittsburgh and Kansas City and even a marriage proposal from a prisoner at Leavenworth. Maybe my work appealed to more people than I thought. That's why Mr. Ritter received an order for three thousand copies. Surely that would take care of the debut edition, and who knew, maybe a second printing and a third and a fourth would come to pass. Cartons of the books arrived on time for a local book festival. With stratospheric expectations, I loaded up the car with one hundred copies. We sold four.

After we scattered review copies in all directions, the investment in postage began to bear fruit, especially this from a *Hadassah* magazine book critic:

> Excursion into the wonderful world of Jewish laughter . . . the poems are little gems that you will wish to read and reread, to share with friends and family. . . . She writes with . . . a sigh for the lost past and an ache for Jewish sorrows, with truth and

> sound sense. And without acrimony, cynicism, defensiveness or moralizing. Welcome to a fresh new voice . . . it should be heard and enjoyed.

But this poet's life, like the policeman's lot, was not an easy one. Fast-running currents swept me far from my destination, and ahead lay gales galeing, eddies eddying, and in the background a hearty chorus of "Britannia Rules the Waves."

The River Cam

There are more relaxing ways to spend the time than launching a book, and I was no well-seasoned captain of my fate. Life becomes hectic, especially if you've just bought a new house and you're selling the old one and find yourself swamped with moving to another suburb closer to where your spouse works, and your first-born is scheduled for his Bar Mitzvah two weeks after the family settles into a new location.

If the Devil and I hadn't been so busy in the details of writing and publishing, I should have realized that choppy waters lay ahead. The previous fall Jerry was invited to present a paper on his work at an Electrochemical Society conference on the passivity of metals.

"How would you like to go to Cambridge next summer?" he asked.

"Go to Boston with you?" I asked, not even looking up. It was late evening; I sat at the dining room table where I stuffed review copies of *Unholy Writ* into plain brown kraft envelopes stamped Fourth Class Mail. It would take only a twelve-cent stamp for each paperback.

"No, England. Cambridge University."

"You want to take me with you?"

"The boys, too."

Jerry had a plan. For our older son's upcoming Bar Mitzvah in June 1970, we would avoid the lavish reception and emphasize the importance of religious aspects, the traditional readings from the Torah and the Haftorah. All year at our synagogue, Lenny had been preparing for the rite of passage with a ferocious cantor of whom our son and his fellow classmates were terrified. So was I.

My husband suggested we ignore the usual commercial frivolity accompanying the milestone event. Instead, we signed on to a dairy lunch served after Sabbath services in the synagogue social hall. It would be open to the congregation. This would be followed by a nighttime private dinner for friends and family at our new house. Like our wedding, our Bar Mitzvah reception would be subdued. Above all, we were determined not to go overboard with wasteful frills like renting Constitution Hall in Washington for a party site or offering Mick Jagger as entertainment.

"Let's control the celebration," Jerry said of the event. "The celebration will not control us. And we'll use whatever money we save to take all four of us on a grand tour of England."

In the Saturday-morning service, our son chanted movingly with no hitches and did us proud. That evening a caterer installed tables and chairs throughout our house, upstairs in the living room/dining room, and downstairs in the recreation room. Our guests at the sit-down dinner included a handful of our son's Hebrew School classmates and friends from junior high. We hired a wandering accordionist for background music and raided Jerry's record collection of Yiddish klezmer and folk melodies. Sadly, the only essentials missing from our Bar Mitzvah joy were three faces, those of my elderly parents and Jerry's father.

Ahead lay London. From the nerve-wracking 747 flight over the Atlantic, I discovered that I was not cut out for international travel. The boys and Jerry accepted it all in wonder, but I was a wreck every air mile of the way. The plane had undergone a two-hour delay at Kennedy Airport, and after hectic weeks of moving to a new house, planning a Bar Mitzvah, and packing for the family in the midst of publishing a book, I was too exhausted to eat the steak meal served at midnight by a stewardess who kept waking me up.

Arriving at Heathrow at about six in the morning, I remember Jerry's advice that we'd be better able to fight off our jet lag if we didn't try to sleep the rest of the day. All I remember was recording on a 3 x 5-inch pad, "Tuesday came in here somewhere. It was very short, and we ate kidney pie, I think."

Comparatively rested, the next day by bus we traveled the well-trampled route of most tourists who flock to London: the boats on the Thames, the majesty of Parliament and Westminster Abbey, St. Paul's, Piccadilly Circus, Buckingham Palace, Trafalgar Square, Regent Street, Tower Bridge, and Oxford Street. They triggered memories of wartime newsreels and stiff-upper-lip royalty in massive flowery hats. The sidewalks spoke to me in posh British accents: Berkeley Square, where a nightingale was reported to have sung; Regent Street, where the doctors flourished. At one point I silently repeated the lines of a favorite Rose Fyleman poem: *Yesterday in Oxford Street, oh, what d'you think, / my dears?* Answer: She saw the fairy queen riding on a motorbus. Passing years have transformed the meaning of "fairy" and "queen," but it remains a charming poem for very young children. Our tour ended at the dreary graveyard of Madame Tussaud's waxworks, not very lively, and neither were we.

I spent the next day in bed while the rest of our family saw Queen Elizabeth riding in a gilded carriage on her way to open Parliament. Jerry brought me a "salt beef" sandwich from Feld's, a venerable kosher restaurant in the heart of old London. Later we ate dinner there. At tables all around us sat, as I noted in my journal, "Jewish faces, but not American-Jewish faces." They reminded me of characters in George Eliot's *Daniel Deronda* or Israel Zangwill's *Children of the Ghetto.*

In the few days before heading for Cambridge, we attended a performance of Agatha Christie's *The Mousetrap,* running consecutively since time began. We took the Underground to Whitechapel for more of that salt beef. The old Jewish section with its pushcarts and open markets recalled to me Reuben, my father's shoemaker brother, who had migrated from Lithuania to England and lived there until he joined other family members in East Baltimore. Did he shop at those same markets? Did he walk Jewry Street? Once again, Zangwill hovered close by.

But of all the sights we encountered, including the Changing of the Guard at the Tower of London, Speakers' Corner at Hyde Park entertained us most. We expected to see English hippies or Beatles worshippers, but instead my 1970 journal described a more eccentric crowd.

> Scattered throughout the greenery is a gaggle of kooks only the British could assemble. All the eccentric characters I've ever read about in Dickens, Thackeray, and the Brontë sisters had been dropped down from heaven or shoved up from hell to their proper place in Hyde Park. Here amidst the well-kept grounds, they were surrounded by puddles of motley people assembled for one purpose only: to heckle the speakers.

We were very much taken with a scrawny woman in a shabby flowered housedress that covered her front except for three missing buttons. She clutched a brown spiral notebook and consulted it every now and then as she fired questions like bullets into the ebbing and flowing crowd around her: (1) How old is the British Empire? (2) What is the tallest hotel in the world? (3) Australia covers how many square miles? What amused us was she never waited for any response, immediately supplied the answer, and continued down the list.

Fascinated, we moved on to a preacher of some sort plagued by one of his listeners who yelled, "Ah, sit down. I've been listening to you for fifteen years and you never say anything and neither does the Archbishop of Canterbury." The speaker, in a black shirt and turned white collar, answered back, "Well, the Bishop of Canterbury is a liar!" And his heckler replied, "That's wot 'e gets paid for!"

"Love thy neighbor!" the self-proclaimed man of the cloth roared with arms raised.

"You haven't seen my neighbor," the same heckler called out. Looking back, I think this was staged, a dialogue that the two had rehearsed beforehand and presented several times each day for the benefit of gullible tourists like us.

A more serious performance included an African blasting American policy in Vietnam. A few yards away a disheveled drunk made pig calls interwoven with rude jokes, as the English called them. A head-shaven Hari Krishna group, preparing to hold a parade, daubed white paint on their noses and lifted homemade signs that read "Peace and Contemplation."

Then on to Liverpool Station and the train to Cambridge and a friendly woman who sat with us describing the breathtaking countryside in her beloved Cornwall and her "dear little dog." "One can become so attached to animals, can't one?" Not a Monty Python caricature of British housewives, she reminded me of Celia Johnson, the sad-eyed actress who appeared with Trevor Howard in *Brief Encounter.*

Although medieval buildings and the greenest of green lawns impressed us at Cambridge, we were relieved to be assigned two rooms in Churchill College, the newest and most modern of the Cambridge colleges. When traveling with boys, ages thirteen and eleven, we American parents learn fast that convenience is more important than roughing it in historic edifices built four centuries before our Jamestown colony in Virginia.

Facing an international gathering of scientists in such an auspicious setting overwhelmed a small-town girl like me. When I closed my eyes that night after a draining day of train stations, tending to our children, and trying to remember the names of Jerry's colleagues assembled from six of the world's seven continents, I half-slept in feverish snatches. All the books, all the English authors I had ever read, from Shakespeare to Fielding to Butler to Carlyle to Kipling to Galsworthy to Mansfield to Amis, swirled around my bed and chanted, "You're here now, old girl. See for yourself."

While Jerry attended endless meetings and listened to papers being read by his esteemed colleagues, the boys and I explored the immaculately kept grounds. We discovered a modest-sized waterway, the Cam River, flowing through the medieval city of Cambridge, and noted the bridges that spanned it. I had never given any thought to it before, but our stroll through Cambridge suggested that it must have been named for the numerous bridges over the Cam River. It started, I was later told, with one great bridge linking land originally reached by ferry. The current town name is derived from Grantebrycge or Grantabridge and later, Cantabridgia, which is what people called the university in its earliest days around 1209. I learned that the abbreviation "Cantab" was used to indicate a Cambridge graduate or degree.

Our wanderings took us through an area known as the Backs, a series of beautifully kept gardens and greenery behind the old colleges that overlooked the river. When we stopped to buy fruit at a street stall in town, the owner in a shabby cardigan apologized to us.

"Sorry, luv," she said. "But those bananas are dear, and I must ask you to pay me one and six." I assured the good-natured soul, "That's perfectly all right," and not knowing how the price tag translated into American dollars and cents, handed her a fistful of British money and informed her to keep the change. We were ugly Americans on holiday and didn't care how much bananas cost.

At a dusty, overstuffed bookstore with wares that spilled out onto the street, I found a series of tiny paperbacks that gave wry advice on how to fake one's way through contemporary British culture. One cover stopped me in my tracks: *Bluff Your Way in the Theater: Know your jargon and hold your own in any company / Instant Erudition*. It belonged to a long line of books called "The Bluffer's Series," copyright by Wolfe Publishing Ltd., London. Here was material to help me make meaningfully outrageous remarks in conversations with English-speaking PhDs at the conference, many of them dons from Cambridge and prestigious universities on the Continent.

Not all the attending scientists were intensely polite Brits. The next day a wild-eyed Romanian physicist offered to take the boys and me on a nautical outing. Jerry was occupied with meetings all morning, and this obviously mad scientist, who resembled the menacing actor Peter Lorre, jumped out from behind some well-clipped bushes. His name was Dr. Lupescu or Ionescu or some such name that ended in the letter *u*, and he refused to accept my refusal to spend a morning in his company.

"I'll take you punting on the Cam," he announced. "Do not make arguments."

Neither my sons nor I knew what punting was. In fact, we couldn't quite figure out just what he wanted to do with us, and did he say "pointing on the Cam"? Or "painting"? Or "panting"?

He insisted on this mysterious excursion even when I pointedly told him we didn't care to go. When we arrived at the water's edge, he found a flat-bottomed boat, acquired a tall pole, hurried us into the bobbing vessel, and proceeded to propel us through the shallow stream by jamming the pole into the river, gondolier style.

"See that spot over there," he said, pointing to a mound of earth next to the water. "When I was a student here at Cambridge, a chorus from the college would gather there to sing madrigals."

It seemed an ideal rustic spot to sing madrigals. "But," he continued, "during the concert, my friends floated a fleet of chamber pots on the river. We put a candle inside each one." He burst into a belly laugh. "One year I climbed a church tower and put a chamber pot on top."

He stopped laughing. "I'm getting tired," he said. "Here," he pushed the pole into my hands, "you do this for a while."

"No, thanks," I said, remembering my clumsiness when faced with unknown gadgetry. "You didn't include this in your invitation."

"The only way you'll learn how to punt," he said, not smiling, "is to do it. If you don't, I'll have to force you to do it."

I wanted to relieve the tension and appear brave to my children. "You'd better not or you'll see what happens to you."

"Is that a threat?" he asked in what sounded like a verifiable snarl.

I lost my head at that point. "Yes. Yes, it is."

He frowned. It amazed me that he took all this seriously. The man expected me to stand up in that flimsy boat and use a pole twice my size to propel us through the water.

"No." Shaken, I fumbled for words. "I-I m-mean, it's not safe." The boys seemed undisturbed by the exchange. To them, this was simply adult banter to be ignored.

"Here." The gentleman thrust the wooden pole in my direction.

"No." Mutiny on the *Bounty*! "What if I lose my balance and fall into the water?" I asked.

"It's not deep. You can walk to shore."

"But I'll get all wet."

He lost his patience with me at that point, abandoned the pole, bodily picked me up, and held me in his Balkan arms. "You'll get wet anyway," he said, "because if you don't cooperate, I intend to toss you into the water."

My sons watched, waiting for the next scene in this made-for-TV movie. There was no way out. I agreed to learn how to punt.

"Just put me down," I said. He released me and thrust that infernal pole into my hands. On my first try, I somehow rammed the thing into an underwater sewer grating. The boat wouldn't budge. Dr. U made no comment and dislodged the pole. Then, without a further word, he quietly taught my sons how to punt. Although they were more adept at it than their mother, the skill has never made a great difference in their lives.

On our last day at Cambridge, while the air was filled fond goodbyes spoken in garbled tongues, a leader of the conference, Mr. Shandy (not his real name), shook our hands and asked about our plans for the remainder of the trip. Jerry spoke of our British rail pass and a possible overnight trip north to Edinburgh.

"If you've nothing better to do," Mr. Shandy said in a casual way, "come to Frinton-on-Sea. My wife runs a summer theater there." At that moment my purchase of the *Bluffer's Guide* seemed a wise move. On the train, I studied hard, skimming through the section on "Jobs in the Theatre," which claimed, "The bluffer must know who's who backstage or he will inevitably get into a nasty tangle." Since having already engaged in a nasty tangle with the damned punting, I was anxious to avoid any more gaffes. It didn't seem necessary to read every word, however, and I doubted that we would be allowed to go backstage anyway. Even if we did, my little booklet warned, "Bluffers should give the impression that they know the names of stage-door keepers . . . keep to Alf, Bert and Fred and you should be safe."

Frinton turned out to be a dismal resort on the North Sea, where shivering but optimistic English folks on holiday basked under a reluctant sun. Approaching the town, I noticed two forlorn palm trees, probably Caribbean imports planted to cheer up tourists brave enough to wear their swimsuits. That night we attended the opening of a play called *Birthday Honours*, directed by Mrs. Shandy, who also cranked the 1930s phonograph to provide mood music. The acting was not the caliber of *Masterpiece Theatre* on our local public broadcasting station but slightly better than the community amateur group to which I once belonged. Mr. Shandy, whose ample measurements (and ego to match) must have been akin to Winston Churchill's, served as impresario and head usher. In a dazzling white tuxedo, he stood at the entrance to the hall, collected tickets, and shook hands with incoming audience members.

Our reception by Mr. and Mrs. Shandy reflected that incomparable British attitude that signals, "Come close, but would you mind terribly not coming too close?" When Mr. Shandy first invited us to Frinton, he didn't think we would come with our two young boys in tow. In fact, he and his wife seemed startled that we showed up, but, stiff upper lip, they made the best of it. After all, we did buy four tickets.

One positive comment on Frinton is necessary here. For years following our trip, the resort provided fodder for conversations we had with smug travelers who had visited remote places like Baffin Bay or the lost continent of Atlantis.

"How nice," Jerry and I would say, playing the final card in a satisfying game of international travel one-upmanship, "but have you ever been to Frinton-on-Sea?"

"No."

"Ah, Frinton is spectacular in July!" Jerry would answer.

Two years later we repeated ourselves when our younger son reached Bar Mitzvah age. Again, we emphasized the religious service at which our child excelled. Our plan provided a dairy lunch for all in attendance and a pleasant dinner and home reception later for relatives and close friends. Although we weathered the criticisms of hard-core family grouches who gossiped about what they considered our miserly approach, we didn't care a whit. A week later, passports in hand, the four of us boarded a plane headed for South America.

Landlocked in the Andes

Jerry had been invited to present a paper and conduct a week-long course at the University of La Plata in Argentina, a marvelous opportunity for a tour of several South American cities. On our way to Buenos Aires we stopped to see the colonial city of Quito and stand on the invisible line that marked the Equator; and then on to Lima, where we soared in a small plane over the Andes and landed at Cuzco, more than thirteen thousand feet above sea level. To help us adjust to breathing air thinner than a spider's web, our hotel served us a nameless concoction that must have contained cacao, because all four of us immediately fell into a deep sleep. My dream was the weirdest, a nightmare about Emily Dickinson surrounded by a herd of white mice. (Kick that one around, Dr. Freud.) Refreshed, we headed next day to the ancient city of the Incas, Machu Picchu, where, according to my journal notes, I walked fascinated through the ruins of a lost civilization and was bitten all over by invisible insects known as no-see-ums.

Then on to cosmopolitan Buenos Aires, still filled with traces of the displaced Perón regime. Although Juan Perón had died, his wife would later return from exile to rule. I saw half-hidden signs that read "Evita Viva!" We toured the European-style city, but while Jerry worked at the university, I hesitated to cover much territory, a woman alone, sightseeing with children and no knowledge of Spanish. In a pervading atmosphere of political unrest, I feared exposing ourselves to kidnapping by violent followers of Perón, his *descamisados*, also known as "the shirtless ones." Jerry and his colleagues at La

Plata laughed at my fears, but I was a mother hen who took no chances when it came to my boys.

We kept to the streets close to the downtown hotel and enjoyed tea and cakes at the nearest *confiteria*. Dinner was served always at nine o'clock, when the streets came alive with crowds out to enjoy themselves. Our kind hosts and dear friends at the university showed us the Casa Rosada, the palatial city hall, and took us on side trips to the Pampas and to a San Martín Day military parade on a damp wintry afternoon. It was during festivities honoring Simón Bolívar that I came down with one of my world-class colds, which introduced me to a local pharmacist who spoke little English, and my college minor in French didn't help a bit. The pervasive inflation and the ever-changing currency stymied me. I gave up trying to determine how many Old Pesos equaled New Pesos.

Final stop was Rio de Janeiro, where we took a cable car high over the waters to Sugar Loaf and Corcovado. The view of Guanabara Bay convinced me that Rio was one of the most exquisite port cities of them all. Since Jerry detested heights, it was his least favorite part of the trip. Later he did enjoy talking corrosion with a Brazilian friend and colleague who guided us across magnificent Copacabana beach. Throughout the South American trip, Jerry managed, as usual, to carry on lively chats in his nonexistent Spanish with friendly cab drivers and waiters. To this day, our sons still joke about his fruitless attempts to use an odd Spanish word he learned for "epaulets." It was not something that popped up in casual conversations. By the time we reached Brazil, my husband was too tired to mangle the Portuguese language.

Anchors Aweigh

Amidst all the hurly-burly transpiring in that decade, my "Unholy Writ" column continued with new verses each week for Washington and New York readers as well as those in other cities. The poems accumulated at a rapid pace. When I reached a total of an additional hundred poems, it was time for a sequel, *More Unholy Writ: Jewish Verses and Vices*. Our printer, Mr. Ritter, was still in business, and he appreciated the order for three thousand copies so much he had his son drive down to Maryland from New Jersey with the precious cargo loaded into the trunk of his Chevrolet.

The second book included more of what an editor once called "rhymed essays." Mindful of the disintegration of European colonialism in Africa, revolutions in South America, and popular books loaded with personal angst and discontent with authority, my work turned outward more often to reflect people, literature, and places that we visited during this decade. The travel increased my hunger for reading old and contemporary authors. In Buenos Aires I located an English bookstore where I found a rare copy of Somerset Maugham's *Cakes and Ale*. I also discovered Gabriel García Márquez and Robertson Davies and Iris Murdoch and Margaret Atwood and Doris Lessing. I even finished reading a tiny volume purchased at a secondhand bookstore when we were in Cambridge. It was the witty novel *Sybil* by Benjamin Disraeli, England's prime minister in 1868 and then again from 1874 to 1880. The gifted politician/statesman/author fascinated me. Inspired by his book and by visits to the United Kingdom, I wrote the following:

Old Westminster Abbey is gray in the rain
And wet with gray mobs from a gray subway train
Or gray as worn pomp, aspiration grown grizzled
Or cloudy as heroes whose vision has fizzled.
The statues line up like live carnival freaks
And here in his robe à la Romans and Greeks
Disraeli, Disraeli, Victoria's pet
Across the road Parliament struggles with debt.
The Irish, the dockers, the Common Mart Crew
While in the cathedral, a lonely stone Jew
Converted by chance to Episcopal ways
First Earl of Beaconsfield named in those days
Forgets a dead Covenant, sips from the Grail
Aloof from Sephardim, the tortuous wail.
Among England's great there is nowhere to hide
As tourists collect around statue and guide
"Our JEWISH prime minister!" booms through the hall
And outside the gray rain continues to fall.

During the upcoming 1972 election year, my newspaper poems turned openly political. "Mezuzah" refers to a tiny scroll of parchment bearing verses from Deuteronomy, tucked into a metal, wood, or plastic container attached to the right side of doorposts in Jewish homes. The mezuzah has a voice and speaks directly to the reader about door-to-door candidates seeking votes. It finishes with the thought that throughout the ages, threatening civilizations have stormed peaceful thresholds and concludes:

Passerby, behold my message
Power stops to pay a call
Pounding at the door, then passing
A mezuzah sees it all.

"Which Way the Wind" also dealt in couplets with the '70s economy and the problem of "stagflation." It suggested that Wall Street emulate the ancient practice in Temple times of burnt offerings. Sages would predict the events of the year ahead by observing how the wind blew:

Should the economists falter or tire
Let's throw another ox out on the fire.
No need for clamping a wage or price freeze
Pry off the ceiling and audit that breeze.

Potomac Fever

One way or another, inhabitants of the Washington, D.C. area can't avoid politics. We are the quintessential company town. Although the Hatch Act prevented my husband, a government employee, from active participation, the restriction didn't apply to me. During the election of 1972, I volunteered to help locally during the Maryland Democratic primary. My job was to offer upbeat Hubert Humphrey pamphlets to all who passed by on their way to our neighborhood polling place.

It was a dark morning, and a certain uneasy pall matched the cloudy weather. One day earlier, Governor George Wallace, the demagogic candidate from Alabama, had been wounded in an assassination attempt in nearby Laurel, Maryland. But so far in my precinct, things moved along smoothly, and black voters rewarded me with affirmative smiles and friendly comments when they noticed Vice President Humphrey's photo on the handout.

"Best man on the ticket!" they said, with thumbs-up gestures.

Encouraged by Americans exercising their constitutional rights, I stayed at my post most of the morning. And then an unshaven, beer-bellied man snatched a pamphlet out of my hand, held it up, pointed to the picture of Humphrey, and shouted, "*He's* the one who should have been shot!"

Horrified, I moved away from him fast. There is never a place for violence in the politics of a democratic republic. That's not the America our immigrant parents embraced in their search for a better life. As the man spouted bigoted reasons to sustain his remarks, he continued to follow me. I tried to put distance between us, not answering him because he might be carrying a gun. When he realized there would be no verbal response from me, he disappeared into the crowd.

That fall, I volunteered to become a judge inside the polls to make sure no fraudulent voting occurred. Democratic candidate George McGovern faced off against the incumbent president, Richard Nixon, and the reader knows what came next. The "Unholy Writ" newspaper column could not ignore the Watergate scandal and its aftermath. Poems on the subject once again piled up on my desk. I wanted to go beyond the confines of an immediate Jewish milieu. The country's disillusionment, enhanced by Watergate and the resignation of a president, touched all Americans deeply. A more patriotic theme awaited around the corner.

With the approach of the American Revolution Bicentennial in 1976, I convinced myself to undertake a commemorative, but lighthearted, poetry collection, based on the country's history. Because my parents had arrived at Baltimore Harbor in 1898, I felt less connection to Plymouth Rock than to the European immigrants, ordinary folks like my own family, who entered the country between the 1880s and the 1920s. Part One of the as yet untitled new book, "A Frontier Past Tense," covered distant historical events between 1876 and 1900, including a contemporary look at post–Civil War robber barons, the invention of barbed wire, do-nothing presidents during the Gilded Age, World War I, and the ambivalence of Woodrow Wilson.

To parallel the events of the late nineteenth and early twentieth centuries, I introduced a peripheral character named Frank, roughly based on my father, born in 1877. As a young man Frank abandoned Lithuania for America, where he joined the U.S. Army and served in the Spanish-American War. Here I blended the life stories of my father and the experiences of my mother's brother Frank, who, unlike my father, did enlist in the U.S. Army and was stationed in sweltering Florida during the war with Spain. In exchange for his services, my uncle became an American citizen. I still remember the old man's description of hardtack, a tooth-breaking biscuit made of flour and water. "Something that wasn't fit to put in your mouth," he said.

Part Two of the book was quasi-autobiographical, introducing Clara, a character modeled after my mother, and memories of a small-town childhood during World War II. It was not difficult to present highlights of my own era, extending from the 1930s through the '70s. I included heroes like Adlai Stevenson and Eleanor Roosevelt as well as references to the short-lived presidency of Gerald Ford. An eight-line poem titled "Fall Out" wondered:

Who'll buy the books on Watergate?
Who'll fill a penitent's pocket?
Ah, Batman insignia, Mickey Mouse ears
Hats à la Davy Crockett.

The point was that human beings would exploit anything to make a buck.

"I need a book title," I said to Jerry one night after dinner, "something broad enough to cover a casual stroll through history."

He looked thoughtful. "It shouldn't be stuffy. It ought to reflect something meaningful to you on a personal level."

"I can't pretend to be descended from Washington or Jefferson," I said. "My family in America goes back only seventy-five years. They came around 1898."

"Pretty impressive," Jerry said. "My father came in 1914."

A hidden memory surfaced. "Wait," I said. "I never told you this before but the last time after the Gordon Conference, remember when we stopped off in Massachusetts and visited the spot where the American Revolution began?"

"Concord," he said, "home of the shot heard round the world."

"I remember looking down at the water and having the strangest feeling that I had been there before. It was all familiar territory to me—sky, trees, the stream, the land on either side."

"We had never visited there. You've seen lots of rivers and streams since you married me. It just reminded you of other places."

I shook my head. "No, this was different. I felt it was home. It was a haunted kind of moment, sort of eerie, mystical. And maybe that explains why I'm writing the book, instructed by a voice from beyond."

Jerry looked at me with a scientist's skeptical eye and then commented dryly, "You're freaking me out, Moll." We stared at each other for three seconds before breaking into uncontrollable laughter. Neither of us believed in the occult. That night I dreamed of my grandfather, father, uncle, and three of their cousins. All of them had been cobblers in Lithuania. After they arrived in this country, they used their awls and hammers to mend boots, and later, one by one, opened shoe stores. When I woke up the next morning, the perfect title wafted into sight: *Yankee Shoes: A Light Verse Saunter Through Our Second Hundred Years.*

Sea Legs

As I continued to research and write, the historical poems flowed at a brisk rate, but we needed an eye-catching cover for the book. Although mail orders for earlier books continued to keep our cottage industry afloat, we couldn't afford a professional artist. Instead, I turned to the in-house miracle worker, who had created covers for the first two poetry collections.

"Can't this time," Jerry said. Ahead of him lay a hectic season of travel to industrial, academic, and government laboratories in cities and towns all over the country. "Got to keep beating the bushes for support these days," he said. "The high interest rates have everybody worried."

He did find time, however, to locate a young Bureau of Standards lab technician, who said he could draw a little, and we hired him. Overnight, he produced the cover, featuring a single oversized shoe. More than an ordinary piece of footwear, he created a fashionable, lace-up granny boot.

Falling back on my advertising background, I created layouts for each of the one hundred pages in a detailed "dummy" for the printer. My older son, a high school senior, typed the final draft of the manuscript. To proofread while I fired off press releases to national and local media, we tracked down the stay-at-home wife of a chemist in Jerry's carpool. Although we enlarged our rather limited mailing list to include museums, college libraries, and Bicentennial committees in each of the fifty states, the competition for publicity in Washington and the rest of the country was overwhelming in 1975 and '76. Most major publishers and authors hawked all manner of books with historic or patriotic themes.

The in-house Maryben Books circulation department, composed of our two teenage sons and me, inundated the post office with what seemed like tons of free review copies. In this dark age before the Internet, I dashed hither and yon to the library reference room, where I hand-copied lists of bookstores, historical societies, libraries, museums, and gift shops. Response was not overwhelming, merely a brief mention in a couple of local newspapers. Baker & Taylor, the wholesale book distributors, sent an occasional order for single copies initiated by stores receiving requests from individual customers. Friends at Jewish newspapers in Washington and Pittsburgh came through with free publicity. Despite all that effort, it was time to broaden the *Yankee Shoes* base, but how?

During that year I received an unexpected phone call. "Would you be interested in joining our Washington-area alumnae society of Mortar Board?" the friendly voice on the line asked.

As a junior at the University of Maryland twenty-five years earlier, I had been tapped for this national college honor society, which highlights leadership, scholarship, and service. It had meant much on campus, but little in the business world. Now after all this time, someone in the local branch had discovered *Yankee Shoes* and recommended me as a potential member.

The District of Columbia group consisted of women originally from all parts of the country. Many had attended exclusive prep schools and Seven Sisters colleges. A few held important positions in the federal government or academia, but most from my generation were content to serve as wives of prominent men, including high-level Foreign Service diplomats. Several lived in exclusive sections of Washington and Chevy Chase, Maryland, places that had supposedly lifted restrictions against letting Jews move into their pristine neighborhoods. The highest-ranking member, their jewel in the crown, was married to a member of Richard Nixon's cabinet. She later enlisted his daughter Julie to speak at the Mortar Board annual luncheon.

The rarefied membership, good Republicans all, was a far cry from Hadassah, Pioneer Women (Na'amat), and the synagogue and temple sisterhoods where I gave numerous readings of the *Unholy* books. Mortar Board alumnae became a perfect market for *Yankee Shoes*. I labored long and hard on producing a monthly newsletter for them, and unfortunately, the following year they elected me president of the chapter. I recall how a lovely lady from a First Family of Virginia held up my new book and introduced me to her high-society friends with the immortal words, "Her family are shoe people." It brought a smile to the face of this immigrant shoemaker's daughter.

As Jerry summarized it, "The Rockefellers are oil people, and Mollee's are shoe people."

Posturing through Passivity

Yankee Shoes struggled to stay alive. I reached out to the American Revolution Bicentennial Committee by sending them free copies. John Warner, later a Virginia senator and husband (briefly) of Elizabeth Taylor, served as chairman of that auspicious group. He said he liked *Yankee Shoes* and would include it in the Bicentennial archive. The Capital Chapter of the National League of American Pen Women, a group of professional women in the arts, invited me to join the Washington branch. I rarely attended meetings, but through them I did attend a White House tea hosted by Rosalynn Carter and another tea at the Hillwood estate, where heiress Marjorie Merriweather Post, deaf, over eighty, but still a beautiful woman, greeted us warmly. Her former palatial home in Florida, Mar-a-Lago, is now more famous than she ever was.

I remember the 1970s as an exhausting decade, a fragmented one for me as well as for Jerry. His mother in her Eastern European accent would often refer to him as "Jerome, the Traveling Salesman." Although we laughed at that, her characterization was apt. He toted Science in his carry-on bag; he shared his findings with colleagues, domestic and foreign. Jerry's professional obligations increased as those years passed. He agreed to serve as co-chairman of the Fourth International Symposium on Passivity of Metals, sponsored by the Electrochemical Society. Now in a position of power, my husband put the question to me gently.

"How would you like to be my First Lady of the whole waxworks?"

At the time, I was swamped with writing my newspaper column, giving readings of *Yankee Shoes* in Boston and New York, creating Mortar Board alumnae programs, and teaching creative writing and journalism classes to senior adults at a nearby community center. On request from a national charity that sponsored an international hospital, I had just finished writing and presenting at a fundraising donor banquet a serious ode to the Israeli heroes of Entebbe, the soldiers who landed in Uganda and rescued hostages held by the Amin regime. And now my man wanted me to play official hostess of another international science wingding?

"Where?" I asked, fearing another unexpected jaunt abroad. "Xanadu? Shangri-La?"

"Airlic," he said. "In October." He went on to describe a remote meeting place in Virginia, a vast estate available to organizations seeking to hold important events near the nation's capital.

"We'll stay there for about a week," he continued. "You'll enjoy taking a break, and you already know a lot of the people who'll be there." He rattled off the names of men whom we had fed and housed at our Rockville home. "Come on," he begged, "the kids are away at college now. You're free at last."

When Jerry saw how reluctant I was to be away from home for a week in the middle of my own commitments, he dangled one more enticing tidbit. "I'm in charge of the program for the banquet at the end of the conference," he said. "You could make your Electrochemical Society debut with a humorous monologue. Or read some of your light verse."

"From *Yankee Shoes*?"

"Whatever you wish. Keep it short and keep it light. Your audience will love it."

"Especially after they've been hitting the wine all evening," I said.

And that was how this English major summoned the chutzpah to deliver a spoof entitled "A Scientific Paper at the Fourth International Symposium on Passivity from the Laboratory of M. Kruger." The good Lord knows I was ill equipped to speak on the anodic breakdown of passive films on corroded surfaces, but writers can be intrepid, and here is what that distinguished body of gentlemen and ladies from the UK, Japan, Australia, Germany, France, Belgium, Argentina, Egypt, Brazil, and Israel, as well as American representatives from industry, government, and academia, heard that evening of the grand banquet:

> Distinguished guests, patient wives, Busy Husband. Earlier this week I had hoped to be able to present to the symposium a paper that I had written. I really don't know anything

about the subject, but for the past twenty-two years I have been married to a physical chemist or chemical physicist or something like that.

Because of him I became acquainted with C. P. Snow's lectures on the gap that exists between the humanist (me) and the scientist (him). And I thought, how can I, as a professional writer, become a little matchmaker and bring these two disciplines together? Well, what better way than for me to write a folk opera based on the noble subject of Passivity?

Now since I am not a scientist, it first was necessary for me to do some serious scholarly research on the topic. So I approached my husband and I said to him, "Can you give me some specific technical scientific background for my opera?" He obliged by explaining to me the Second Law of Thermodynamics. I was impressed. And having in this manner completed my basic research, I went off to write a passivity folk opera in thirteen acts.

I had hoped to bring my opera here tonight to perform it for you. But I couldn't find it. Like the twenty-nine missing plays of Aristophanes, my opera is unfortunately lost forever. (My husband threw it into the fire and burned it.)

Frankly, I can't see why anyone would want to burn a thirteen-act folk opera which deals in a shockingly realistic way with the Second Law of Thermodynamics. You see, it's the story of a boy corrosion scientist and a girl corrosion scientist who fall in love. But throughout the story the boy, Don José, and the girl, Agatha, are competing to see who can publish the most scientific papers over a thirty-day period.

As it usually happens in folk operas, the heroine, Agatha, was stolen by a band of wandering corrosion scientists, who carried her off to a meeting of the Electrochemical Society at the Warrenton Howard Johnson's.

Thirty years later she meets Don José, a Scotsman, and there is a passionate seduction scene, as in Bizet's *Carmen*, between Agatha and her lover. It takes place at the nuclear reactor. Later Agatha stuns the scientific world with a paper on the Second Law of Thermodynamics. (I had to include that somewhere.) She delivers this paper at the National Academy of Sciences.

Unfortunately, her hot Mediterranean blood is her undoing. She comes to the lectern in an off-the-shoulder blouse, colorful beads around her neck, and between her teeth a Luggin capillary. Then she walks through the audience composed of her distinguished colleagues, rumpling their hair, and singing sexy songs, one of which is entitled "Is There No Hope for My Wrong Tafel Slope?"*

But she is thrown out of the National Academy of Sciences. And then the hero, Don José, surges ahead with still another paper on the Second Law of Thermodynamics . . . because that's the only science I know anything about. He comes out in his white laboratory coat and kilt (remember, he is a Scotsman), strums his electric guitar, and sings (to the tune of "The Wabash Cannonball"):

Dear friends, I tell a story
Of Science on the run
Things are getting hectic
It's this phe-nom-e-non.
Low Entropy is order
High Entropy is not
Low Entropy is chilly
High Entropy is hot.
The more the competition
The worse it gets to be
The greater the disorder
The higher the Entropy.
For Energy is constant
And that old Entropy
Is seeking maximum value
For all the world to see.
And all of us poor creatures
Including you and me
Are running in that rat race
Building up our Entropy.

*"Luggin capillary" and "Tafel slope" were terms suggested by my husband. I had no idea what they meant and still don't.

For this paper he is awarded the Palladium Medal and later the Nobel Prize for Chemistry, also Physics, Economics, Medicine, and Literature.

In the final act he appears in Sweden, where he clutches the Nobel prize money to his heart and sings his acceptance aria. He steps into the spotlight, which is a powerful laser beam, and delivers the paper he has been spending his entire career to produce:

"Aria for a Famous Artist"

I'm a star
I'm a name in the field
I'm a star
Bunsen flame in the field
And my name will be known to the man on the street.
I'm an Einstein
I'm a Pauling
I'm complete.
I'm a star
I've attained the sublime
I'm a star
With my picture on TIME
And I'll wave to the crowd
From the President's car
And he'll give me his ear
(He's been briefed I'm a star)
And foundations will toss boundless grants at my feet
And prestige universities compete.
My pre-eminence is permanent
A Fermi in the firmament
I am stellar
Edward Teller
I'm a star.

JOURNAL ENTRY: OCTOBER 20, 1977

Did monologue for Electrochemical Society. Left audience agog.

A Metric Mallard

That whirlwind year quickly twisted away as all years do. More could have been done to promote *Yankee Shoes*, but my cottage industry was a one-woman operation, seriously understaffed. Although national distributors handled a few stray book orders for independent stores in other cities, local stores remained lukewarm to my book. An old college friend invited me to present a reading of *Yankee Shoes* at the University of Maryland Faculty Club. The professors seemed to appreciate the work more than other audiences, although one English professor approached me with some apprehension about my use of the word "cope" in the final poem.

Meanwhile, the *Unholy* books did much better. The Women's League for Conservative Judaism held a Family Tree Contest in which I stressed the immigrant experience and entered a scrapbook of old family photos interspersed with homey verses like "Sunday Afternoon," "Saving Graces," "Cousin Jake," "Gifts," and "Who'll Have the Seder?" At their national convention in the Catskills, the group awarded the entry a gold ribbon and a bronze plaque. Another women's organization agreed to sell the *Unholy* books at their national convention's gift boutique in exchange for my services as a volunteer at the shop. Emily Dickinson didn't have to put up with this kind of excrement.

JOURNAL ENTRY: DECEMBER 1977

> It's time to change course. After seven hectic years, the comedy must end. Only a closed circle of powerful people to whom I have absolutely no access whatsoever can elevate my work to the next level. Publishers, drowning in manuscripts from all sides, have their own inside circle of writers. Influential publications have grown even less accessible to people like me with no recognized backing or connections. No more freelancing. I crave a steady paycheck that proves my worth. Resolved: find a full-time job. Behold, this is my better-late-than-never resolution as I steer into the New Year ahead.

A port of call is not necessarily a port of entry. It is a stop along the way where cargo may be taken aboard or unloaded before a vessel lifts anchor and continues the journey. That would categorize my excursion into the wilds of the federal bureaucracy.

JOURNAL ENTRY: FEBRUARY 1978

> Last month Jerry told Madeleine, a Public Affairs section chief at the National Bureau of Standards, that I was interested in applying for a writing job there but didn't know what positions were available. She asked for a résumé and SF171, which in government gobbledygook stands for Personal Information Form.
>
> "You're in luck. There's an opening for a writer/editor in her division," my husband said. "Hop to it if you're interested."
>
> "Don't I have to take a Civil Service exam or something?"
>
> "Not for a job like this," he said. "It's considered creative."

I mailed Madeleine the necessary documents and entertained my usual doubts. At the age of forty-nine, was I too long in tooth to be hired? Twenty-four years had passed since my last full-time job. And could a liberal arts–tainted writer bluff her way through science and technology?

"It has been done," Jerry said.

"Even so," I said, "will this put an end to my literary dreams? What effect will the federal bureaucracy have on me?"

"What effect will you have on the federal bureaucracy?" he answered. "Look, when Nathaniel Hawthorne, Herman Melville, and Walt Whitman were government workers, it didn't cramp their style. It needn't ruin yours."

Two weeks later I reported to the National Bureau of Standards for an interview in the Public Information Division. In truth, it was rather fun supplying renegade answers off the top of my head to a pair of young supervisors in their early thirties, women almost twenty years younger than their job applicant. Delighted to be entertained on a dull weekday morning, they sat almost transfixed, their shiny, unlined faces beaming.

Right through that interview I sailed, not giving much of a damn about anything. I drew on years of experience as a freelance writer who slants material toward the market. What's more, these youthful potential bosses reminded me of my nieces, two little girls with whom I babysat. In my mind I was still hanging out with my sister's children. There were no "self-made" men like Mr. Kamenetz to intimidate me. (Random thought: Why do we rarely refer to ourselves as "self-made women"? Answer: All women are self-made; we renovate ourselves in each minute of the day.)

The Public Information Division hired me. I swore allegiance to the U.S. Constitution and the metric system, and took my place as an official writer/editor at NBS, a venerable institution established by Congress in 1901, the very first scientific laboratory of the federal government. It had already moved from Washington, D.C. to the distant suburb of Gaithersburg in Maryland. The verdant 578 acres, 234 hectares for metric mavens, are dotted with temples devoted to Science and Technology. The grounds even provide a haven for deer, raccoons, squirrels, skunks, chipmunks, mallards, and Canada geese, as well as an outdoor duck pond and an indoor one in the open courtyard of the Administration Building.

Government laboratories like this, however, are not free spirits. They are molded by the usual bureaucratic limitations, benchmarks, monthly progress reports, grant forms, departmental inquiries, requests from academia and industry, Congressional oversight, and other time-consuming escapades. Stereotypical scientists with wild hair do not pour potions of green liquid from one crooked glass vial to another and shout, "Eureka! I've found it!" They take their children to the movies, make mortgage payments, and suffer indigestion frequently.

My job centered around editing a biweekly in-house publication called the *Standard*. Madeleine, my intrepid boss, was a remarkable young woman with a background in chemistry and an affable, creative personality. She supervised several other official scientific publications as well as mine. A fellow writer, she shared my desire to make the *Standard* less stuffy and to avoid bureaucratic gobbledygook whenever possible.

An incident during my first week on the job set the tone for my entire tenure as editor. At a man-made pond adorning a courtyard inside the Administration Building sat a lone mallard, a patient female duck waiting for something momentous to happen. A few days later she hatched six ducklings. Earlier in the month before I arrived on the job, Madeleine had already assigned this story to the official bureau photographer and a writer in the *Standard* office. She sent me to observe as part of my on-the-job training.

I watched as an armed Bureau guard walked to the edge of the pond. He squatted and gently picked up a fuzzy duckling, placed it in an empty cardboard carton, and continued until he had collected all six. The mother mallard protested and then flew off in a maternal snit. Meanwhile, the guard lifted the carton and carried it down the corridor past a cluster of meeting rooms and offices, through the lobby, past the reception desk, to the front entrance, and then carefully walked down the outside steps. He held the box of tiny birds close to his heart until he reached the bottom step, where he unloaded the precious cargo with loving care.

Mama Duck landed to supervise the operation. After counting tiny webbed feet to make sure no baby was missing, she efficiently led away her brood. With military precision, they headed for the duck pond in a remote part of the campus. The staff photographer recorded all this; the writer took notes, and it became the *Standard*'s best centerfold story.

I learned much that day. It was possible to include human-interest articles in the *Standard*, stories that would center on personnel in all areas of the agency, even ducks. We should aim for warming the cold, rigid world of impersonal laboratories and sterile offices. We should bring joy to hard-working government employees, from the lowest paid to the highest. Yes, include dry figures, facts, and descriptions of vital work performed in the laboratories, but there was no need to duplicate subject matter already efficiently covered by other publications in our division. These included an award-winning magazine, official brochures, pamphlets, calendars, and directories available to the public. It seemed to me that human-interest stories and maybe even a dab of light verse would liven things up a bit.

One of my earliest assignments was to cover a rare visit from a delegation representing the People's Republic of China. The day of their arrival, I dressed in my most business-like glen plaid suit and took pen and note pad down to the main lobby of the Administration Building, where the top brass would officially greet the Chinese. Although President Nixon had officially "opened up" Red China, the diplomatic relationship between the United States and the Communist nation was tenuous, and the atmosphere reflected the gravity of this unusual visit.

There they were, the Bureau director and other leading lights of the administrative staff plus higher-ups from the Department of Commerce. They formed a tense receiving line that stretched across the lobby and waited impatiently for the visitors to appear. I stood off to the side scribbling cryptic notes, which I most likely wouldn't be allowed to use. At best, mine would be a superficial kind of article, a bird's-eye overview. A low-level GS-7 scribe like me had to remain invisible, not authorized to speak to these Chinese bigwigs. Nor would I have a chance to interview their lofty NBS counterparts before or after the meeting. I was there merely to absorb atmosphere and possibly insert a colorful word or two into the cut-and-dried official statement that would eventually turn up on my desk from the Foreign Affairs office.

Wearing identical black suits, a dozen stern-looking Communist gentlemen entered the spacious lobby. A Foreign Affairs official led the guests to the stone-faced American greeters, standing, glued side by side, as if they were playing a children's game of Red Rover. Our visitors worked their way down the receiving line, shaking hands, rendering tight smiles, and although the atmosphere seemed cordial enough, a certain restraint loomed over the hosts and guests.

The first of the Chinese dignitaries finished gripping all those American hands, and then an odd thing happened. Instead of stepping aside until the others finished, he saw me standing about four feet away from the line. He broke into a broad smile, moved in my direction, seized my hand, and shook it as if we were long-lost cousins. Since he considered me part of the entourage, I gripped his hand with hearty warmth, and gave him a friendly "Welcome!" Then instead of breaking away because I really wasn't supposed to be playing an active part in this historic meeting, I stayed on, smiling the placid smile of a Washington society doyenne, as each member of the visiting delegation, one by one, paused to shake my hand.

If I had been a sweet young thing just out of college, I would have bolted after the first Asian hand-squeeze, but that might have caused an international crisis. Besides, it seemed the most natural thing in the world for me to remain, paying individual attention to each guest who came my way. In my experience as a scientist's frau, I had many times greeted foreign visitors like this and often cooked them a decent meal when warranted.

In the meantime, the NBS pooh-bahs noticed an extra person in the receiving line, a woman whom they had never seen before, certainly someone not authorized to be there fraternizing with Beijing's scientific elite. I overheard one puzzled senior executive mutter as he gestured toward me, "Who the hell is *that*?" It was time for Cinderella to return to the hearth—in this case, the cubbyhole office of the *Standard*. But Jerry raised his glass and toasted me at home that night: "Here's to Moll Flanders. She was only a humble editor, but she performed nobly in the service of her country."

Almost most two years later, I submitted my final monthly report to a new section chief. Madeleine had left for a better job, and it was also time for me to bid aloha to my days as a government worker. Even so, I was proud that the *Standard* had won an Award for Excellence from the Society for Technical Communication.

JOURNAL ENTRY: JANUARY 2, 1980

> I sit here at the barely cleared top of my desk in this rain forest I call my home office. During the twenty months at the National Bureau of Standards, I have neglected cherished aspects of normal living and now I'm catching up. A sense of calm pervades this room. I may write all day, and no one will interrupt. Working on the *Standard* took its toll; I felt like quitting every week. Most of all, I hated waiting around for a half dozen higher-ups to approve and sign off on the contents of each item, each article, and each entire issue.
>
> As a publication, the *Standard* did develop a sense of humor. We conducted a successful Bureau of Standards limerick-writing contest, the subject matter limited to (what else?) Science and Technology. Some of our most brilliant physicists, chemists, engineers, and mathematicians participated with witty entries. And our December "People Issue" attracted attention from all the Centers and from the NBS Director himself. I did an interview with a cafeteria worker who also served as minister of a local Baptist church. It was gratifying to highlight the unpublicized lives of ordinary citizens who do the gritty, unglamorous, low-level work that has kept this mammoth agency running since 1901. For every Nobel prize winner produced in the labs, there are masses of barely noticed

workaday souls. They wash dishes, vacuum laboratories, serve food, plant azaleas, cut grass, wash windows, repair lighting, paint, hammer, answer phones, type papers, guard the gates, and deliver abandoned ducklings to their mothers. Vital as the scientists and engineers may be, they are not the only people toiling in the field of Science.

Best of all each morning, I liked riding to work with Jerry in our own private carpool. He would switch on the radio for a classical music station, and we imagined ourselves performing a gavotte to Mozart or a minuet to Chopin or a Hungarian folk dance to Liszt.

"Now we're bounding over the fields, hand in hand," I said, directing our joint madness to the music, "and now high over the trees into the forest." We laughed as we pictured ourselves dancing in appropriate costumes across farmland that has since been covered with high-rise apartment buildings, shopping malls, and neo-Victorian houses. We belonged to the same work gang; we shared our impressions of co-workers, their glories and their imperfections. Jerry's lab was located not far from the building where I worked; he knew all the characters in my charade, and I knew his. We played "Can You Top This?" with our frustrations and triumphs.

He had talked me out of leaving many times, but I realized my quest to transform the *Standard* into a scientific version of the *New Yorker* would soon end. Ronald Reagan vowed to cut the cost of government by downsizing all departments of every agency. The people of NBS expected massive budget cuts, whole sections wiped out via the dreaded "RIF" policy. I thought that was a jazz term, but Jerry explained it meant Reduction in Force.

"The most recently hired personnel are always the first to go," he said. To avoid being riffed, I left on my own, still a free spirit. The *Standard* was well liked by the readers, including the top brass; why not leave the party at its height?

On my brief watch, did I bend the bureaucracy to my will? Not really, but a single defining accomplishment remains with me. During my tenure as editor of the *Standard*, a co-worker informed me of a suicide in one of the laboratories. He mentioned the name of the person, a serious young woman just out of college, a physicist or chemist, I didn't know for certain. She and I often exchanged a friendly hello at the cafeteria or in the Ladies' Room.

"Should we get to work on the obit?" I asked my office mate.

"Of course not," he said. "The top screws forbid any publicity on this."

I was incredulous. "Nothing at all?"

"No. They really feel it's better to keep it quiet."

"But won't people want to know how . . ."

"Everyone either knows about it already or will soon find out. Word of mouth travels fast around here."

This was the official reaction? It upset me. Madeleine was still section chief at the time. I went to her, complaining about such a cruel and impersonal policy.

"She was a scientist, a member of the staff here, someone we saw every day," I said. "We don't know what triggered this, why she did it, but out of respect for a human being, a fellow co-worker, she at least deserves some mention in the *Standard*. We can't act as if she never existed. We owe it to her and to her family."

"We do," my young boss said. "I'll plead the case to the powers that be. They damned well better let us run something."

"Tell them," I said, "that we won't go into how she died, where she died, or even when she died. But the article should say we are saddened to learn of her recent death, give a few details about her background and education, and add that she'll be missed by many at NBS."

Fired up, Madeleine agreed that it was the paper's moral obligation to acknowledge the passing of a colleague. It surprised our entire division when she convinced the bigwigs to change their minds. I wrote the piece as tactfully as possible, and it ran in the following issue of the *Standard*. I was proud that two females in this predominantly male bastion stood firm for a moral principle. In reaffirming the human condition, we lent dignity to the loss of a troubled young woman who had chosen Science as her calling. Who knows what vital contribution she might have made to her profession had she lived?

PART TWO

Ports of Call

Potomac Fever Redux

MAY 1980

To the Editor of the *Washington Evening Star*
Dear Sir:
One of the best kept secrets hereabouts is the upcoming selection of delegates to the Democratic National Convention this summer. In the 8th Congressional District of Maryland, the selection will very quietly take place in Rockville tomorrow. This countywide caucus, designed to involve all registered Democrats of the district, is especially important to the 17 percent of Montgomery County voters who voted "uncommitted to any presidential candidate" in the May 13 Maryland primary.

It is important that this outpouring of dissatisfaction with both presidential candidates will not pass into oblivion. The caucus has been so poorly publicized that not a single registered county Democrat I have spoken to has heard or read a word about it.

In previous years, delegates' names have appeared on the ballot used in the primary. Under Maryland's new Democratic Party rules, mandated for all states by the Democratic National Committee, the names of those running for office were removed. Instead, a presidential candidate who received a certain percentage of the popular vote also received a proportional share of the delegates. Kennedy won three of the district's six delegates; Jimmy Carter, two; and "Uncommitted," one. Selecting these individual delegates is what tomorrow's caucus is all about.

The unpublicized system works to the advantage of the party machine. What this means, especially to voters who mark their ballots "uncommitted," is that party regulars will quietly elect one of their own pro-Carter or pro-Kennedy delegates, who have infiltrated the uncommitted ballot. The person with the highest number of votes will represent the uncommitted voters of our county at the Democratic National Convention. If you are a registered Democrat in the 8th Congressional District, vote from 7:00 a.m. to 10:00 p.m. tomorrow at Rockville's Educational Center.

Mollee Kruger
Candidate for Uncommitted Delegate to the
Democratic National Convention

Why was I, a freelance writer, delving into politics? Potomac Fever is contagious in Washington, D.C. and environs. For the past twenty-five years as the wife of a government employee, I followed closely the escapades of the U.S. Congress, especially the effect of budget cuts affecting federal workers. In 1980 neither Jimmy Carter nor Ted Kennedy thrilled me. Perhaps I could dip a toe into the surf and make a minor splash.

My SOS to the family brought mixed results. "I'll be out of town all next week for an American Society for Testing and Materials conference," Jerry said. "Getting involved in the election would be great fun, but there's the Hatch Act. I'm a government worker and can't risk getting into trouble." He saw my disappointment and added, "But I'll be back in time to vote and lend you moral support."

Our younger son at Cornell had just left for a summer semester, but our older son, now out of college and job hunting, was available part-time. The official campaign staff now numbered two. Not only a candidate, I planned to serve as my campaign manager, publicist, and dogsbody. Number One Son would be on tap periodically to save me from myself.

At that time the *Washington Post* ran a feature called "Company Town" to which readers could submit a day-by-day description of whatever was happening in their lives over an entire week. Desperate to be published anywhere at all, I sent the editors the following about my plunge into the upcoming presidential election:

SUNDAY, JUNE 1, 1980

It's the final week before the Maryland selection caucus. As an uncommitted delegate to the upcoming Democratic National Convention this November, I think there's a chance for someone like me with no previous political experience. Government workers were among the nearly 13,000 dissatisfied D.C. area folks who voted "uncommitted" in the recent primary. That's why I spend morning, afternoon, and evening addressing envelopes that contain an explanation of the revised delegate selection process plus my own humble qualifications. For dinner, husband prepares roasted chicken basted with Tulkoff's Tiger Sauce to fire me up for the battle ahead and then leaves town on business.

MONDAY, JUNE 2

I withdraw campaign funds from my bank account. I pocket a cool $30 in cash, my total campaign budget from which I immediately reimburse myself for money already spent: $15 for stamps, 89 cents for envelopes, and $6.62 for printed flyers. At the instant printing place, I pick up an additional 100 flyers. Another $3.31 bites the dust.

At night I attend an unpublicized candidates' forum. Beginning at 7:30 we uncommitted folks are scheduled to speak, each one for two minutes. Arriving late, I find a row of no-nonsense uncommiteds already seated at microphones and an audience of twelve citizens, mostly mothers and wives of would-be candidates. When my turn comes, I shake things up by reading one of my *Yankee Shoes* poems about the wife of President Rutherford B. Hayes, "Lemonade Lucy," who refused to serve liquor at the White House. Why? It strikes me that I have no chance whatsoever in competition with the articulate lawyers, women's activists, and labor leaders running against me. I drive home alone, laughing hysterically at the memory of puzzled looks evoked by my eccentric performance.

TUESDAY, JUNE 3

Expecting no results whatsoever, I send off more dire letters to local media warning against voter apathy. Deep in my heart, I know that although Jimmy Carter has the national convention all wrapped up anyway, Ronald Reagan will beat him. If so, what am I knocking myself out for? Chalk it up to grist for the writer's mill and a barrel of laughs (maybe).

WEDNESDAY, JUNE 4

The *Washington Evening Star* calls saying they may or may not run my letter. Terror grips me. I remark to my son, "This is the nuttiest thing I have tried yet." Wearily, he agrees. At night I am sleepless again and read Doris Lessing's *The Golden Notebook*, which is about women as sex objects on the fringe of political activity while men pull all the strings. An outsider, though not a sex object, I wonder who pulls what strings in our county politics. Whoever it may be, they're going to fall into a snit if my critical letter ever hits the papers.

THURSDAY, JUNE 5

I nap and am awakened by the damned phone. It's a fellow "Uncommitted," who congratulates me on getting a letter published in the county paper. While complimenting me on the free publicity, he mentions a competitor who has bought expensive newspaper ads. The *Jewish Week,* where my weekly poetry column appears, publishes a blurb about my campaign with a godawful photo that may win me a large sympathy vote.

FRIDAY, JUNE 6

I do essential laundry, three loads. (Does Teddy Kennedy ever wonder where his next clean shirt is coming from?) The

Washington Star runs my letter about the unannounced caucus. A strange lady calls and promises to vote for me. An unidentified gentleman phones informing me that the previous caller is now making calls for me in her precinct. Another caller wants to learn more about my presidential choices. I mention a desire for an open convention and the appearance of a compromise candidate, possibly Walter Mondale. It satisfies the questioner. My husband, back from his trip, promises to cheer me over the finish line.

SATURDAY, JUNE 7

Caucus time. I stash away mimeographed flyers in my pocketbook and head for the polls. A mad confusion of candidates, cars, signs, and posters awaits. I'm reminded of Melville's *The Confidence Man*, a cynical book about human gullibility and nineteenth-century Americans on the make. Skimpy crowds materialize under a broiling sun. The day grows muggier, the air hanging heavy like a damp quilt. I don an unbecoming floppy sunhat and find a spot on the front lines, where candidates are lined up like carnival hawkers. We buttonhole perspiring people as soon as they leave their cars. Voters will choose from twenty-six "Uncommitted" wannabees. An irate voter attacks us for surrounding him. "Get away from me, you pack of idiots!" he shouts.

Relatives arrive, complaining that I have no signs posted. After a sudden thunderstorm which destroys the other candidates' expensive placards, a makeshift sign appears, mounted on a broken yardstick. It bears my name and underneath, these immortal words: "Sloppy sign . . . good Uncommitted Delegate. Moll's no pol! Vote for her!" Stars appear in the sky; candidates grow punchy. At 10:00 p.m. I go home to sleep. My husband awakens me with news that a popular attorney has been elected Uncommitted Delegate. The runner-up, another influential local Democrat, is chosen Alternate. I score third place, losing the Alternate position by fifty votes.

The *Washington Post* never ran this account in "Company Town." "My life in politics is over," I told Jerry afterward. "It's even harder than getting something published."

"Don't let the bastards wear you down," Jerry said. "You probably inspired more women to run for office next time."

Sink or Swim

At its beginning, the new decade, 1980, was a time to take personal inventory: a loving husband, two admirable sons, three poetry books under my belt, and the "Unholy Writ" column still running weekly in Washington, New York, Pittsburgh, and other cities. Entering stage right, the Reagans and their supporting cast of characters dominated the Washington arena. I wrote light verse that was tinged with politics but only if I could find a biblical or contemporary Jewish connection. Our sons grew up, the older graduating and taking a magazine job in Cleveland, the younger finishing high school and college and then playing drums in a rock band. Surely, now I'd find more time to turn myself into a bona fide author.

Not so fast. Those years were often weighted with family obligations, hospital and cemetery visits, traditional home-cooked holiday dinners for relatives, numerous houseguests, including college friends of our boys, and the usual procession of scientific notables. The musical wing of the family from Georgia continued to grace us with visits a couple of times a year until all three of my brother-in-law's children went away to college. It resulted in little time for significant writing.

In fact, it was easier not to write at all. Local government people asked me to conduct a county-sponsored workshop for citizens interested in creating light verse. I agreed, certain that no one would want to register for this fiasco, but a considerable number of adults signed up, including newsletter editors, songwriters, general freelancers, and even technical writers, most of them retirees. This sort of thing can get out of hand. Soon I found myself teaching senior adult courses in journalism and creative writing to an adoring, elderly throng. I supervised a monthly newsletter put together by my students and spent long hours editing two anthologies of their work.

JOURNAL ENTRY: APRIL 1981

Although I should put an end to these classes, they're catnip for the ego. They boost confidence and give me a sense of mastery over the material, my own private refresher course based on the words of Dorothy Parker, Phyllis McGinley, and Victorian light versifiers Edward Lear, W. S. Gilbert, and Lewis Carroll. With the annual stress of getting our house ready for Passover and the Seder, all the planning, shopping, cleaning, cooking, and switching to special Pesach plates and pots, I have fallen victim to what some brilliant copywriter has termed "tired blood." Where is a magic elixir when I need it?

JOURNAL ENTRY: MAY 1981

Another mindless detour. I received a call from a woman who runs an ad agency in the National Press Building. In a weak moment I allowed her to hire me. Now a couple of times a week, I'm writing humorous radio commercials for two popular radio disc jockeys named Harden and Weaver. It's trivial and why continue? I'm reading *Journal of a Solitude* by May Sarton. The poet describes her detached world, the realm of gardening, isolation, country life, cats, flower arranging, and writing. Her milieu is not mine, and yet maybe I can learn more about the battle against futility, which, at one time or another, hits every writer. Never should have taken this silly advertising job. Jerry hints there is a way out. Time to pack the suitcase again and flee to exotic shores.

The Nebulous Nile

We snuggled into the soft cushions of the sleek French-built train that would carry us from Cairo to Luxor. Parallel to the rail tracks flowed the Nile, the country's lifeline. Where we would stay upon arrival we had no idea. It was July of 1981, and that month is amazingly hot in Washington and even more so in Egypt.

"Do we need to make reservations?" Jerry asked his Egyptian colleagues at the government laboratory he had just visited.

"No, no," they said, "there are many fine hotels along the Nile. The first one you see will welcome you and your wife."

We had boarded the luxurious Wagon Lit at the chaotic station in Cairo. It was late afternoon before the night dropped like thunder over the landscape and all the countryside turned an inky black. The farther our speedy train shot into the countryside, the fewer the lights until there were none left anywhere.

"Wasn't darkness one of the biblical plagues to force Pharaoh into letting the Hebrews go?" I asked.

"That particular plague went nowhere," Jerry said, peering out the train window. "Can't see a thing. Try to get some sleep. We don't know what we'll find when we get to Luxor."

I closed my eyes and tentatively dreamed, off and on. Our voyage to the Land of the Pyramids came as a surprise. When Jerry was invited to Israel for a visit to the Technion, Israel's MIT, I welcomed the chance to go with him. Another journey abroad, I thought, might revive my sluggish imagination. And we would have one more chance to see Jerry's elderly uncle in Ra'anana and his sons, living on a nearby *moshav*. We had first visited this part of the family in the 1970s and were fascinated by their lives as active farmers who tended an orange orchard. They also raised chickens and grew roses for European city markets.

The Camp David Accords and the uneasy peace between Egypt and Israel had become a fait accompli. Now travelers could fly directly from Tel Aviv to Cairo. A more relaxed atmosphere led to Jerry's invitation to visit the laboratories at Egypt's National Research Center. Since El Al still had no permission to land on Egyptian soil, we took Nefertiti Airlines, which kept a low profile to avoid attracting too much attention. Our Israeli cabdriver had never heard of it; the plane itself was unmarked. I didn't feel comfortable in such a tense situation, but Jerry said it would be considered an insult to his Egyptian colleagues if he didn't come. We would stay in Egypt a few days before returning to Ben Gurion Airport and then start the long flight home.

JOURNAL ENTRY: SUNDAY, MARCH 8, 1981

> There was a dusty haze over the city when we landed in Cairo today. All buildings sported the same beige color, even the mosques. It's quite warm, over eighty degrees, masses of impoverished people in the streets and horrific traffic jams. After an exhausting hassle with long lines and passports, Jerry's colleague and a driver took us to a hotel in Dokki, a Cairo suburb. We relaxed a bit at the hotel (our clothes were dirty and smelly) and then we were collected, as the Brits say, by an attractive woman scientist, our host for this visit. She was as kind and thoughtful as she was beautiful. I was impressed by her fashionable suit and especially by the unique jewelry at her neck and on her wrists. Her rare collection, she told us, includes a necklace that is two thousand years old and a bracelet of ancient coins going back to the reign of King Tutankhamun. My oldest possession is a high school ring that doesn't fit anymore.
>
> When the lovely lady, a Copt, took us sightseeing, we stopped at Dr. Rahab's Papyrus Museum situated on a Nile riverboat. It was here we saw how the papyrus plant is grown and the dried strips made into paper. Other boats sailed by, replicas of the same durable barks once built by

> ancient Egyptians. Thor Heyerdahl, the Norwegian ethnographer and intrepid adventurer, duplicated the design of these ancient boats for his world-startling oceanic voyages. The year I finished college in 1950, he made his famous trip across the Pacific on a primitive vessel called the *Kon-Tiki.*
>
> Traffic in Cairo is insane and noisy, much honking of horns for no good reason. While we stopped at a light, an insistent peddler stuck his head through the car window and tried to sell us something. Our driver told him in Arabic to buzz off or less polite words to that effect. The woman brought us to her apartment, where we met her daughter and husband, a professor at the University of Cairo. They were hospitable and charming at a dinner prepared especially for us: hummus, flatbreads, a meat and rice dish, baba ganoush, and tamarindy, an apricot-flavored drink popular in Africa and Asia. I learned about husband-wife relationships here; she and I spoke about the difficulty of being a professional woman with a husband and family to care for. I also discovered a valuable Arab saying, *Inshallah bukra malesh*: God will provide tomorrow, possibly, but it really doesn't matter. The vagueness resonated with me. It seemed to describe perfectly my writing career up to this point.

Because Jerry's Muslim and Coptic associates spoke with such enthusiasm about the magnificent treasures of Luxor, we made a split-second decision to see for ourselves. Our Wagon Lit arrived at daybreak in time for us to see the sun rising amid clouds of pink and lavender high over a row of gigantic columns that must have been four thousand years old, give or take a millennium. We didn't know what they were. Cairo friends had given us no English-language guidebooks to Luxor. No one met the train. We were on our own.

The sleepy town wasn't bustling with activity at six in the morning, not a taxi in sight outside the train station. We waited on a barren platform with our single suitcase and looked for transportation of some kind. A shabby cart appeared, drawn by a donkey on its last legs and with a cantankerous driver, who spoke a bit of English and wanted an enormous amount of money to take us to the nearest hotel on the Nile. We turned him down, and shortly afterward another man arrived in what looked like the same cart drawn by the same emaciated donkey, except that the driver charged even more. Wearily, we succumbed.

The first hotel, a Hilton, turned us away, no rooms available. The second, third, and fourth did the same. All the Western-style hotels were filled. A clerk advised us to head for the Tourism Office, where we could find more information, and we hailed another cart drawn by an elderly horse and driven by an entrepreneur who charged us even more than the two earlier fares combined.

"I don't ask for much," I pleaded silently with Ra, the ancient Egyptian sun god, "just any place with no bedbugs."

The clock read 7:30 a.m. by the time we reached the Tourism Office. It was closed and wouldn't open until later, *Inshallah bukra malesh*. We sat on a bench in the town square and fought off other aggressive drivers and their downtrodden animals. At 9:30 when the Tourism Office opened, a skinny clerk with a bushy black moustache informed us that all hotels on the Nile were booked (really?), but if we wanted to venture deeper into town, he would recommend the St. Antonia. "Clean and comfortable," he said.

I was nearly prostrate with fatigue. We paid a pharaoh's ransom to reach the hotel, run by friendly Egyptian Christians. Many cats roamed through the lobby. Our suite, crowded with heavy Levantine furniture, faced a dirt road filled with braying donkeys and freewheeling poultry. Although not air-conditioned, our rooms were spotless; we slept for the rest of the day.

The in-house restaurant obviously hadn't been in business long. Three waiters, all handsome young men with sparkling dark eyes and welcoming smiles, knocked trays of dishes to the floor and tipped over glasses of Omar Khayyam wine onto the laps of the few foreigners who ate there. Service took about as long as building the pyramids. At the next table a quartet of Germans pounded the table, chanting, "Beer! Beer! Ve vant our Stella beer!" After our dinner arrived, I watched fascinated as a dead fly dropped from the ceiling into my soup.

Luxor and Karnak, we explored it all, the crumbling statues and towering columns, and then rejoined our friends in Cairo. What do I remember of this remarkable trip to Egypt? The genuine warmth of our hosts and the Egyptian people we met, the pyramids of Giza, the Sphinx, the enormous statues of pharaohs and their indifferent blank stares. In the Valley of the Kings we saw the physical decay of glory, human vanity buried in dust. Lying abandoned on the ground, scattered like trash, were massive heads carved in stone, the dismembered legacy of forgotten monarchs long dead. It was the same kind of debris in the Valley of the Queens, where the form of Hatshepsut, a female pharaoh, stood in immortal defiance. Her face had been destroyed by her enemies.

Thanks to our Egyptian friends, books on the art and literature of the Coptic people kindled my interest in this branch of early Christianity. I admired its modern-day followers who maintain their church amid neighbors growing less and less religiously tolerant over the years. The Copts are a national treasure, the direct descendants of ancient hieroglyphic figures on the walls of the tombs we visited. The almond-shaped eyes of our hostess, outlined in heavy black, duplicated those of ancestors who regarded us from panels of art created thousands of years ago. When I returned home, our travels inspired two poems, "The Copts" and "A Chat with Ramses II":

They tell me you're the Pharaoh
Who refused to let us go,
I stand here at your colonnade
And catch the gusts that blow
The hieroglyphs and callous heights
At Karnak. Is it so
That Rameses, master-builder king
Was vanquished by us slaves
The maker of Ramesseum
Demolished by such knaves?
And now we whisk away the flies
At Karnak. Do the waves
Of silent Hebrews in your halls
Instill a granite fear
That kings don't get a second chance
But Freedom blooms each year?
(A message one can find inscribed
At Karnak)

Travel sections of newspapers were not terribly interested in our trip to Luxor. An editor returned my manuscript with the note, "Lots of people go to Egypt these days. It's no big deal." Slightly miffed, I returned to the themes of Washington and politics. That summer I sold a piece, "Signatures, Writ by Hand." In the article, I referred to imaginary autograph books filled with the rhymed sentiments of classmates at my rural elementary school. Those simple verses that we girls exchanged could easily be used by political leaders when fans sought their autographs. I suggested, *Way back here / Out of sight / I write my name / Just for spite . . . Richard Nixon.* Or, *I luv ya, I luv ya / I luv ya so well / If I had a peanut / I'd give you the shell . . . Jimmy Carter.* Or more contemporarily:

There are silver ships / And there are gold ships / But there is no ship / Like a chairmanship. (Here the reader may sign the name of any powerful Senator or House Representative currently in office.)

Taking advantage of an election year, I dumped this brand of nonsense on the Weekend section of the *Washington Post.* They bought it but nothing else from me for the next ten years. Meanwhile, Jerry beckoned with another enticing itinerary, and once more we embarked on a voyage to a faraway land, reached by flying down to Rio de Janeiro and then across the Atlantic to a place once known as the Dark Continent.

Parsing Pretoria

"I can't sleep, can you?" I asked Jerry in a whisper. We huddled together at midnight in an African hut covered with what looked like an authentic straw roof.

Lions roaring, hyenas laughing, and elephants trumpeting did their best to keep us awake. Would the stockade fence around our compound protect us from wild beasts who might enter for an evening snack composed of two well-fed Americans? We were thousands of miles from our quiet suburban home in Maryland where even the tiniest dog was forbidden by law to run free without a leash.

"They wouldn't build cottages for tourists out here if it wasn't safe," Jerry said. "It's not a jungle. It's a South African preserve, and besides, it has our name attached to it for good luck."

"I don't want to wake up devoured."

"What could possibly happen to us in Kruger National Park?" Jerry said. "My cousin arranged for a safari tomorrow. Our own private guide will pick us up tomorrow afternoon for a preliminary drive. If the light is good, we'll be able to get some good shots."

"You don't know anything about guns."

"Cameras. They don't allow tourists to kill animals here. Go to sleep."

Who knew that the man I married would have relatives living in Johannesburg or that a branch of these cousins from the land of the Boers would arrive in Atlanta, Georgia, to meet U.S. family members for the first time? Who knew that his kinfolk would later visit Washington where we took them on our standard capital city tour for foreign visitors? Or that they in turn would issue us an open invitation to come to Johannesburg and spend a week with them in a spacious house designed by his cousin, an outstanding South African architect?

"It may be our only chance to see my father's brother," Jerry said. "Uncle Morris is eight-three. I've never met him. Besides, I have another international meeting in Athens this July."

"Greece is nowhere near South Africa," I remember saying.

"So we'll sidetrack a little bit and drop in on our relatives. Look, we'll be out anyway," Jerry said with his usual hard-to-resist enthusiasm. "Call their embassy and find out about visas."

That became the easiest part. When the person at the other end of the line heard our name, we were treated like royalty. Paul Kruger, sometimes called the George Washington of the Republic of South Africa, was revered there, as evidenced by all the towns, boulevards, stamps, and currency that bore his hallowed name.

"We're not in any way related to him," Jerry said, but in the Johannesburg of 1982, it didn't hurt to be known as a Kruger.

Tommy, our park ranger, was a former citizen of Rhodesia, now known as Zimbabwe. On our first afternoon, he arrived dressed for the part in pith helmet, beige safari jacket, matching shorts, and knee socks. This great white hunter out of Central Casting drove a Land Rover filled with cold drinks and snacks. "Keep your windows rolled up at all times, please," he said in his best semi-British accent. "I intend to show you a whirlwind view of dazzling African flora and fauna." He would also reveal his views on apartheid in the Republic of South Africa.

As we passed African pedestrians on the road, Tommy wasted no time in revealing what his politics were. "I know the black mind," he said. "They live only for now." Black people formerly worked with him in the Salisbury government, he claimed. They had forfeited their pensions in order to leave the country for more freedom and later returned empty-handed to beg for their jobs, which had been given to others. Not only did his co-workers lose work and money, he said, "they had been beaten and forced into hard labor in Mozambique by the Communists. Now they're back home in Zimbabwe with nothing."

Tommy also worried about the massive amount of red tape that prevented him from receiving his Rhodesian government pension since his move to South Africa. He planned to confront Harare officials by threatening to mail them a small packet of hyena fat, a frightening symbol of bad luck. "That ought to get my check deposited in the bank speedily. All those chaps are deathly afraid of magic."

JOURNAL ENTRY: WEDNESDAY, JUNE 30, 1982

> We met Tommy for breakfast at the preserve restaurant and began our odyssey to track the White Lion and the White Rhinoceros. No success there, but feathered friends galore. At home, Jerry and I could identify only sparrows, robins, and crows, but here Tommy treated us to tropical birds of all colors and sizes: parrots, storks, guinea fowl, sunbirds, egrets, and herons. We delighted in the glories of the bushveld and snapped photos of giraffes munching on the tops of acacia trees. When an angry jackal charged at our van, Tommy barked, "Go back, you twit!" and the animal ran off. An irate male baboon wandered up to the car, bared his sharp teeth, and put his hands on the closed window next to where Jerry sat.
>
> "They can fly into a rage and kill," Tommy said, "but he'll go away soon." As the animal shuffled off, we were treated to full viewing of his rear end. "That's the worst case of hemorrhoids I've ever seen," Jerry said.
>
> Over the next few days we encountered elephants, lions, masses of wildebeests, giraffes, gazelles, zebras, kudus (an antelope-like creature with antlers), impalas, gazelles, warthogs, a mother baboon with a baby riding on her back, and a dead monkey hit by a car. Angered by the accident, Tommy stopped two tourists feeding the baboons. "If we catch you doing it again, you'll be subject to a heavy fine," he said. He turned to us. "Baboons sit at the roadside all day and wait for litter from passing cars. They never go looking for natural food anymore. Recently a baboon died of starvation, and junk food was all that the park rangers found inside him. A damned shame."

Tommy loved the animals, but his attitude toward the dark-skinned population all around us did not equal his respect for the jungle beasts. When he would speak in Swahili or Nguni to local people, his manner seemed arrogant and condescending. And yet, in the comfortable suburbs of Johannesburg, Jerry's family members could not have been more hospitable to us. They wanted to make our visit as perfect as possible with meals of "cottage pie," a mixture of ground potatoes and meat sweetened with syrup, served by their full-time cook/housekeeper who, with a sullen handyman, lived in the servants' quarters, a tiny house on the edge of the property. Each day we were treated to sightseeing trips during which our architect cousin pointed out traces of colonial culture like Cape Dutch buildings, some with thatched or red tile roofing.

We drove to Pretoria and Witwatersrand University for Jerry's visit to a South African colleague's laboratory. We drank something called milk stout, a heavy dark beer, and met Jerry's elderly uncle. He was a lively man past eighty, who in his youth left Lithuania and trekked his way through Mongolia to follow the girl he loved when her family moved to South Africa. Uncle Morris intrigued us with stories about his grandfather Lemach, the same hot-tempered man who had once been my father's *melamed* (teacher) long ago in Vabolnik.

At parties in our honor we learned that in Johannesburg, a Vabolnik Society existed, founded by people who had emigrated from that tiny Lithuanian town. It amazed the members to hear that both Jerry's father and mine had been born there, although they were a generation apart and never knew each other in Europe.

"I can't believe it," Jerry marveled. "All these descendants have ties to an obscure *shtetl* called Vabolnik, a place no one else has ever heard of. It's nowhere on my map, and here we are, two Americans with the same roots, discovering our fellow Vabolnikers in Africa of all places!"

One afternoon our hosts drove us to the Crown Gold Mine, a re-created 1890s town with its corrugated-iron rooftops and rococo Victorian parlors heated by iron fireplaces. The white mine workers once lived here, far from the black laborers in their ramshackle log cabins located dangerously close to the mine shafts.

After the tour, we entered an amphitheater where Nguni people in leopard skins performed tribal dances. They wore white feathers tied to their wrists and upper arms; fuzzy pom-poms dangled from their knees. As they menacingly flashed cardboard shields and thrust wooden sticks in our direction, they didn't hide their true feelings toward the audience. A cheerful brochure assured us, "Our workers dance for recreation," but I wondered. How much did it hurt these obviously resentful dancers to display the secrets of their culture for the amusement of ogling white foreigners? And how many of the smiling, applauding foreign audience realized that Nelson Mandela still languished in prison as punishment for his crusade to end apartheid? Or that the growing power of the African National Congress continued to spread anxiety throughout the staid government halls of Pretoria?

Wherever we went, a gray cloud of uncertainty hung over this beautiful country. I couldn't forget what happened the evening we arrived in Johannesburg. As relatives drove us from the airport to their home, we were trailed by police, who motioned for the car to pull off to the roadside. An officer illuminated each of our white faces with his flashlight and asked, quite politely, for the driver to step out of the car for an identity check. The interruption lasted only a few minutes. "Sorry for the delay," he said in his Afrikaans accent. "You people have a nice visit."

"Probably looking for an escaped political prisoner," our cousin said, but he didn't go into detail.

Most upsetting of all was an unexpected trip to an infamous place we had read about in the newspapers at home. "Why on earth do you want to take them to Soweto?" our cousin's wife asked her husband. "It's too dangerous."

He scoffed at her remark. "No, it's not. Why shouldn't people see it?"

"The day of reckoning is coming. It's only a question of time," Jerry said to me earlier that day. He was upset because the surly manservant of the house kept calling him "Master."

We didn't expect a carefree paradise on this South African trip. We came prepared. In Washington we had been moved by Alan Paton's *Cry, the Beloved Country* and Athol Fugard's *Blood Knot*. Author Nadine Gordimer stirred me with her stories that emphasized the injustice and bigotry of apartheid. One afternoon on their shady verandah, our cousin's liberal wife handed me a battered copy of Olive Schreiner's *The Story of an African Farm*, published in 1883. "It's the first and greatest South African novel ever written," she said. "There's much one can read between the lines."

Although Jerry and I were aware of increasing racial tensions, it wasn't until we entered the township of Soweto that reality struck home. Now forty years later, looking back, I can remember only a handful of things about Soweto. Our cousin had not obtained the required pass or any special permission to enter. That alone put Jerry and me on edge, but his relative laughed at us. "Don't worry," he said, "we'll be fine."

As we drove slowly through the wretched streets, I recall thinking, this is more than a disadvantaged neighborhood. I had seen the miserable poverty of city slums in Baltimore and Washington, but this affront to human dignity surpassed them all. The narrow, soot-blackened streets were lined with wooden shacks. In almost every doorway stood a woman holding a baby, surrounded by toddlers. Expressionless, they stared at us as we drove by.

The segregated town had been built for laborers in the nearby mines. The men were away at work and the younger women were off somewhere in Johannesburg cleaning houses and tending to white children. Their commute from the city to this hellish place had to be long and exhausting, but they weren't allowed to live closer to their jobs.

The overpowering pollution from the nearby industrial plants made our eyes water. Domestic coal fires heated each house. We wondered how residents could live breathing coal-fired air month after month, year after year. On crowded streets, open markets thrived; uncollected garbage filled dirt ditches nearby. We did not see a single white face or a smiling child or an adult whose expression didn't register hopelessness and degradation. We left before dark. It wasn't a place people of our color wanted to be at night.

Apartheid in the Republic of South Africa ended in 1994. Life may have grown somewhat better for the citizens who lived in Soweto and its replicas throughout the country. Now in the twenty-first century, travelers can find packaged tours of Soweto listed on the Internet. I wonder how the story is told. Tourism always tends to disinfect history.

A Shifting Wind

After we returned from Africa, I learned that my sister Eleanor, at sixty, was battling lung cancer. She hadn't smoked in thirty-five years, and even before then only occasionally. A brief half year after the diagnosis, she died on a hospital respirator. She was my defender, my protector, who had watched over her little sister and kept her from running into the street. It was she who obtained a library card for me and introduced me to *A Child's Garden of Verses.* Growing up, before we fell asleep together under the same quilt, she read me Robert Louis Stevenson's lines about the little shadow that went everywhere with him. "That's you," she often said to me. "I see you jump before me when I jump into my bed."

JOURNAL ENTRY: AUGUST 1982

> The end of summer, and I fight an urge to cry long and loud at the unfairness of death. How will I be able to visit Mom and Pop's graves this fall without Eleanor? I'm trying to pull myself together after the pain of shiva and the feeling that all this is happening to someone else. Or maybe the person I thought I was has been pruned down to reveal the forlorn stump I really am.
>
> On NPR, I listened to Elmer Rice's *The Adding Machine,* a remarkable play with insights that come to a playwright

> once in a lifetime. When he wrote this in 1923, it lodged in his head all at once. With little revision, he got it down on paper in seventeen days. It makes me think he had help from some supernatural essence that invaded his subconscious, sowing the message that we enslave ourselves, that most of us little people don't know how to break out of our bonds even in Eternity. We are doomed as souls to be reborn, he writes, into the same petty lives that we led previously. Did this crystal truth come to Rice from beyond himself? How else to explain the overwhelming mystical quality of it?

Around this time, a Gotham publisher of Jewish feminist books, Biblio Press, offered me a contract to write a collection of verse about Jewish women. She had been reading my "Unholy Writ" column in a New York paper and thought I could unleash amusing but trenchant poetry on women's liberation. I felt late to the game. In the 1970s I had been too busy to follow the adventures of those campfire girls, Betty Friedan and Gloria Steinem, and their push for female equality. Why jump into the fray now, pretending to be a latter-day suffragette? I was a child of the Depression, a female whose duty was to make-do with whatever life offered. I was hardly in the mood to immerse myself in womanly hurts and harassments. Did a market really exist for a lighter touch, one that younger, more militant women would tolerate? Biblio Press assured me it did.

The editor/publisher, Doris Gold, pelted me with material from feminist publications. She scribbled in the margins, "How about this as a subject for a poem?" Or, "A topic perfect for your light touch." The woman was a veritable snake pit of ideas, some doable, some too off-the-wall even for me. I dreaded her letters from New York. Every time I thought enough poems had accumulated for a book, she loaded me with heavier cargo.

"Time out," I wrote back to Doris. "I have to make a historical detour."

The Free State Beckons

A competing opportunity had washed ashore. My home state planned to celebrate the 350th birthday of Maryland, founded in 1634 by Lord Baltimore and first settled by colonists arriving in two capital ships, the *Ark* and the *Dove*. Local citizens were already forming a committee to launch a year of commemorative activities. I discussed it with Jerry.

"*Yankee Shoes* in 1975 stirred the pot for me," I said. "It was fun to revisit the past and then pass it on to others."

"In a palatable form," Jerry added.

I went on to explain that here was an opportunity for me to become an actual part of Maryland history. "And this might be a chance to adapt history for the stage. That way it can reach entire communities."

"It's worth a try," Jerry said, "but you shouldn't let Biblio Press down."

On deadline I finished ninety feminist poems and sent them off to the publisher with a note: "The Biblical canon is hereby closed." And that's how *Daughters of Chutzpah: Humorous Verse on the Jewish Woman* materialized in 1983. The dedication page read: "In memory of my sister Eleanor, Poet Laureate of the Baltimore County Community Library." Working there for many years as a member of the office force, she wrote lighthearted birthday, wedding, and farewell verse to delight fellow staff members. Eight years older than I, an honor roll student all through high school, she had not gone to college but stayed home during the war to help in our parents' store. Chronology and world cataclysm mold our futures more often than we care to admit.

Daughters of Chutzpah derived its title from an introductory poem about three generations of mothers who complain that their rebellious daughters are too independent to attract husbands. Another poem, "Ancient ERA," related a tale from the Book of Numbers about five biblical daughters who won equal inheritance rights in a patriarchal society. Having temporarily cleared the decks until the first proofs would arrive from the publisher, I officially signed up for that Maryland 350 Committee and the celebration just ahead.

Meanwhile, back at the laboratory, Jerry approached the peak of his government career with publication of research papers, prestigious awards, and involvement in the Electrochemical Society. Even so, he always found time to support my fantasies. At first, the strain of serving on a committee of cantankerous Maryland citizens discouraged me.

"Everybody seems so competitive and touchy," I told Jerry after the first few meetings.

"That's the way committees are," he said cheerfully. "You should hear some of the soreheads I have to work with."

Always a loner, I represented no established community organization like the League of Women Voters or the Chamber of Commerce. Although the group vaguely classified me as an Idea Person, I was destined to be elbowed out of the way by articulate folks with better vocal projection. Eager to earn respect as a historian, I toted free copies of *Yankee Shoes* to distribute at those meetings. It somehow generated goodwill from this mélange of aggressive civic doers, professors, and genealogy gurus. In a brainstorming session, our 350 Committee chairperson suggested we schedule a Gala as our first project.

"We need a big public event that will kick off festivities for the year," she said. Everyone except me jumped in with grandiose plans, but when the question arose, "Who wants to take on this opening project?" the room grew quiet. All heads turned toward the Idea Person.

"How about an original show based on state and county history?" I heard myself ask, and then babbled on about recruiting talented local citizens, all creeds and colors, for a theatrical production that would include dancers, singers, actors, musicians, and artisans willing to donate their talents to such a worthy community endeavor. At the end of this impassioned speech, the entire committee broke into wild applause, voted "Aye" unanimously, and insisted that I take charge of the noble venture. They even chose the date: February 4, 1984.

For me, it was an open invitation to contribute to the community with whatever talent I had to share. Jerry was reaching retirement after more than thirty years at the National Bureau of Standards. He had just received a Lady

Davis Fellowship to do research and teach at the Technion, the MIT of Israel. It would begin in the fall of 1983 and extend into the winter and spring of 1984. How could I undertake the Gala and accompany Jerry on a journey that meant living in Haifa during the year ahead?

"You'll find a way," Jerry said, breaking into that broad grin of his. "Unless I can change your mind, Molkalini."

"Don't call me that," I said. It was a pet name he sometimes used, not terribly romantic. It reminded me of the departed Fascist dictator, Mussolini. "When we were young and foolish, you referred to me as Moll Flanders. I liked that better. It sounded more literary."

My husband laughed and recalled the first year of our marriage when I coaxed him into appearing with me in an amateur theater performance of *The Curious Savage*. He also recalled my having drafted him to don a bedsheet and fake beard in his portrayal of Rabbi Hillel, a famed sage of the first century BCE.

"You and your scripts for *The Jewish Community Hour.* That crepe hair on my chin was hell to remove," Jerry said. He could always get a smile out of me and took my hand. "It's your decision to make. Tell me what I can do to help."

"You'll be thousands of miles away. You won't be here to run interference."

"Then forget it and come with me," he said. "Now you're free to enjoy yourself for a change." It was true. Our sons were young adults; they no longer lived at home. The "Unholy Writ" column still ran in Washington and New York papers. A stay in Israel would supply grist for the mill; airmail could carry new poems to the States each week.

"I've always wanted to see a show of mine produced on stage," I said. "This could be a revue with humorous sketches based on Maryland history and whimsical lyrics I'll write for the songs, and maybe we can even find a choreographer to stage a serious ballet based on a Civil War battle."

Jerry interrupted me. "You've already drawn a blueprint in your head," he said. "Tell you what, go ahead and give them your script before we leave in October. There's the whole summer ahead to knock it out."

"That won't work," I countered. "The 350 Committee is depending on me to see the job through." The show couldn't be written until I knew what kind of volunteer talent was available, amateur and professional. That meant holding open auditions to attract performers. Once we had a general idea of which groups and individuals qualified, and once I finished researching historical background, only then could I produce a draft. With that done, the committee could easily secure a state grant to cover production expenses.

"Okay," Jerry said after hearing me state the case, "suppose I leave by myself. After you write and cast the show, work out a few preliminary details and then join me as soon as you can."

"You mean not stay here to see how it all turns out?"

"Yes."

"I can't just cut and run like that," I protested. "Besides, once it's written, I may want to direct it."

Jerry sighed. This was just as difficult for him as for me. "You really think you have the experience and stamina to handle a full-length production like this? Sounds like a hell of a lot of work."

"What about the TV show I handled when the kids were little, all those scripts I researched and wrote, and then finding actors, even putting together costumes? And my Play Direction class at Catholic U, remember? And that three-act S. N. Behrman play I directed for the Cheverly Players during the Cuban missile crisis?"

"I remember," he said. "You were so involved in that one, you forgot to worry about being wiped out by a nuclear war."

We were both weary of the discussion. "Okay," Jerry said with a tone of finality. "Do you want to stay here until it's all over?"

"Yes." By now I was in tears.

He put his arms around me. "Then you should stay."

"Really?"

"You won't be satisfied unless you do the whole job. It will be a smash hit. And in February, you'll join me in Haifa. Deal?"

"I love you," I said. But nothing is ever easy for a guileless navigator like me who, more often than not, sets sail without a compass.

JOURNAL ENTRY: JULY 1983

> The past four weeks have been jam-packed with 350 Committee meetings, Jerry's Georgia cousins visiting Washington for the first time, and a family wedding on Long Island. I've found little time to tackle the Gala script, which should be completed before open auditions in mid-August. Last week, I researched Maryland history at the local library and even drove downtown to the Library of Congress in search of authentic seventeenth- and eighteenth-century music.
>
> Armed with extensive notes and 78-rpm recordings, including "The Roast Beef of Old England," I now have enough fodder for an opening sketch on land grants in

colonial Maryland and the arrival of indentured servants. I'm acquainting myself with English ballads of the 1600s and then substituting my own lyrics. Maybe we can unearth a nearby musical group of classically trained singers to perform this kind of music. I also wrote press releases announcing tryouts. Everyone else on the committee seems to be at the beach. Completed back-up poems for the "Unholy Writ" column to have on hand in case I get too bogged down with show biz. I must find time to finish the Gala script.

JOURNAL ENTRY: AUGUST 1983

I'm hopelessly behind. It's a frantic time of preparation involving Jerry's upcoming departure in October, arguing with two boozy housepainters who goof off too much, and dealing with a hyper real estate agent. I doubt she'll find a tenant to rent our house because we'll be away less than a year. My poetic mishmash, *Daughters of Chutzpah,* came out a couple of months ago, and I haven't had a free minute to promote it. The publisher spread the word in feminist circles, resulting in some favorable newspaper reviews. She hates me because I'm not doing any readings or plugging the book.

I began writing bits and snatches of the Gala script. At our first organizational meeting, six helpers from the 350 Committee arrived to give their all to the cause, but they didn't know what to do. It was an Agatha Christie setting, bewildered strangers assembled for undisclosed reasons in that deserted mansion on Rockville Pike, a who-done-it that hadn't been done yet. I delivered a pep talk but could supply no finished script to show anyone. Meanwhile, I was called for jury duty.

JOURNAL ENTRY: SEPTEMBER 1983

A whirl of activity, including my mother-in-law's two-week visit and the High Holy Days with its lavish family meals of roast turkey and potato kugel provided by this frazzled chatelaine. Somewhere in between cooking and praying, Biblio Press squeezed in an interview for me on station WEVD in

New York. I took the train north, spent the night at the publisher's house in Queens, and woke up sleep-deprived from flailing about all night on a lumpy sofa-bed in her un-air-conditioned den. The host of the radio program read selected poems from *Daughters of Chutzpah* and stumbled badly over the lines, fracturing the meter. It was embarrassing.

I struggle to finish the Gala script. Committee members are breathing down my neck and asking where the hell it is. Finally, after three all-nighters I finished two comic sketches: "Namesake," about indentured servants; and "Birthday Roast," inspired by a yellowed program I discovered in a collection of library memorabilia left over from the Maryland Tercentenary in 1934. My latest sketch is about participants of that 300th birthday celebration as they battled the sweltering heat of Southern Maryland in their authentic woolen seventeenth-century costumes. According to an old newspaper article, they were dropping like flies. I tried to make it funny.

I conducted our first open auditions alone because our artistic director didn't show up. Neither did any real actors. Instead, stumbling into view came a parade of off-key sopranos, each one belting out her version of "Memory" from the musical *Cats*. Also taking center stage were a lonely tuba player, a ukulele virtuoso, an entire class of giggling nine-year-old girls from a neighborhood dance school, and an eighty-year-old baritone singing "The Impossible Dream." How am I going to mold all this into a musical show based on Maryland history? Is it too late to back out of this fiasco?

A couple of happenings, one good, the other a disaster. First, an excellent review of *Daughters of Chutzpah* in a Yonkers, NY feminist publication. Second, my Washington Jewish newspaper was sold to a new publisher, who is replacing the entire staff with hotshot out-of-town editors and reporters. In ordinary times, I'd be worried sick about the demise of the "Unholy Writ" column, which has run weekly in that paper for the past sixteen years, but right now I'm too harried to think straight. The new editors immediately discontinued my column, and they owe me money.

In October Jerry left for Haifa. Our Rockville house seemed lonely except for the family of raccoons who decided to keep me company. They settled comfortably in a crawl space under the roof just above my bedroom. If they stayed in the attic, I could live with them, although the pitter-patter of little feet overhead kept me awake nights. Feeding them popcorn seasoned with arsenic was against the law. A protected species, they had to be trapped (expensive!) and delivered to freedom in a more rural area. I wished some humane group would trap me, too, and ship me away to Tahiti. Pressure mounted on me to finish the still-untitled script. After researching seventeenth-century literature for archaic vocabulary, I came up with *Prithee, Happy Birthday, Maryland!* Best I could do.

VIA AIRMAIL: OCTOBER 17, 1983

Dear Mollee and Boys,
My Technion office here is very nice. It's probably larger than my old one at the Bureau of Standards and has curtains and a rug on the floor. There is a guy here (sort of helper, janitor, dogsbody) who speaks to me in Yiddish and provides me with a glass of tea.

The trip over was relatively smooth although I had a few bad moments. When I arrived in New York, the footlocker looked like it was going to come apart any moment, but it didn't. Worse was the carry-on bag which started leaking some liquid on the other bags while I was waiting for transportation to Kennedy Airport. Since I had four bottles of whiskey in it (gifts), I expected a mess. It turned out to be a bottle of hair lotion. The leaking was confined to one side. Most leaked out before the bus came. I kept moving it to new places on the sidewalk until I didn't see much of a wet spot.

When I checked in at New York with El Al, I was told that I could take only two bags plus one carry-on. Since I had three, they said I would have to pay $89 extra. I got excited and said two bags were not enough for my ten-month stay. I told them that I was a visiting professor at the Technion . . . so the woman said okay and let it through without my paying. Perhaps, Mollee, you should take only two bags plus a carry-on.

I arrived at our new place in Ahuza around 8:30. It's attractively furnished with many conveniences. It has a TV set, a stereo with records, a set of the Talmud, separate milk, dairy, and Passover dishes, a large refrigerator with a freezer, a modern stove with oven and grill, and a bathroom scale, metric of course. In some ways the place is better furnished than our own house. It has a nice garden and a place to park the car. Well, this letter is getting over-long. Miss you.

Love,

Jerry

Not Exactly Shipshape

After I handed the manuscript of *Prithee, Happy Birthday, Maryland!* to our 350 Committee chairwoman, a member of an old Maryland family, she took it home to the beloved plantation or wherever she lived. If she didn't like it, I planned to hop a plane and join Jerry for a glass of tea in Haifa. Unfortunately, the woman was ecstatic. At the next meeting she read aloud parts of the dialogue to a somewhat disgruntled committee, many of whom previously had shown mutinous signs of stripping the Idea Person of her credentials and feeding her to the fishes. They welcomed the script with a vibrant "Huzzah!"

NOVEMBER 1983

Dear Jerry,
Never did I expect "Prithee" would embroil me in county politics and the classic struggle between the executive branch of local government and the legislature. Our 350 Committee is under the jurisdiction of the County Executive's office, but to receive funding, we must engage the County Council, which looked down its nose at the entire idea of the commemoration because they hadn't thought of it first. A 350 Committee member wrangled a few minutes for me to appear before the County Council to plead our case. Shamelessly, I promoted the

> show by reading them my iambic pentameter Prologue along with the modern lyrics I've written for the antiquated state song, "Maryland, My Maryland." The legislators appeared startled and vaguely uncomfortable to hear poetry resound through their august chamber, but at the end, the county representatives rallied to our cause. We even won over their workhorses, the cynical staff people. I was told later that when secretaries in the County Council office typed, proofread, and reproduced the manuscript, they fought over it. One young office clerk said, "At least it's more fun than typing another rezoning report."

Everything had its price. I felt guilty that there was no time to promote *Daughters of Chutzpah* for Biblio Press. It's depressing to have a book published and not do anything to promote it. The publisher sent unhappy letters in which she blasted me for abandoning her, but I was struggling to stay afloat. According to Aristophanes (or maybe it was Neil Simon), plays are not written, they are rewritten. And rewritten and rewritten. Every line in *Prithee, Happy Birthday, Maryland!* became expendable. A fluctuating amateur cast necessitated constant revision of sketches, lyrics, scenes, and entire acts. Performers swore their allegiance and then dropped out. It hurt because I had spent hours in search of historical authenticity. Much to my delight, the dusty attic of a local nineteenth-century house yielded a stack of crumbling sheet music, written around the time of the Civil War. These songs became the perfect lead-in to a dramatic scene about the Underground Railroad, the secret route by which enslaved people escaped north to freedom.

That slavery scene gave me a few more gray hairs than needed. The script originally included three fugitive slaves and one German peddler, who rescued them from a Quaker's barn where they had been hiding. It was based on a TV script I had created twenty years before. The actor playing the peddler dropped out when he found a day job; I had to cut the part. Another nerve-wracking problem: finding local persons of color to portray slaves. It was my job to phone complete strangers, county citizens whose names were suggested. They refused immediately. A community church leader agreed to take the part, but after I rewrote the dialogue to include only two speaking parts, she withdrew to care for a sick relative.

This serious episode of history had to be retained. Maryland was a conflicted border state in which the Underground Railroad played a vital part. I shrank the scene to a dramatic monologue but still couldn't locate anyone to do it until a drama professor at Howard University in Washington saved us. She had been inspired by the 1977 TV miniseries *Roots*, based on Alex Haley's novel, and she admired the memorable cast of LeVar Burton, John Amos, Leslie Uggams, Cicely Tyson, Louis Gossett Jr., Maya Angelou, and Ben Vereen.

"I told my best student," the professor said, "that thanks to those fine actors, the award-winning drama introduced white viewers to the most realistic portrayal of slavery ever presented on television. And that's when this gifted young woman agreed to join your cast."

I slept soundly that night. It would have been an enormous mistake to commemorate Maryland history without reminding our audience that not everything in our past was glorious.

NOVEMBER 1983

> Dear Jerry,
> I miss you every day. The euphoria has worn off; the exhausting grind of "Prithee" begins to strike home. Enthusiastic people promise to help and are never seen again alive. I'm constantly rewriting, blocking, and directing the continuity scenes with a stable of unreliable amateurs who don't know stage left from right.
>
> Another political wrinkle for me has arisen in convincing the County Council president that he is an ideal person to deliver the show's Prologue in colonial attire. Although I expressed misgivings, the 350 Committee wants him in the cast. It's part of their political strategy to win the unanimous endorsement of his fellow Council members, who, when informed, promised they would all attend opening night. ("Bill in velvet pantaloons and a white wig? This we gotta see!") Flattered, he accepted the role and has never come to a single rehearsal. It does not bode well.

VIA AIRMAIL: NOVEMBER 1983

Dear Mollee and Boys,
Sunday is the day my Moroccan cleaning woman comes, but she didn't show up so I'm having servant problems. It's very annoying anyway because when she comes early in the morning, she always catches me while in the bathtub and I put on my raincoat to open the door while soaking wet. ("Oh, monsieur, le bain, pardon!") . . . Friday night, still one more invitation from a colleague and his wife. At dinner, another professor's wife looked out for your interests, Mollee. She told me, "I noticed you were talking a lot to a very attractive woman, Jerry." Well, that was true. I was talking to a doctor at the party who was originally from England and her husband is away in the U.S. for a year at Harvard. She is attractive, but I was mainly talking to her because she spoke English and I didn't have to sit around like a dummy when everybody is speaking Hebrew.

NOVEMBER 1983

Dear Jerry,
The chorus director keeps calling me to ask about the musical keys her sopranos must sing in. How should I know? I can't read music and don't know what to tell her. It never occurred to me we needed arrangements for the music. I guess we're lucky someone dragged in a retired music teacher from the community college to do that job. He is an American Revolutionary War enactor and really didn't want to help unless he could wear his bright red brass-buttoned uniform in the show. I had to rewrite the finale to include him in his damned uniform. Several late arrivals to the cast don't understand the purpose of our show. To prevent a full rebellion on my hands and to establish a feeling of esprit de corps, I took time to send each participating group a letter explaining what we're doing and why. It would be useful if someone would write me a letter telling me what I'm doing and why.

VIA AIRMAIL: DECEMBER 1983

Sweetie:

This is a little private letter to you. Of course I miss you! I don't know how long I can last all alone. I hope my weekly letters get to you. You really are going gangbusters. I'm proud of you on how you engineered the presentation for the County Council! Please don't work too hard and overdo it! Miss you terribly. Love you!

Jerry

DECEMBER 1983

Dear Jerry,

Mavis, our artistic director, is absent when we need her; she's been ill with flu. She has just told me she will be in England between December 15 and January 10! The show is scheduled to open February 4! Now I must shorten the Prologue speech of the County Council president, who says he can't memorize all those lines. Not one of my better months. On radio I heard a country-western dirge titled "If I Can Just Make It Through December," which said it all. We have not been able to rehearse with the entire cast, and that includes the marching band from the community college. Before our artistic director vanished, I hoped she would leave the Civil War ballet she promised to choreograph. Not so. She arranged for a high school senior to serve as my assistant, but this kid left on a road trip to Miami and forgot to come back. My voice has deteriorated from yelling too much at rehearsals.

Waterlogged and Listing

We were lucky to find actors from two excellent semi-professional community theaters. One group tackled with gusto the comic sketch about the Maryland Tricentennial celebration fifty years earlier. The other group consisted of classically trained singers who specialized in Gilbert and Sullivan and could easily manage the eighteenth-century melodies in the sketch about indentured servants. Over the weeks, I developed a recurrent pain in my left arm, but I thought it came from unloading props from our car trunk.

JOURNAL ENTRY: DECEMBER 1983

> Pains up and down my left arm are increasing. Dr. K prescribed nitroglycerin tablets. They threw my whole system into a tizzy, and then he sent me to an arrogant young cardiologist who gave me a stress test and coldly informed me of a heart abnormality. When I told him no doctor had ever diagnosed me with a heart problem before, he looked at me with disdain and snapped, "Well, you have one now. If you take two pills ten minutes apart and it doesn't help, call 911."

Escape from the Storm

As the El Al plane flew over the Atlantic Ocean, I closed my eyes and fell into a half-sleep. The 350 Gala had taken place as planned. Three days before my flight, *Prithee, Happy Birthday, Maryland!* played to a full house. The audience stood in unison as the costumed cast poured onto the stage to take the curtain call. Voices cried out, "Author! Author!" and a person, purported to be me, strolled into the lights and gestured magnanimously toward actors, singers, dancers, and musicians, encouraging more recognition for their efforts, not mine.

Now all that lay behind, forever gone. The motor of the Boeing 747 lulled me into another semi-dream. What price glory? My reverie floated back to mid-December and that persistent arm pain. One Saturday night our sons drove me to the Emergency Room of George Washington University Hospital, where nurses hooked me up to a dense forest of tubes, wires, and blinking lights. Although the boys wanted to call their father in Haifa, our family doctor advised them to wait. Two days of intensive testing told the tale: false positive. The diagnosis of that insufferable young cardiologist had been wrong about my heart.

"Too much stress," our primary care physician said. "You have to cut back on all your activities."

"I'm delighted to cut back," I told him. And all at once, Divine help came roaring in from all sides. The County Executive's office found a spirited young director to assume my chores. A retired history teacher volunteered her assistance as coordinator. As I recuperated with bedrest, she visited each day to relieve me of worrisome details like phone calls to remind truant actors of rehearsals, promotional letters and invitations to Maryland officials, press releases and copy for flyers advertising the show, the ever-changing lists of backstage volunteers, and the correctly spelled names of all two hundred fifty Gala participants. Then, finally, came my phone call to Jerry.

"I'm okay now," I said. He, of course, asked, "What do you mean NOW?"

"Oh, nothing. You'll be getting a letter from me about it."

Glory, glory, hallelujah. As my plane flew through mists of clouds over the Mediterranean Sea, I dozed and awoke with a sense of achievement. Doing the show didn't kill me. I was proudest of the young African American student's portrayal of a resilient slave in search of freedom. Her monologue received a standing ovation. And although our young brass band sounded a bit off-key, the uniformed players marched with unexpected professional confidence down the center aisle for the grand finale. Those show-stopping little girls from the dance class waved their miniature black-and-gold state flags and led a jubilant audience singing my updated version of "Maryland, My Maryland." What author in her right mind could ask for more?

It had been a gratifying moment in time, our humble, sometimes pathetic, grassroots extravaganza. Relatives, friends, and local politicians applauded until their hands blistered. They even laughed at the funny lines. Someone threw a bouquet of roses over the footlights; the 350 Committee awarded me with an engraved silver tray. *Prithee,* with all its flaws, became a part of history that night, representing the intrepid, do-it-yourself American Suburbia of the latter twentieth century. These days, I'm not sure one would find this kind of hometown effort on such a broad scale as that departed Gala of long ago. One thing is certain. They won't get me to do it again in 2034.

With my head in the clouds, I took a deep breath, sank my head into the pillow given me by the plane's stewardess, and visualized a placid harbor with Jerry smiling and waving me ashore. Instead, more stormy weather lay ahead.

Anchored in Haifa

Experience is overrated. Victorian writer Samuel Coleridge had the right idea in *Table Talk* when he wrote, ". . . experience is like the stern lights of a ship, which illumine only the tract it has passed." True. As our plane taxied across the tarmac at Ben Gurion Airport, reality held up a sign with my name printed on it in bold black letters.

The sweet reunion with Jerry, the genuinely warm welcome of his Technion colleagues and their wives, and the human vitality all around us could not blot out something that became clear to me at once. I was not the same person who had bid my husband a tearful goodbye in October of the previous year. At age fifty-five, I could not ramp up the same degree of youthful enthusiasm for my surroundings as I had on our first trip to Israel a decade before. Worse still, I had squandered ten months on a localized project that had little to do with advancing as a writer.

A maelstrom of ill health sent me spinning the first month. Every virus in the Middle East sought refuge in my battered hulk. To put it in purely unmedical terms, I quickly morphed into a sickly, coughing, aching, unapologetic middle-aged grouch with a fractured voice and an attitude that didn't ingratiate me with anyone. I had expected there would be a rude awakening once *Prithee* ended. What I wasn't prepared for was the onslaught of sore throat after sore throat, a severe sinus infection, sleepless nights, daily stomach upsets, nausea, and a touch of food poisoning. My entire body had finally rebelled against those demanding months of *Prithee*.

Jerry had already settled into the new surroundings; he enjoyed his research and interaction with students and professors. Always optimistic, he faced life in Israel with a sunny disposition. He arose each morning to drive a newly purchased Opel to the lab every day. He worked, joked, and laughed with an inner circle of distinguished scientists. Evenings, he took an Ulpan course enabling him to speak at least rudimentary Hebrew with his relatives who lived in Ra'anana, a suburb of Tel Aviv. The family were farmers, raised chickens for the market, and owned a large orchard where they grew oranges and grapefruit. In 1934 Jerry's aunt and uncle fled the pogroms of Eastern Europe to become pioneers in what was then a British mandate called Palestine.

"Why don't you join me in the Ulpan class?" Jerry would ask, always bent on bringing good cheer. "You'll meet people and get to feel at home there."

"That's the last thing in the world I want to do right now," I muttered, weighted down with woolen sweaters and two pairs of pants on top of bulky thermal underwear. Winters in Mediterranean countries are deviously damp and chilly. Our garden apartment, which Jerry had praised so highly in his letters, featured no central heating. We huddled around a space heater for warmth as we watched old reruns of *Bonanza* on a flickering TV set.

"The Ulpan is fun," Jerry said. "This week we're learning to talk about clocks. The instructor asks us, 'What time do you get up in the morning?' Now we know what time everybody gets up in the morning. My friend Eddie from Pittsburgh always gives a different answer because he says it doesn't make any difference as long as he answers something that's in Hebrew."

I had no patience to sit in a class with strangers or twist my brain trying to tell them in a foreign language what time I got up in the morning. Sometimes I didn't get up at all. Instead, I returned to a favorite complaint. "It's too damned cold in here," I said. "The only warm spot is the bathroom with that heat light in the ceiling. I hate taking baths in that stupid bathtub." The apartment building may have been constructed in the 1920s or '30s or possibly earlier to accommodate King Richard and the knights of the Crusades. Our bathtub was only three feet long with a seat built in at one end and an eighteen-inch ledge to sit on while soaking knees and feet. Folded up like a jackknife, I tried to avoid grazing my chin with my kneecaps.

Jerry, ever the loving problem-solver, used his technological expertise. "Try using the shower," he said.

"I wouldn't dare. It spits out in all directions and drenches the floor." Clumsily attached to the vinyl shower curtain with a piece of waterproof tape hung a hand-printed sign that read, BE CAREFUL OR U MIGHT GET WET.

I was in no mood for these oppressive surroundings. Our absentee landlords were German-born immigrants who rented out this furnished apartment to visiting professors and other foreign guest workers. The chilly rooms were overstuffed with humorless black furniture left over from the Weimar Republic. Brown brocade drapes and heavy wooden shutters blocked any sunshine from hitting this northern exposure. Our place looked like a stage set for John Van Druten's play *I Am a Camera* before it became the musical *Cabaret*. Both shows were based on Christopher Isherwood's novel *Goodbye to Berlin*, which I had read as a freewheeling, single young woman in Baltimore, which at a distance was beginning to look better and better.

JOURNAL ENTRY: FEBRUARY 1984

> Our bathroom has no toilet. It sits all by itself in a dreary room overlooking an enclosed mildew-smelling back porch and an ancient washing machine. The john is not a bidet in the glamorous French style but a bleak water closet flushed by the metal chain hanging from the ceiling. If I yank it hard, it will work. (Cue Judy Garland: *Clang, clang, clang, went the trolley.*) Wherever we go here and in Europe, the toilets confound us. I'm never sure whether to flip a lever, press a button, crank a handle (upward or downward), turn a faucet, stamp a pedal, or jab away at the porcelain in search of a magic button.
>
> "Thank God I am a child of the Depression," I often say to Jerry. "I remember how to make do." All utensils in the dank kitchen have to be washed by hand. Each dripping paper bag of garbage must be carried outside down a long and winding path to the Big Can, which disappears periodically. Ants invade the sugar bowl. Our gas range is not exactly on the cutting edge of technology either. Jerry orders bottles of gas when it runs out. Although one must light the burners with a match each time, the oven is electric. Since the toaster is broken, one can use the oven to make toast. One doesn't want to do this.

Fortunately, a Jewish-Moroccan woman named Seima arrived each week to scrub floors, vacuum, and do laundry. She composed her own songs based on the work instructions I gave her. For instance, she asked if Jerry's thermals were *propre ou sale*, clean or dirty. She spoke only French, but having minored in the language at college, I could connect with her better than with the Hebrew-speaking populace around me. If I answered *c'est sale* (dirty), she proceeded to go about the flat singing her own original tune to *"C'est sale, c'est sale!"* Or once when Jerry was home with flu—*il est malade,* I told her—she warbled *"Il est malade! il est malade!"* for the rest of the morning.

It was difficult to slam on the brakes after months of independence alone in our Maryland house. Now housebound in a foreign city, I feared going out, worried I'd get lost and find myself wandering helplessly in the Arab quarter of the city. From day to day, I never knew what social commitments were being made for us. Which of Jerry's friendly colleagues, whose names I could neither remember nor pronounce, would invite us for dinner with their families? How could I spend another evening trying to look pleasantly engaged while I didn't understand the language into which the conversation always lapsed after the first few English formalities? Although Jerry commiserated with me, he had his own struggles at work.

When we weren't having the traditional Friday-night dinner with an assortment of well-meaning Technion people, Jerry's uncle and aunt insisted that we dine with them on the weekend and sleep over in their tiny bungalow so that we could spend the Sabbath together. That was pleasant. Jerry's uncle, his father's younger brother, spoke only Hebrew and Yiddish, his mother tongue. Jerry, who had attended a Yiddish school in Atlanta, could easily converse with the old man. Although I wasn't fluent in the language, my parents spoke it, and I had a general idea of what the conversation was about. Younger members of the family were bilingual.

In the spring we were invited to a Passover Seder at the home of one of Jerry's cousins. The warmth and genuine hospitality inspired me to throw off my negativity and resolve to break out of the cheerless dungeon into which I had cast myself. I wrote this advice to my inward eye:

> You are here, gazing at the Mediterranean Sea, where the Phoenicians, the Greeks, the Romans once sailed, the Mediterranean, where the water is stretched out like a wrinkled blue-gray rug and then the lights of Haifa Bay, each one glowing, shouting, "Look at Me! Look at Me!" all the way up Mount Carmel. Embrace it. See, over there, Mount Hermon with a bit of snow on top like a balding old scholar. Look into the distance and know that all antiquity is captured in the rock formations of the Negev and enjoy the first real desert you've ever seen, the godlike desert where the Sabra cactus,

> in green, brown, and golden robes, rise for the Amidah, the Silent Prayer. And here is where Joshua fought the battle when those walls came tumbling down, and over there the Sea of Galilee, the lush greenery of the Kinneret, and somewhere, chasing history around in circles, blows the red desert wind and the crimson blossoms of sandalwood trees, can you smell them? Thrill to it, treasure all you see. In a few months, after you're back home, it will be a half-forgotten reverie, just like everything else in life that passes by whether you want to hold onto it or not.

Seeking a new friend for me is like making a left turn on a busy street. It's hard to break into oncoming traffic, and will your choice be the wisest one? In our airless living room, I found, stacked away in a black china closet, shelves of well-weathered books, including *The Life and Adventures of Martin Chuzzlewit.* The Dickens novel became my solace and best friend. I identified with one fictional character, the man who is not pleased with his life unless he can be in a situation where he proves to be jollier than all those around him. I, too, can shine when competing with negative people. I become miraculously positive, but left with no one to outshine, I become as dull as a hunk of steel wool. And confronted by someone striving to be more positive than I, something ugly happens to me. The person inhabiting my body turns into a bitchy horror, tight-lipped and grim.

Jerry, the most perceptive soul ever to walk the earth, sensed my Jekyll and Hyde changes of mood and became more concerned about me than his work.

"You'll be all right, Molkalini," he said as we huddled together for warmth near the space heater and watched old reruns of cowboy movies from a Christian TV station in Lebanon.

I shivered in my fleece-lined raincoat. "I doubt it. Haven't been able to write a sensible word ever since the plane landed."

He kissed my frozen cheek. "Know what I think it is?" he asked. "Chalk it up to the damned *khamsin*." He was referring to the dry wind that blew in from the desert. "People here blame it for anything that goes wrong. They say they're more nervous, more irritable when the khamsin blows. A woman at the lab told me her nose bleeds only at that time."

"Does it bring on menopause?" I asked. "Because that's what may be hitting me right now in addition to everything else."

"It could be you feel very tired, worn out from the khamsin. It's messy, and it leaves sand on the car."

"And in the house. Seima is always running the vacuum."

Pleased that he had my attention, Jerry continued. "There's a whole canon of lore about the khamsin. One belief is that it blows only every three days. And you can call it the khamsin in winter, spring, and fall, but not in summer."

"What do you call it in summer?"

He shrugged. "In summer you call it a very hot dry wind."

"It always blows?"

"On fifty days out of the year. The religious guys somehow connected it to the fifty days of counting the Omer between the Pesach and Shavuot holidays, but that's debatable. In fact, deciding whether something is or is not a khamsin causes violent arguments. If an outsider like me says it is, Israelis say it isn't and vice versa. My friend Eddie said a man from Morocco told him the khamsin was over, and Eddie said, 'But it's only lasted two days, and you said it has to blow three.' And the Moroccan man said, 'So I guess it isn't over.'"

"I'd rather not hear any more about it," I said. "It must be forty-five degrees in the apartment now."

But Jerry was teasing me and pretended not to hear. "Did you know the khamsin is bad for chickens?" he asked. "My cousin who raises them on the moshav said you have to pour water on the roof of the chicken coop or they die."

"Get me out of here," I said, crying and laughing at the same time.

He grasped my icy hand. "Let me take you away from all this," he said in a mock dramatic voice. "I can get off a few days from work. What are they going to do, fire me? Sunny Italy isn't that far away. Let's just pack a few things and fly over there."

"I love you, my mad scientist," I said.

"Even when the khamsin blows?"

"Especially."

And so we took off for Rome, Amalfi, Ravello, Positano, the Isle of Capri, the Bay of Naples, the Bay of Palermo, Milan, Florence, Venice, Pompeii, Siena, the works. We marveled at a natural rock formation purported to be the face of Garibaldi, and the tour bus nearly left us behind among the ruins of Pompeii when we got lost looking for the toilets. We were mugged by thieves in Rome. And because Italy as a Mediterranean country has winters not unlike Israel's, we were treated to cloudy skies and chilly raindrops almost every day of our trip. I caught another cold, but it wasn't so bad this time because Jerry caught it too. Our Italian trip did inspire me to dash off "The Venice Ghetto," where a fellow sightseer inspired the poem's final lines: *A tourist comments with a grin, / It's better outside looking in.*

JOURNAL ENTRY: APRIL 12, 1984

> I have an urge to jot down impressions on paper, possible seeds that may sprout eventually. Today while visiting the Museum of the Jewish Diaspora (Beit Hatfutsot), I watched a band of German tourists at a display that highlighted the work of a Torah scribe. "Torah sheiber," announced the guide, and she described what a Torah scribe does. Their next stop was a documentary about World-Renowned Jews; I heard the Germans laugh at the mention of Henry Kissinger. How could they laugh at anything? Watching the film, I choked back tears at the thought of those who did not escape the horrors that befell them and the injustice of so many compelled to leave their native lands, forced to make new lives for themselves elsewhere. These were some of the most creative minds of all time, novelists, poets, playwrights, composers, painters, physicians, professors, statesmen, actors, filmmakers. As they looked at the photographs of these gifted souls who gave so much to mankind, I wondered what the Aryan visitors thought of their Ultimate Solution now.

The weather grew warmer outside but not inside our Arctic flat. I spent time on a park bench with the Hebrew poems of Nathan Alterman translated into English by Robert Friend. A British-born Technion scientist and his wife had lent me books of Alterman's verse. I especially liked "The Olive Tree" and his lines: *When you wish your mountains to die /. . . It [the olive tree] will stand watch on the wall, your solitary bridegroom / And you will know your life is in its keeping.* Through these new English-speaking friends, I also discovered Yehuda Amichai's poem "Jerusalem, 1967," in which he describes "a port city on the shores of eternity." It inspired me to return to write impressionistic verse about another port city, Haifa, the harbor sitting "like a blue porcelain teacup below Mount Carmel."

In late April after Jerry and I visited a crumbling amphitheater left behind by the intrepid Romans, I described it in a poem called "The Ruins at Bait She'An." Closer to home, I immortalized in verse "The Cats of Ahuza," our roaming neighborhood felines, whose yellow-green eyes "could read Hebrew from left to right." The two Israel-flavored poems were published by small literary magazines after we returned home. Thirty-three years later these travel impressions appeared in the *Kosher Salt* collection.

After Jerry was invited to deliver a paper for an Electrochemical Society meeting in Toronto, we said shalom to Technion co-workers, sold the car, packed, and spent a week in Canada before returning home to Maryland. Without Jerry's patience and optimistic support in Haifa and the kindness of his relatives and colleagues, this ailing traveler probably wouldn't have stayed the course. Still, I profited from undisturbed hours with books and meeting resilient survivors like Sheina Sachar-Gertner, a Lithuanian-Jewish schoolteacher from Vabolnik. In her book, *The Trees Stood Still*, she described how she escaped a firing squad during the Holocaust by pretending to be dead. She told us that she lived in constant fear of betrayal by her Lithuanian neighbors and later joined an active partisan group living in the nearby woods. Her courage and sacrifice put a pampered American like me to shame. I vowed then to enjoy more fully the sheltered life into which I had been born.

The Tide Turns

JUNE 18, 1984

Dear Barney Bragin,
Thank you so much for your kind words. It's gratifying to receive appreciation from a fellow artist. The poem you referred to, "Jewish Clockworks," first appeared in my book *More Unholy Writ*, published in 1973. Since then that poem has been reprinted in publications and presented at poetry readings throughout the East with excellent response from the listeners, so I know it would make a winning song.

Your credits sound impressive, and your idea for the song is intriguing. You know, I've been searching for someone capable of writing good music for my lyrics. Like everyone else, I have an idea for an original musical in the back of my head.

Yes, Barney, I know I am a lyricist although it was nice of you to remind me. And my answer to your request is okay, you may use my lyrics in "Jewish Clockworks." The copyright on the words is in my name, and you must list in the credits "Copyright, 1973" on the special form that the Copyright Office provides. Please send me a copy of the song.
Best wishes and good luck,
Mollee Kruger

The remainder of 1984 saw the defeat of the first woman ever to run for vice president of the United States. I was upset that Walter Mondale's ticket with Geraldine Ferraro failed against Reagan and Quayle. Obviously, our country was not ready for a female in its second highest office. The national election results would have been more depressing if a local government official, an admirer of *Prithee,* had not awarded me with an appointment to a newly formed county project, the Commission on the Humanities.

The nonpaying position meant working directly with university professors, public school teachers, and artists seeking grant money for worthwhile projects. I would help make decisions on literary, historical, and sociological programs funded by county taxes. The challenge would be to publicize the humanities and make them more palatable to the general public. I saw this as my way to become a teacher-at-large, fulfilling at last my mother's dream.

Meanwhile, Doris Gold at Biblio Press forwarded a belated review of *Daughters of Chutzpah* which ran in Yonkers, New York. Critics liked it. While I was out of the country, the book of feminist poems underwent a second printing, Doris said, and had been included in Women's Studies courses at a handful of colleges. The publisher suggested that I now write a biography of Emma Lazarus, author of the stirring lines inscribed on the Statue of Liberty. I had already used her work as inspiration for a poem called "The Statue Speaks Again." The words are as timely today as they first were when I wrote them in 1976 to mark the American Revolution Bicentennial:

Give me your tired, your poor (she said)
And never fear abuse,
The new blood feeds my arteries
I put it to good use.
You brought me your European dregs
Rejected and despised,
And soon they mainstreamed in my blood
A land revitalized.
Give me the incandescent core
That keeps my lamp ignited,
For they belong like all of you
Who came here uninvited.

The Cape of Dystonia

Unfortunately, a threatening health situation scuttled all upcoming plans. My voice was misbehaving; it took greater effort for me to utter more than a sentence or two at a time. Still, I pretended nothing was wrong; writers live in a world of make-believe. I convinced myself that Emma's life story no longer fit into my schedule. Politics called. Serving as a county commissioner could bring me closer to my neighbors and perhaps reveal unexplored territory to conquer.

Not facing up to the voice problem, I plunged into creating poems about Maryland history and entered one in a contest held by an exclusive liberal arts college on the East Coast. The poem, "Henry Harford," was a narrative about the colonial inheritance lost after the American Revolution by the bastard son of Frederick, England's sixth Lord Baltimore, proprietor of Maryland. I imagined Henry in Annapolis, hat in hand, trying to restore his lost legacy or at least collect reparations from unsympathetic American citizens. Sealing the envelope, I muttered to Jerry, "There's no way in hell of my getting even a bloodless Honorable Mention from this gang."

"It has substance," my loyal husband said. "Who wouldn't like a poem about Henry Harford?"

"Who would?"

Once again, Henry lost out. The manuscript didn't win, but the returned entry bore this note from an unknown judge: "Delightful and well-crafted." I felt vindicated. Poets take whatever they can get.

* * *

That unidentified malady continued to plague my vocal cords. Even so, I agreed to read selections from *Daughters of Chutzpah* for a group of Virginia women. A gifted Jewish-Malaysian-Chinese poet named Hilary Tham told me she had discovered the feminist book for sale at the Writer's Center, a hub for Washington-area writers of all genres. It was she who invited me to entertain at a luncheon.

I read, but it didn't sound like me. The voice that had done my bidding for years rebelled and lodged halfway down my throat where, for a full forty-five minutes, it struggled to escape. The resulting sound was a half-whisper that faded into nothingness and returned in sporadic gasps. The sympathetic audience thought I was struggling with laryngitis. Although they responded with enthusiasm and generously bought numerous copies of the book, the reading frightened me. I didn't have laryngitis.

JOURNAL ENTRY: APRIL 20, 1986

> My voice continues to take flight, and I'm afraid to learn why. Small talk is a luxury I can't afford these days; words stick in my craw, sounds come and go. Dreading the worst, avoiding doctors, I hope it will all go away. Last week I began voice exercises from a book written by a speech specialist. Maybe if I practice for fifteen minutes three times a day, things will improve. Forcing the sound does more harm than good, and the unreliability worries me. My voice is like a workman who doesn't show up for work when needed, and then even when he does, botches the job.
>
> Jerry is alarmed. "Don't neglect this," he said. "I'll make a doctor's appointment for you. If necessary, I'll drag you there."

We turned to Dr. Feggleman (not his real name), a reputable ear, nose, and throat physician in Washington. His laryngoscopy examination consisted of a tube thrust down into the throat through my desensitized nose. The test revealed no malignancy.

"It could be a disorder called spastic or spasmodic dysphonia," Feggleman said. He explained that perhaps an involuntary muscle condition affected the way my vocal cords opened and closed to admit the passage of air. "Breathing vibrates the cords, or vocal folds, as we call them," he said, "and that produces voice. An inadequate amount of air passing between the folds creates poor voice quality."

He confessed that doctors didn't know much about spasmodic dysphonia. "We have no idea what causes it, and there's no cure," he said, adding that surgery could possibly alleviate the condition. "A surgical procedure is available. I've recommended it to several of my patients."

The operation involved cutting a nerve adjacent to the vocal fold. This would ease the restriction and allow air to flow through more freely. At least that's what I think the doctor said. As soon as he talked about cutting a nerve, he lost me. And the risks? The size of the area where the food went down would become reduced. In other words, I might have trouble swallowing for the rest of my life. When he noticed my lack of enthusiasm, he quickly added, "The operation is reversible, and the nerve will grow back." He paused. "Eventually."

I shook my head. Dr. Feggleman reached for his prescription pad. "Here's the name of a speech pathologist who can give you further diagnosis."

It was not a cheery office. I listened to patients whose larynxes had been removed; they communicated robot-like through electrical voice boxes. It was difficult to understand what they were saying. The specialist taped my voice and then said, "Do you think you sound like any of these patients who have spasmodic dysphonia?" He played another tape. What I heard was depressing, men and women making tortured sounds with great effort. One patient, who had already undergone surgery, could speak faster than the others but with a dismal hoarseness. It was terrifying to hear.

"There's another way to determine whether or not you have spasmodic dysphonia," the speech pathologist said. He could recommend me for clinical trials at the National Institutes of Health. Later, when I phoned for details, they told me that by injecting botulinum toxin into the muscles near the larynx, the researchers hoped to relax the nerves that control the vocal mechanism. This might help a patient produce a better voice with much less effort.

"But isn't this the same botulism you get from eating poisoned toadstools?" I asked.

The NIH person assured me the dosage was minute and had worked wonders in relaxing eye muscles. The doctors weren't quite sure whether it would do the same for my voice. I was leery of the procedure. During this time in the mid-1980s experts and the public in general had no inkling that one day Botox shots would be used cosmetically like cold cream or moisturizer to erase wrinkles on aging faces.

"What's the risk? What will the long-term effects be?" I asked, and of course, no one knew. "How will letting them inject that poison into my body every three or four months affect my lungs or kidneys or heart?" I asked my primary care doctor.

"I'd wait a while before doing this," he said.

When the permission papers arrived in the mail for signing, I refused to serve as a guinea pig for the injections but agreed to other tests to see whether my problem was indeed spasmodic dysphonia. Assured that I could quit at any time, I submitted to a videolaryngoscopy. It was strange to watch my vocal folds on a screen that pictured the reaction of my voice as I repeated phrases and sentences. I was seeing an internal display of body parts hitherto unknown to me. There they were on the screen, the little darlings, my very own vocal cords, resembling two forlorn scoops of half-melted vanilla ice cream.

The medical crew wired me for a laryngeal electromyography to determine which muscles might be having spasms or abnormal movements. "We are going to insert these electrodes into your laryngeal muscles," they said. I expected my hair to stand on end like the Bride of Frankenstein. Instead, prickly sensations sparked through my throat as I repeated sounds and sentences like a toddler learning to talk.

After two days of testing, which included analysis of laryngeal, respiratory, mouth, and facial speech functioning, my NIH friends told me that all they could see was an incomplete closure of the vocal folds when I spoke. They recommended a trial period of speech therapy.

"It's not life-threatening," I told Jerry. "I can live with my silence a bit longer."

He looked sad. "It's okay," I said. "Many husbands would welcome this as a reprieve."

Perhaps delay of further testing was foolhardy, but we had already made reservations for a northern cruise to explore inland waterways and, along the way, dock at exotic places like Ketchikan, Juneau, Whittier, Wrangell, Valdez, Sitka, and Anchorage. We were scheduled to take the good ship *S.S. Universe* on one of its highly recommended educational tours in conjunction with the University of Pittsburgh.

Seward's Folly and Mine

A speech disorder was not the best thing to pack for an Alaskan cruise. I had no burning desire to strike up tortuous conversations with others, especially older passengers with hearing problems. Our first day out was not promising. When the ship's public address system announced a tea party on the promenade deck, Jerry and I hurried to a sweet table set with all manner of cakes, pastries, and fruit pies. We selected magnificent slices of German chocolate cake, and then we rushed to find deck chairs, most of which were already taken. We grabbed the last one. While I stretched out on the lounge chair, Jerry placed our cake on a nearby wrought-iron table and pulled up two wooden folding chairs for us. He hastily devoured his cake before remembering hot tea was available nearby.

"Stay put. You look too comfortable to be disturbed," he said. "I'll get us some tea."

"Perfect," I said. "You can sleep on this lounge when you get back. I'll have my cake later."

Pulling a wool blanket up to my chin, I settled down for a quick nap, but not before I noticed, hovering close by, a heavy Slavic-looking woman in a curly red wig. When I opened my eyes after nodding off, I found her sitting in Jerry's vacated chair. In horror I watched as she bore down on my luscious uneaten piece of cake, grabbed it with her bare hands, and wolfed it down in three undainty gulps. I parted my lips in protest, but no audible sound came out. Nothing. Without glancing at me, she wiped her nose with my napkin and lumbered off. When Jerry returned with the tea, I cried out in a voice that could have been heard all the way to the Klondike, "That woman stole my cake!" Passengers turned to stare. The culprit disappeared.

"Hey," Jerry said, "you sound pretty good today."

What I liked about this trip were the daily lectures on such topics as the culture of Aleuts, Eskimos, and coastal Indians. I enjoyed the talks by art historians explaining the intricate designs carved on native totem poles. A professor spoke of Vitus Bering, who discovered the Bering Sea in 1742. We learned that the Russians held Aleut kinfolk hostage until their hunters turned in a required number of furs. If they didn't fill the quota, their families would be killed. I had heard of gold rushes, but there was even a Fur Rush in search of skins from the Bering Sea otter.

"Alaska was peripheral to the Russians," the lecturer informed us. "There was always the difficulty of keeping their struggling settlements provided with food. The domestic problems of the mother country were always more important. In 1867 the United States bought the territory for $7.2 million. That's a real bargain, just two cents an acre."

When we weren't listening to lectures on Alaskan geology or to concerts by a string quartet, we assembled on deck to marvel at bottlenose dolphins, fin whales, breaching humpback whales, blue whales, and sperm whales, kin to my good friend Moby Dick. We gloried at the sight of porpoises, bald eagles, and seals with remote expressions on their faces. Always scribbling notes, I kept to myself, mindful of my uncooperative voice and the futility of engaging strangers in strained conversations.

JOURNAL ENTRY: AUGUST 15, 1986

> We headed into Glacier Bay this morning, and now I'm on the starboard side of the promenade deck to listen to a Park Ranger. We're approaching Margerie Grand Pacific Glacier, birds ahead, tufted puffins, black-legged kittywakes representing the seagull family. It's about fifty degrees F outside, but I'm blanketed and cozy in the deck chair, a cup of Irish coffee in my hand. We passed a spot called Johns Hopkins Inlet. "Can't get away from Baltimore, can I?" Jerry said.

Whoops, I just saw an ice ball fall from a glacier. It startled the birds so much they flew off their nests. The surrounding hills look like the bald pates of very old elephants, rough, wrinkled, and dullest of gray. There is an ancient quiet hanging above the mountains. I've struck up a conversation with the mist. No one can hear it except the mountains and me.

Captain's First Mate

Returning home, I tried to put my spasmodic dysphonia into perspective. Voice loss must be worse for politicians, actors, lawyers, teachers, singers, salespeople, and clergy. In the year that followed, I pared down my words, using as few as possible, each syllable carefully planned. In restaurants I pointed to items on menus instead of ordering them aloud. All telephone messages to the plumber, the doctor, or the airlines were written out ahead of time, word for word, with all the economy of a thirty-second TV commercial. It was easier for me to read from a prepared script than to speak extemporaneously.

After discovering a certified speech therapist in a nearby neighborhood, I visited her home office twice a week. Months passed, filled with progress one week, regression the next. I longed to drop the voice sessions and return to full-time writing without these distractions. Jerry became quite concerned with me, although his own career was blooming as a professor at Johns Hopkins University.

Despite the hourly commute to Baltimore, Jerry enjoyed working with young people. In his earlier years as chief of the Corrosion and Electrodeposition Section at NBS, he hired a lively group of budding scientists who led fascinating social lives. One summer they organized a Casino Night with roulette and card tables paid for by fake currency featuring the faces of mice called Cor-rodents. The corrosion crew even distributed T-shirts that read "In Rust We Trust." Jerry always had fun working with the younger crowd, who liked him because he never took himself too seriously. At Johns Hopkins, he became involved in university activities and tried to engage me in the new social world of his academic colleagues and their wives. My attempts to join him were half-hearted. It was too difficult to explain myself to overly sympathetic strangers.

I did make inroads with his students. When they invited us to a Halloween party, we appeared in full costume, I, all in white, as a silent Emily Dickinson, and he, with clawing fingernails and scary makeup. He wore a sign identifying him as Freddie Krueger, a menacing serial killer in movies we had never seen. Jerry was popular with the young people. Each fall at the beginning of the term, he treated his graduate students to a Sunday breakfast at the Hopkins Faculty Club. I always joined them because students are seldom eager to hold long conversations with their professors' wives unless the lady happens to be Deborah Kerr in *Tea and Sympathy* or Elizabeth Taylor in *Who's Afraid of Virginia Woolf?*

My metallurgical spouse made his biggest hit with students when he posted on his office wall "Rust Never Sleeps," a poster of a Neil Young and Crazy Horse album cover. Jerry and I were mid-level insomniacs. After learning about the poster, I issued a wisecracking remark, which tickled him for some reason. "May I quote you on that?" he asked. He keyboarded my words in a gigantic bold font and attached it to the poster so that it read "Rust Never Sleeps . . . and Neither Does Mrs. Rust —Mollee Kruger." Not many people appreciated the joke, but I was pleased to receive this honor from the JHU Department of Materials Science and Engineering.

"The name Mrs. Rust seems grungy," I told Jerry. "If necessary, I prefer to be called Mrs. Corrosion."

"Right," he said. "It sounds classier."

In early 1985 Jerry learned of an upcoming Summer Writers Conference on the Homewood campus of Hopkins. He told me he would also be working there on a special assignment before classes started in the fall.

"This is just what you need," he said. "You'll live on campus for a couple of weeks, and I'll be there too. You can make new friends and contacts."

"I'm a journalist at heart," I said. "I don't feel comfortable around pretentious English Department academics."

Jerry handed me an application. "Don't be so pessimistic," he said. "Fill this out and send them an example of your stuff." I shook my head. "Please?" he said. "Do it for me?"

But what about my voice? Would I be able to battle criticism of my work in open discussions at this writers conference? Or would I suffer needlessly, crawling into a silent shell and hating everybody around me? How could I be outgoing when my voice sounded like air leaking from a punctured tire?

As the deadline drew near, I relented and scribbled a check for the registration fee. I sent them "Forsythia," an ill-fated short story rejected innumerable times.

"That Hopkins bunch is not going to accept me into their rarefied circle," I said to Jerry. "I'm not that kind of writer."

"Give it a try," he said.

On the application form, in the space where they asked for age, instead of fifty-six I scribbled, "Nobody's damned business."

"That's telling 'em," Jerry said.

Briefly invigorated, I made another wild stab at freelancing and mailed off a flurry of poems to *Modern Maturity*. The magazine surprised me by purchasing two light-verse poems. This acceptance by a national magazine emboldened me to think it was the beginning of a beautiful friendship. After publishing the first one, "Imbalance," the editorial staff modernized the publication's layout and content and reconsidered running the second poem. They paid handsomely for both, but with the revised format, the editors stopped buying poetry of any kind. All was not lost. Another sample of my verse, "Author! Author!" was accepted by an obscure writers' magazine in Michigan. It paid twenty-five cents a word.

"Better than nothing," Jerry said. "You're on a roll now, Molkalini."

Bits and pieces of my work continued to find their way to editors who did not know me and didn't care to. Meanwhile, Jerry, invited to a meeting in Tokyo, lobbied me to accompany him. "How often do we have a chance to go to Japan?" he said.

Escape made sense. Even if my voice defied me, the Japanese would be polite and act as if they understood every word.

"Do you think taking a break in routine will recharge my vocal batteries?" I asked. "Maybe I've been trying too hard, overdoing the deep breathing and the daily exercises."

"Only one way to find out," Jerry said. "Come with me. I'll introduce you to one of my esteemed Tokyo colleagues who belts out a Japanese version of 'I Dream of Jeannie with the Light Brown Hair.'"

It didn't seem like a compelling enough reason to travel from East to West Coast and then across the Pacific Ocean. What appealed even less was a silent week at home with indifferent rejection slips as my only companions. I compiled a list of Things to Take Along, packed a barely closable suitcase, and off we flew via Chicago and Seattle to the realm of Madame Butterfly.

Tokyo Transients

After our punishing twenty-four-hour flight, we managed to wake up at the Shiba Park Hotel in Tokyo. That first bleary-eyed morning, I vaguely recall a hazy demonstration in the lobby on how to open oysters when looking for pearls. A beautiful young woman materialized out of the mist to conduct a contest among the guests. I didn't draw the magic number to win a free pearl. No loss. In my Zen state, I would have swallowed it with my vitamin pills.

I always take notes on trips, but in Japan, spelling was a problem. Although the English-speaking guides identified each site, by the time I figured out how to spell and write down the name, our bus would speed ahead to still another gorgeous pagoda, blotting out whatever we had just seen. Ill-prepared, not having studied a guidebook beforehand, Jerry and I joined forces, constantly asking, "What did she say that was?"

It became necessary to use American-style phonetics to record names and places. I chopped up the sounds into manageable syllables and printed out everything in capital letters. I don't trust the puzzling notes I kept, but let's just say we took a bus to HA-KO-NE and KA-MA-KU-RA to view the famous Great Buddha.

On the way to the temple, we laughed at an English sign that advertised "Delish Curry." We eventually landed at the HA-KO-NE Hotel, a mountain resort that smelled of sulfur from the hot springs. Although Jerry usually avoided heights, we took an aerial cable car up Mt. KOM-A-GA-TAK-E for the fantastic view and couldn't see a thing because it was snowing. The weather turned damply bitter. Almost everywhere we went, I dressed in the same woolen suit jacket, blue wool slacks, fleece-lined raincoat, heavy turtleneck jersey, and thermal underwear left over from our winter in Haifa.

Our conservative Japanese guide spoke wistfully about the change in male-female relationships in his country. "Men take out the garbage," he said. "Some women work, some stay home and watch soap operas and acquire wisdom while men get very tired." He warned us about women who drive motorcycles. "If you see one, you be very careful. Stand back." The following day, an unmarried female guide clarified the generational divide. "Japanese men use only three words when speaking to their wives," she said. "Dinner, bath, bed." In the thirty-odd years since that trip, Japan's birth rate has dropped; numerous career women prefer to remain single.

A human mind can absorb a limited amount, and then it shuts down. I felt this way in Tokyo on an expensive cab ride through the Ginza section. The garish neon lights seemed like an unfathomable puzzle designed by a madman. Nothing seemed to connect with anything else, no two pieces fit together, no pattern existed. In Ginza, false gaiety was ominous and harsh, the lights as blinding as a migraine. I found this freewheeling, anything-goes section of town out of keeping with the rest of an exquisite country, laden with quiet rivers and welcoming harbors, pine-draped valleys, and a tradition which prided itself on order and discipline.

I quickly became overwhelmed with playing the part of a tourist in a culture that raised enigmatic questions everywhere we looked. One morning I resisted taking another tour and discovered in the lobby an English-language magazine published in Tokyo. It was sponsored by the PHP Institute, founded a year after World War II ended. The goal of the organization was to promote peace, happiness, and prosperity.

Despite the precision of bullet trains, the crazy-quilt lights of the Ginza, and the humorless Kawasaki factory tour, I sensed around us a certain empty sadness, a cultural stalemate despite the obvious technical progress. I knew nothing about the emotions of ordinary Japanese citizens. Where would I find clues to deeper feelings behind the polite smiles and dignified bows?

One of the most impressive articles in the PHP publication described Enka, a popular kind of music enjoyed by everyday folks. Written in minor key, the melancholy tunes were performed by vocalists in a style that blended singing and sobbing. The songs reflected desire, indignation, and unhappiness. This was more like it. Universal human feelings interested me far more than gimmicky tourist traps or lectures on the country's industrial advancement.

The magazine article offered English translations of Enka lyrics, simple words that expressed the pain of the country's ordinary people. The style was handed down from an earlier period of their history. Songs written in the turbulent 1920s revealed the misery and fatalism of the working man. One depressing ballad addressed the lack of change in "this endless stream of life" and the hardship of "living through eternity as Tone River boatmen, as withered pampas grass."

Earlier Enka songs were often sung by wandering street minstrels, who tried to whip up some protest among the downtrodden masses. A 1931 melody, "The Carefree Warrior" by Ichimatsu Ishida, bemoaned the sacrifice of the "sons of the poor," who honored their emperor while being killed by the Chinese in Manchuria. After the penniless die for their country, the poet wrote, "the rich shall buy all the salt," meaning they would profit from the war. And then he commented with sarcasm, "Oh, what a carefree life!" Ishida was arrested for daring to express such thoughts. He later amended his paean of frustration by admitting it was better not to complain. His clever song might please his customers, he wrote, *But I would only go right back to jail / Oh, what a carefree life!*

His irony struck home. Sometimes an identical sardonic approach to politics and tradition appeared in my own poems. I absorbed enough of this magazine article to refer to Enka in conversations with Japanese hosts at cocktail parties and dinners sponsored by the country's universities and businesses. My listeners seemed stunned that a woman from the United States had heard of Enka. It was a superficial ploy on my part; a little bit goes a long way when diverse languages clash, and everyone is struggling to find something to say. Just before we left Tokyo, a thoughtful young scientist handed me a recording of Enka music to take home.

After viewing shrines and palaces in Kyoto, Jerry and I headed for Nikko in a people-stuffed train, the aisles thick with humankind. In the aisle next to my seat, an expressionless little man tried to maintain his balance while the crowd pushed him into an absurd angle that forced him to lean over me. I cringed away from him, but he extended so far that he could touch the window beyond Jerry's seat on my right. There the Japanese gentleman busied himself by wiping off the moisture accumulated from the panting throng around us. Corners of his black raincoat kept swinging into my face. Meanwhile, Jerry and the man began a lively conversation because he knew a few words of English, and Jerry could fake any foreign language that confronted him even when he didn't know a word of it. The passenger ended his journey with a "Goodbye" in exchange for our "Sayonara." We parted the closest of friends. Literally.

Seated behind us was Bob, a New Jersey colleague, concerned we wouldn't know when we reached Nikko because we could neither read Japanese station signs nor understand the conductor's announcements. He had a point. Fortunately, Nikko was the last stop on the line, which ended at a stone wall. We found our hotel, a rickety place built one hundred years before by the French, and here we met a New Zealand colleague also on his way to the corrosion conference. All of us devoured an edible meal of god-knows-what and retired early after watching a Japanese TV version of *Laugh-In* with blackout skits performed by actors making bizarre noises at each other.

Located high in the mountains, Nikko turned out to be a holy place. I felt we were trespassing in areas where we didn't belong. Before Jerry's meetings began, we toured with our friend Bob, and began our ascent to the Nikko Toshogu Shrine, a sacred spot venerating Tokugawa Ieyasu. A shogun born in 1542, he unified the country and led it to peace and cultural progress.

"My Japanese colleagues tell me that 'Nikko is *kekko*,'" Jerry said. "That means spectacular." He nodded his head at the grandeur before us. "They spoke the truth."

The son of Toshogu built the shrine to honor his father; a grandson rebuilt it. More than four million laborers completed the project. Gilded carvings of peacocks, dragons, birds, and monkeys surrounded us at every turn, and this constituted only the Outer Shrine. Although neither Jerry nor Bob's wife felt up to climbing the 233 steps to the Inner Shrine, equivalent to twenty stories high, Bob talked me into it, saying, "Perhaps we'll even find a holy man living at the top." He finished by telling me a joke about a Jewish mother who climbs up a mountain to reach the sanctuary of a sainted guru and then says, "Enough already, Sheldon, come home."

Why we wanted to reach the top I'll never know. The higher we climbed, the more penetrating the cold, which filtered through layers of my woolen clothing. At journey's end, we found a hollowed trunk slashed open to reveal a holy tree branch inside. The Inner Shrine was as plain as the outer one had been elaborate. Nearby hung a twisted rope adorned with cowbells, which tourists were invited to ring. I yanked the rope, tossed ten yen into an earthen pot, and said an impassioned prayer for a safe trip down those perilous stairs we had just climbed. We were due back at the hotel for a six o'clock reception to welcome all scientists attending this auspicious international meeting. I dreaded the meal ahead because already my digestive system had sent me a dire warning in Tokyo.

"Eat lightly," Jerry said. "Remember, less is more." In this case even less was risky.

When we awakened the next morning, snow was falling gently and would continue all day long. The whitened landscape around us duplicated every lovely Japanese print we had ever seen, pine trees heavy with snow, purplish mountain crags outlined in gleaming alabaster. After breakfast, Jerry and his predominately male scientific chums departed early to present their papers and conduct those endless discussions afterward. "There's always some sorehead who doesn't agree with anybody," Jerry said, "and the comments drag on ad nauseam. Wish I could go with you on the trip the ladies are taking."

A lively, Japanese-speaking Brazilian member of the conference committee volunteered to lead us women on a tour of the former imperial summer villa of Tamozawa. It may have been a delightful summer vacation home for the nobility, but during the raw March weather, the palace couldn't have felt chillier. Two shivering California women, wearing cotton pedal pushers, flip-flop sandals, and T-shirts, had accompanied their husbands to Japan without thinking ahead. I looked dowdy in my bulky fleece-lined raincoat, a heavy bandana knotted under the chin, and a droopy rain hat anchored into place with a woolen wraparound scarf, somewhat moth eaten. I may not have appeared chic wearing King Kong–size mittens and ugly black rubber galoshes to keep my shoes dry. But as I expressed motherly concern at the discomfort of the young fellow travelers from San Jose, I felt smug. Sometimes there is glory in the cautious foresight that accompanies middle age.

Outside again, we passed through drifting snowflakes, our feet almost frozen from walking on Tamozawa's unheated wood and tatami floors. The last stop included the Kanaya Samurai House, former home of a leading Nikko family. When we entered, a guide asked us to remove our shoes, then led us to a room where we sat on the floor, our feet dangling over a charcoal pit. To shield us from drafty walls, an enormous hanging quilt surrounded us on all sides. Solicitous ladies served hot tea and shiny, tasteless crackers. They told us that General Ulysses S. Grant had once been a guest there. We were embarrassed when one of our women asked, "You mean he was sober enough to come all this way?"

Back at the hotel while waiting for Jerry in the lobby, I heard a frightening roar, felt a shake, and saw snow sliding off a nearby roof. I thought the noise came from a heavy snowdrift, but it heralded a brief earthquake. Detailed instructions were posted everywhere, advice to stay away from windows and cover the head. That was the least of my worries. Although I tried to limit my Japanese diet, something was getting to me, and I had to miss the evening activities.

"It must be the dashi soup with dried bonito floating in it," Jerry said. "Take my advice and avoid all soups while we're in the Land of the Rising Sun."

"I feel something rising in me," I said in an unhappy voice, "and it's not the sun."

Additional tours for the ladies included the mausoleum of the third shogun Tokugawa, the ornate Gates of Paradise, and Lake Chuzenji. Streets had been cleared, but slippery spots still posed a potential danger. We poked along behind a snowplow on a narrow mountain road leading to the tomb.

"I counted forty-eight hairpin curves," our Brazilian guide said. Later at the Kegon Falls, we marveled at magnificent red cedars, boughs laden with ten inches of snow. The topiary resembled ghost-like figures draped in robes of white, half-hidden in shade.

During the five-day conference, other wives went shopping, but I sought more information about love poems we had seen painted on a scroll in the Toshogu Shrine. They were written in the seventh and eighth centuries, and English translations were available only in Tokyo. I doubted there would be time to find them. Instead, in the lobby reading room, I discovered the work of a woman writer named Sawako Ariyoshi and promised myself to find her books, one of which had been translated into English. I always enjoyed tracking down books by foreign writers previously unknown to me. When available to buy, these were the only souvenirs that ever accompanied me home.

Curse of the Sneaky Sea Cucumber

Our return to Tokyo seemed smoother than the anxiety-fueled journey to Nikko, although I was feeling tired and grumpy on the trains and pretended to sleep, avoiding conversation. Under my bulky layers of wool, I wore a black cocktail dress to circumvent the frantic last-minute wardrobe change when we arrived back in Tokyo. I could rest a full fifteen minutes before the exhausting farewell banquet that night.

I have been sick in all the Great Capitals of the World. Tokyo was no exception. It doesn't reflect on the Japanese, who were attentive and helpful, but their food did not sit well with me. The tasteless beige-colored broth I could manage to swallow and also a glue-like porridge. Horlicks, a white malted milk served hot, was good if the traveler didn't look at it. Even so, almost every day I chewed four lovely pink Pepto Bismol tablets to battle the chaos in my doomed interior.

Perhaps that's why fear and gloom cast a dark shadow all around me on the train ride back to Tokyo. The dinner would be lavish. If they served any Western food at all, even a measly Ritz cracker, I intended to devour it and consider it my evening meal. While we were eating at the banquet, someone sneaked a sea cucumber onto my plate. For the uninitiated, let me describe this greenish-brownish marine animal, also known as a trepang. It resembles a cucumber except for the black prickly needles on the outside, which later I discovered were tiny tentacles that surrounded the mouth. A few sips of sake must have gone to my head. I ate the entire eviscerated creature.

"Not bad," I said, swallowing fast before I could reconsider what it would do to my inner machinery.

Our Japanese hosts were flabbergasted. They took to murmuring among themselves. "You like it?" they asked. "Americans don't want to eat this."

Four sheets to the wind, I smacked my lips, and when I answered, "It's delicious," they responded, "Are you American?"

"No," I said for some unfathomable reason, "I'm Chinese."

Everyone laughed uproariously. One of the Japanese professors told me he treasured a copy of the satiric lecture, "The Ballad of High Entropy," I had delivered at the Airlie passivity conference banquet seven years before.

"You're very big in Japan," Jerry said later. "Ever consider doing stand-up comedy there?"

The sea cucumber didn't kill me. The following day, after our arrival at the New World Hotel in Jiulong across the water from Hong Kong proper, everyone in our tour group immediately lit out of the place to go shopping. An excited woman from Texas said to me, "I'm going to get in there and buy, buy, buy. I can hardly wait, can you?" I could wait.

In Hong Kong, we rented a sampan and expressed sympathy for the poverty-stricken fisherfolk who live on humble boats in the harbor. "They're not as poor as they look," our Japanese pilot said. "Most of them are richer than you are."

Jerry found something else disturbing. "In 1997, according to a treaty, the People's Republic of China will take over this democratic city from Britain," he said. "A cabdriver yesterday told me that everybody here is afraid of what's next even though the Chinese promise not to change the style of government." The city exchanged hands as planned. Now in the twenty-first century, the population still struggles to remain free.

On our last evening, when we walked through Hong Kong streets teeming with insatiable shoppers, I noticed a young girl no older than twelve, alone without an accompanying adult. She was beautiful, possibly Scandinavian, with perfect features, long curling blonde hair. Her face bore an expression of anguish strange for a girl that age. She didn't appear to be lost, but she didn't seem to belong there all by herself either. Before I could give her a second look, she vanished into the crowd. Even now forty years later, I still see the haunted look in her eyes and wonder whether she was a youngster forced into the horrific sex trade that flourishes in cities all over the world. I have this chilling notation in my journal for that day, March 17, 1985: *The vulnerability of Hong Kong scares me. The potential for evil here is overwhelming.*

Go with the Flow

Returning home, I found a letter of acceptance from the Summer Writers Conference at Johns Hopkins. The brochure offered fiction workshops and lectures by established authors on the faculty like John Barth, whose novel, *The Sot-Weed Factor,* I had liked. It was a marvelous satire of seventeenth-century life, and I sympathized with a hapless character serving as poet laureate of Maryland. The poor man suffered criticism of his poems by every nitwit he met, many of whom couldn't even read but freely gave him tips on how to write.

I was certain the entire two weeks at the writers' conclave would be a disaster. Arriving at the conference without my typewriter, I was scolded and told I should have known better. I did at least remember to bring those essays that the *Washington Post* ran back in the 1960s and '70s as well as two unpublished short stories. Our freewheeling instructor at the conference was a professional with an impressive number of short stories and novels under his belt. A minimalist, he urged us to use as few words as humanly possible in our assignments. His advice registered with me because that's exactly how I managed to cope with spasmodic dysphonia day by day. If I could pare down every sentence that issued from my lips, surely it would be easy to shrink my output in print. The next morning Jerry brought my typewriter from home.

In the dormitory, I shared a suite with three young women who were awed by my advanced years. I was probably the age of their parents. They treated me as if I were Willa Cather or Eudora Welty, which did wonders for a deflated ego. Although they admired my work, they especially respected me because I was the only attendee with the foresight to pack a tube of something to cure athlete's foot.

Our classes throbbed with scribes of all ages, authentic writers as well as dilettantes. I avoided hanging out with a gang that preferred to talk about writing rather than spend time doing it. In the quiet of my room, I produced a short story based on an actual visit to the 1978 White House where Rosalynn Carter once gave a tea for us Pen Women. The instructor proclaimed, "Your story should be in the *New Yorker*!" My euphoria disappeared when I overheard him compliment two others with the same magic words.

His assistant, a female English professor, found my oft-rejected short story, "Forsythia," "well-written and worthy of publication. Send it to the *Paris Review*." Alas, no sale. Attention all practitioners: Effusive praise doled out at writers conferences should be taken with a grain of sodium chloride. Even if your stuff is as fantastic as the instructor says, editors may not agree. After undergoing transformation from nonfiction to fiction, and then back again, "Forsythia" eventually survived. Stripped bare of all fictional excesses, it later served as part of a chapter in *The Cobbler's Last*. Waste not, want not encore. The Hopkins conference became a pivotal point in my haphazard career. It gave me confidence. Getting published was a coin toss, but even if an editor detested my work, I knew that somewhere over the rainbow there existed someone who wanted to publish what I wrote. The problem, of course, was to locate that person in just the one lifetime allotted to me.

Anchors Astray, My Lads

JOURNAL ENTRY: JANUARY 1988

> Instead of spinning out another book of Jewish poems, I've decided to commemorate the five hundredth anniversary of Christopher Columbus in what he called the New World. In his diaries he readily used references to events and characters in the Hebrew Bible. I could use a similar approach by reworking some of my newspaper poems on Jewish themes. This book ought to appear well before the official commemorative date. I have months of research ahead of me. After all, 1992 is only four years away.

Ronald Reagan's years at the White House ended and George H. W. Bush took the helm. And the voice predicament that had bedeviled me for seven years? Doctors officially diagnosed it as spasmodic dysphonia. There still had been no miraculous cure and no foolproof treatment. Nor did I find solace in joining a support group, although I made them a hand puppet named Sir Larynx Olivier. In a squeaky, ragged voice, I had him give a humorous monologue on coping with voice disorders. It went over well, but I risked being elected president of the group. I had learned my lesson from the Maryland 350 Gala.

"I've decided not to let support groups swallow up all of my time and energy," I announced to Jerry. If I couldn't easily communicate with my voice, an active imagination via the written word would suffice. It had to.

My feminist book of poems, *Daughters of Chutzpah*, continued to receive favorable reviews, especially when its publisher, Doris Gold in New York, gave proxy readings, which I was happy to have missed. Biblio Press sold all the copies and even went into a second printing, an act of Providence that provided me with some lightweight royalties. I found time to write "Superfrog," the tale of an unhappy young woman visited by the ghost of Emily Dickinson, but that little short story kept coming back like acid indigestion. I received a request from a religious magazine in California to reprint one of my poems, and I planned future ironic short stories to inundate the desks of formidable editors. Although I had promised myself to settle down and tackle more serious writing, I didn't get around to it. Instead, surprisingly, *Writer's Digest*, a national magazine for hopeful scribes, ran a humorous article of mine, "What Rhymes with 'Sincerely Yours'?" It resulted in a mailbox overflowing with light verse from frustrated poets in the hinterlands seeking advice on how to publish their masterpieces. What could I tell them? What could I tell *me*?

Swimming the Moat

We pause here for a somewhat humorless aside. My health had deteriorated again after the Japan trip. A gynecologist discovered a mysterious mass that had invaded my ovaries, and he ordered me not to delay a hysterectomy. "Probably isn't malignant," he said, but still . . ."

Undergoing major surgery had its bright side. Cards, flowers, charity contributions, and rare delicacies surprised me. Jerry, bless him, made Hanukkah latkes, potato pancakes. "I heated them up in the hospital microwave," he proudly told me. In his first post-operation visit, he brought me a letter from a young New Jersey woman who befriended me at the Hopkins writers conference. We had been exchanging unpublished short stories and mailing intense critiques to each other. Her stories often featured juvenile delinquents who terrorized the New Jersey countryside by tipping over unsuspecting cows. Because she had recently married a Sikh, I suggested she describe problems of a mixed marriage in a setting that reflected her husband's background. She did this and immediately sold her story to *Mademoiselle* magazine, much to my unadulterated envy. Most important of all, that ovarian tumor was benign.

A shakily scribbled journal entry for December 1985 reads: *Still recuperating. New Jersey pen pal in her recent letters bids me, "Write! Write! Write!" but weeks have passed, and to quote Walt Whitman, I am undergoing "a period of sloth."*

In the healthier months that followed, our county Humanities Commission kept me hopping with assignments to write brochures and press releases, and to edit a newsletter announcing programs dealing with literature, psychology, music, drama, and history. I contacted actors who impersonated Lincoln, Clara Barton, and Edison as well as literary figures like Mark Twain and Emily Dickinson. To engage our diverse community, the commission planned a yearly Ethnic Festival. A state-sponsored group requested my services as a judge in creative writing contests. During one of these competitions, I urged support for a poem written in Spanish by a local immigrant poet from Central America. Against a dark cloud of resentment and racism, his entry won first prize. Proudly, with tears in his eyes, he read his original verse, followed by the English translation. As a commissioner, this was my finest hour.

In the late spring of 1987, a community group suggested that I write a series of Bicentennial Minutes commemorating the two hundredth birthday of the United States Constitution. It was a challenge for me to link our local politicians with James Monroe and other delegates who labored in the heat of a Philadelphia summer two centuries before. I loved drawing parallels between past and present. Whenever possible, the minutes concentrated on Daniel Carroll, a Maryland delegate to the Constitutional Convention and a champion of strengthening the power of central government over the individual states. In 1787 our feisty delegation was split between two conflicting factions in a struggle for power, reflected in the following lines:

The little states are much upset
They fear the mammoths will forget
A Maryland or a Delaware
Deserve their legislative share.
Should size on map or population
Determine who will rule this nation?
If such is what this act will bring,
My Maryland won't sign the thing!

And so the battle lines were clearly drawn. As Ben Franklin put it, with proportional representation, the smaller states "feared their liberties would be in danger," and with equality of votes, the larger states "felt their money would be in danger." Who would win? More next week in our next exclusive Constitutional Minute!

Even today in the twenty-first century, the conflict remains a thorny subject; the battle for more equal representation continues unabated in the United States Congress as well as in state legislatures across the country. I was pleased that my local government officials read these minutes aloud at each County Council session and later published the work in a pamphlet available to all constituents. Note to my mother: Mom, I *did* become a teacher but in my own fashion.

Beyond the Blue Horizon

Miracles great and small took place during the latter years of the 1980s, restoring battered self-esteem, helping me change course. In June of 1987 an interview by reporter Rebecca Boroson appeared in a New York newspaper that had continued to run the "Unholy Writ" column. Her article outlined in detail my life and poetry, which she generously described as "light, lyrical rhymes that mirrored foibles of modern times. Critics have compared her to the Pulitzer Prize winning poet Phyllis McGinley, whose work was similarly freighted lightly with messages. They have also characterized her poems . . . as American Jewish folk poetry because of its simple style, a chronicle of American life in the last part of the 20th century."

Cheered on by such kind words, I sought other ways to stay in the game without depending too much on untrustworthy vocal cords. But connecting with the public at large has always invigorated me. At a folk festival in suburban Washington, our entire family set up a booth to announce the twentieth anniversary of the "Unholy Writ" newspaper column still running in New York. We offered birthday cake, Kool-Aid, and a gratis copy of *More Unholy Writ* to any passerby who volunteered to read a poem to the crowd. To amplify my fickle voice, I hawked our generous offer through a homemade megaphone, a gray cardboard tube removed from a roll of paper towels. Although I felt like a shill at an amusement park, it worked. Once a sizable audience gathered, we had to fight off freeloaders who returned for second and third helpings of cake. "That's one sure-fire way to bring poetry to the masses," Jerry said.

Soon after that minor accomplishment, a Courage Award from the Dystonia Medical Research Foundation arrived in the mail as the result of a published essay of mine about coping with voice loss. Even more satisfying was "Brotherly Breach," a wry poem based on the biblical tale of Joseph and Isaac, which earned first prize in the humor division of a Virginia Poetry Society contest. Jerry and I journeyed down to Charlottesville, where a local actor read the verse to a good-natured audience. As a Wandering Jew in the Bible Belt, I was deeply touched afterward by a kind woman who took my hand and said, "You really know your Scriptures. I can tell you're a good Christian."

These mild successes increased my determination to finish the Columbus project. It was fascinating that some scholars believed he may have been a Marrano, a Jew converted during the Spanish Inquisition. My book title was based on these words attributed to disillusioned former colonists to whom he owed money: "There go the sons of the Admiral of the Mosquitoes, of the man who discovered the lands of vanity and fraud." I gave myself a 1990 deadline and outlined ways to connect early with the national Christopher Columbus Quincentenary Jubilee Commission as well as state celebrations throughout the country. On another trip with Jerry to New Hampshire, I planned to finish research and buckle down to writing a first draft.

All of Jerry's international corrosion buddies were at the Gordon Research Conference in New Hampshire that summer, older colleagues and a few new faces. One friendly young man when introduced to me said, "In the lab I speak your name every day. We call molybdenum 'moly.' Believe me, Moly, we couldn't get along without you."

"Thank you," I murmured. "That's indeed a compliment." After he walked away, I consulted Jerry. "What's he talking about?" My husband patiently informed me that molybdenum is a pure element that resists corrosion well. "It has one of the highest boiling points of all pure elements," he said. "It's used in alloys. In case you're curious, the atomic number is 42 and the symbol is MO."

"Don't start calling me Mo," I said. "It sounds like someone who works in a Jewish delicatessen."

All I wanted was a quiet retreat where I could finish reading a couple of reference books, jot down notes, and begin to season the well-known history of Columbus with a contemporary view of the facts. At the conference I deserted my role as Mrs. Congeniality to become a stiff-necked Hermit Lady, avoiding any activities planned for companions of the attendee scientists. That wasn't easy. We were all lodged cheek by jowl in dormitories at Colby-Sawyer College. In the available classrooms, peer-reviewed papers of note were aired all morning long by Jerry and his colleagues. The period after lunch was left open for hiking or swimming in a glacial lake nearby. After dinner, our menfolk again occupied themselves with matters scientific. But on this trip, I did not join the other wives slapping away at insects as they waited on lawn chairs for their spouses to adjourn and join them for drinks at 10:00 p.m.

Although the ladies may have considered me an obnoxious snob, I couldn't simultaneously devote myself to the Admiral of the Ocean and double as everybody's friend. One woman even remarked in a loud voice, "We don't like it when people would rather read than socialize with the rest of us." Too bad. Ferdinand and Isabella beckoned. During one escape when I wandered into a Thoreau-like woodland, I found an artist busy at work on a watercolor of the surrounding landscape. I watched how easily she managed the paint on her palette, and I appreciated the colors she used.

Here was Yolanda Frederikse, a soul mate, another wife who had refused to go on the tour of the day. I learned that she, too, lived in the Washington suburbs and headed a local branch of the National League of American Pen Women. Although I was already a member, the meetings were held in an inconvenient city location where parking space was hard to find. I had always liked the idea of an exclusive organization for professional women writers, artists, and composers. It was founded back in 1897 by a handful of women journalists, including the niece of Henry Wadsworth Longfellow. The ladies decided to create their own organization after being denied membership in the all-male National Press Club.

"Why not switch over to our branch?" Yolanda asked. "When we get home, I'll sponsor you and mail you an application." A brilliant watercolorist, she had won innumerable international awards for her art. Her invitation became a turning point for me.

In the Wake of Don Cristóbal

During the following months, *Admiral of the Mosquitoes: Columbus and America in Light and Dark Verse* topped my agenda. Yolanda Frederikse agreed to design the cover and illustrate the poems.

"No one knows what Columbus looked like," Yolanda said. "I'll just draw him as I imagine he looked. Who'll know the difference?" As soon as she had some poems to work with, she put herself wholeheartedly into the project and produced seven memorable drawings in black and white. She knew instinctively how to capture perfectly the lightness and darkness of a hazardous theme.

The more I worked on the new book, the more doubtful I became. Was it wise to pursue a dusty topic like Columbus? If so, what fresh insights could possibly sail into view after five centuries? Certain lines and phrases could be recycled from my Watergate-inspired verse addressing the abuse of power, governmental corruption, and political arrogance. These were universal themes, and human nature had not changed. Reaching back to the Second Law of Thermodynamics, I found a suitable title for a group of poems describing the tragedy of the Great Navigator's fall from grace.

"The Entropy of Success?" Jerry said. "Your impressive scientific background has finally come in handy."

"True," I said, "but where do I go from here?" Columbus succeeded because of his connections in high places, but I had only one remote possibility. Through projects sponsored by the Maryland 350 Committee nearly a decade before, I had encountered Mickey Reed, an aide to the Honorable Constance Morella, U.S. House of Representatives. Congresswoman Morella was a first-generation American like me, a former English professor at the local community college, and a liberal Republican.

"Do I dare beg her to write an Introduction?" I asked Jerry. "We have something in common. We're both first-generation Americans. And people of Italian descent love to claim Columbus as their own."

"Along with the Spanish, the Portuguese, the French, and a half dozen other nationalities," Jerry said.

"I doubt that someone like her would take the time," I said.

"Who knows? Write your friend Mickey a friendly pitch and ask her to pass it along to the boss. What have you got to lose?" He was right. Shortly before we went to press, the Congresswoman asked for a draft of the manuscript, read it, and sent back this foreword:

> What better way to celebrate the Quincentennial than by engaging in a pastime that is quintessentially American: humor. One look at the gifted author and historian, Mollee Kruger, is evidence enough that her talents are aptly suited to take on the task of bringing Christopher Columbus into our home . . . to better understand and appreciate our earliest American Heritage. In the tradition of Mark Twain, Will Rogers, and Garrison Keillor, [she] gives us *Admiral of the Mosquitoes*. Typically, we don't think of Columbus' travels as particularly funny . . . but after all, it is amusing that in 1992 what we are celebrating is really the celebration of a navigational error committed half a millennium ago. It does point out that the journey to America was both a drama and a comedy just like life itself.
>
> [Her] depiction of Columbus' travels is much more than a comic endeavor. Through light verse, Ms. Kruger has managed to convey with remarkable aptitude a sense of the mystique of Columbus in the new world. This volume enables readers . . . to replace the drudgery of textbooks with the pleasure of poetry. And what a pleasure it is. How better to describe the creative wizardry of words . . . than in the definition that Robert Frost once gave: "A poem begins in delight and ends in wisdom." In [the book] Ms. Kruger places the protagonist in a timeless milieu: between the biblical prophets

> and contemporary clichés. Abraham and Elijah are juxtaposed with civil servants, whistleblowers, and press releases. We are all part of the continuum.
> *Constance A. Morella – 8th Congressional District*
> *Congress of the United States – House of Representatives*

I was grateful to the Congresswoman beyond words.

Just as Columbus immersed himself in lobbying the kings of Portugal and Spain for royal support, I engaged in local political intrigue to find support among federal government figures and members of state commissions connected to the Quincentenary. With little success, I courted the national chairman, a political appointee of President George H. W. Bush. I sent copies of *Admiral* to famous Italian-Americans like Governor Mario Cuomo of New York. I circulated review copies and wrote press releases for national and regional magazines and newspapers. Bush left Washington, and Bill Clinton took his place in the Oval Office. A new era had begun.

Crashing the invisible wall around big-time publishers and national media seemed beyond my reach, no matter how many free books, letters, quoted reviews, and freewheeling flyers were fired into the Great Unknown. Getting support, that's what Jerry and his scientist colleagues talked about all the time, finding support from grants, public and private, monetary assistance from government, industry, and academia. But a wee publisher like Maryben Books had to hustle for the tiniest amount of backing—financial, media, or moral.

What's more, perceptions had changed since the American Revolution Bicentennial in 1976. Our country didn't respond gung-ho to a commemorative event in 1992 that would mark the discovery of a "New World." Those white-faced foreigners who sailed across the sea to exploit and destroy entire populations? They were devils, not heroes. Luckily, my approach to this painful subject resounded with the *Baltimore Sun*. Under the headline "Columbus-Bashing Gains Ground," journalist Samuel Goldreich wrote:

> Christopher Columbus doesn't get the respect he used to. . . . American Indian groups across the nation have complained that elaborate plans to celebrate the 500th anniversary next year insult the memory of the indigenous people who were enslaved and killed by Columbus and those who followed.

> Poet Kruger has added to the fray by publishing a book, *Admiral of the Mosquitoes*, whose title mocks the mariner's failure to find the elusive westward passage to India. One section, "The Entropy of Success," features Maryland artist Yolanda Frederikse's Renaissance-style drawing of a stern, dignified Columbus holding a huge mosquito, which many of his contemporaries said was all he had to show for his four voyages. . . . Kruger includes a . . . lament for Columbus' misadventures and harsher indictments of the rule of Queen Isabella, including the expulsion of hundreds of thousands of Jews whose seized property helped fund the explorations.

Another article in the *Washington Post*, "Rhymes for an Ancient Mariner" by Leonard Hughes, touched upon the influence of Ogden Nash on the poetry but didn't mention the underlying tragedy of the explorer's life. In "The Poem He Never Wrote" I tried to capture the admiral's obsession with biblical figures and his bitterness toward enemies he blamed for his failures. Unrhymed, it was the only poem where I slipped into a disjointed, free-verse style that hints of the madness that overtook Columbus in his final years.

An unrelenting ego destroyed Columbus. One newspaper article quoted me as saying, "He was so many different things: a mystic, a religious fanatic. He believed he had been ordained to discover his new approach to the Indies, and he used the Bible to justify it. . . . What do I think of him? An enigma . . . the more I studied him, the less I knew." The interviewer ended her article with this quote from the book:

His apparition haunts me still
a fitful residue
which gives no other choice but this:
to foist him off on you.

Admiral of the Mosquitoes broke no sales records, but it remains a favorite of mine. A couple of years later, I wanted to present Columbus in song and dance, a poignant musical version of my book. By this time, our changing nation chose to forget him, and besides, I couldn't find a composer willing to invest time in a longshot like this or a producer to supply needed venture capital. Meanwhile, I began collecting Social Security. With the rise of social media, a new era took hold, but my past was still catching up with me.

Culling Old Salts

Something else enticing often distracts me at critical moments, especially when one of my books is on its way to publication. It happened again. Our student publications crowd had flourished during golden days at the University of Maryland. Over time, the youthful friendships dwindled down to occasional Christmas cards or no communication at all. After forty years, only one couple, Charlie and Liza, remained among the old friends living nearby. College sweethearts, they had worked together on the staff of the campus magazine and married soon after receiving their diplomas.

At a dinner one evening, we spoke mournfully about how the old gang had disintegrated. "Maybe we should have a reunion," I said, realizing that at one time our cynical little circle would have scoffed at such a bourgeois idea. Jerry, a University of Virginia man, who met and enjoyed my friends back in the early 1950s, approved heartily, but not Charlie. Formerly a reporter with the Associated Press and now editor of an aviation magazine, he freelanced in his spare time and sold lighthearted essays to *Esquire* and other national magazines. He and I had been editors of our college humor magazine, the *Old Line*.

"No one will come," Charlie said. "They're off somewhere in a drunken stupor." We paused reverently to recall an Oscar Wilde quote posted over the entrance to our shabby student headquarters: "All of us are in the gutter but some of us are looking at the stars."

Liza and I pushed the idea of a reunion. She volunteered to reach people and pointed out that our dispersed group since graduation had taken journalistic, television, or academic jobs everywhere in the country.

"Look, we're talking dangerously here. I don't think we should bring this on ourselves," Charlie said. We wondered how much everyone had aged since we last assembled. By the 1990s, most of the women were sixty years old or more. The males, mostly veterans, were four to ten years older. Liza hoped we had reached a time in our lives when nostalgia would have mellowed the testy, dispassionate clique we once imagined ourselves to be. "I doubt it," Charlie said with a gloomy sigh.

I expanded the mailing list to include stars of University Theater during our era. Though not a drama major, I worked backstage on makeup and even trod the boards with them as Mrs. Soames, the neighborhood gossip, in Thornton Wilder's *Our Town* and as Dora, a pregnant Cockney maid, in Emlyn Williams' *Night Must Fall*. My fellow actors were legendary campus extroverts who knew how to liven up a party.

Our immediate task was to fire off broadcast letters written in college humor style to attract this mishmash of oddballs. "They're all still hung over from our last party," Charlie said, then added, "You're not going to hear from the journalists. They would never turn up for something like this."

He was wrong. The young cynics had mellowed. In the avalanche of responses, we found ecstatic acceptances and mournful regrets but not one snarling dismissal or nasty retort.

"Yeah, they say they'll come," Charlie said, "but wait till they find out how much it will cost them for the whole weekend."

The No-Class Reunion was the name we gave to our bacchanalia. It would distinguish us from (ugh) generic college alumni celebrations. We saw ourselves as an unofficial cadre, an ingathering of doubters, naysayers, and durable soreheads who avoided reunions at all costs. Undaunted, we targeted our weirdest and most whimsical classmates from the late 1940s through the mid-1950s. Our provocative brochure inquired, "Do you have no class? Join us."

I mailed out reams of No-Class Reunion information and a request, "Give us the story of your life in twelve and a half words or less." Maybe Charlie was right, I thought. It was foolhardy to devote so much time to this sentimental tryst. And yet, in a warped way we couldn't resist those nostalgic feelings we once ridiculed. At last, even Charlie weakened. "I guess it might be bearable for one lost weekend," he said, "but I can't take anything longer."

JOURNAL ENTRY: APRIL 10, 1990

> I look forward to seeing how much we've changed in forty years. It's a laboratory experiment. What has time done to everyone, including me? From whence cometh my own bouncy good cheer, speaking on the phone to laconic men, most of them introverted writers, some of whom I never bothered to talk with even in olden times. Yet there I am, babbling away, Miss Big Woman on Campus once again, bursting with girlish joie de vivre. What's lacking is my old black blazer jacket with a golden chrysanthemum pinned to the lapel. In all this pregame excitement, even my wayward voice does passably well.

Charlie and I relived old times as we worked side by side to produce a newsletter, which we called the *Old Throwback*, a satire of our student publications. I wrote a tongue-in-cheek article about our aging attendees barricading Route 1 and rocking a Greyhound bus ("No-Class Reunion Rioters Rampage"). Charlie at age sixty-two remained a gentleman editor of discretion. In editing biographies from our crowd, he deleted the forbidden word "menopausal" and censored a former drama major's graphic description of her sexual triumphs in New York. And he continued to predict a dismal finale.

"We won't meet the caterer's minimum of seventy-five victims foolish enough to pay for this kind of nonsense," he muttered into his Scotch and water.

We attracted ninety people. As it happens in life, the work of paving the way delighted us more than the actual event. At a preliminary cocktail party that weekend, as I flitted through the guests, now all nonsmokers, I sensed on the sidelines a pudgy little man watching me. He looked familiar but I couldn't think of his name. He nodded and smiled; I returned his greeting, and it wasn't until he spoke that I felt queasy. It was either my college sweetheart Zach or a bald sixty-six-year-old grandfather pretending to be the man I almost married. He still observed me analytically with those dark inscrutable eyes. He informed me that he was retired from the World Health Organization and had lived for several years in Malaysia. "We eradicated smallpox from the face of the earth," he said. "I helped make it happen."

"Congratulations," I said, lacking a sharper comeback.

"And at the end of the Vietnam fiasco," he added, "I was one of the Americans on the last plane out of Saigon."

He seemed to enjoy the expression on my face when he told me that. I have no idea whether I looked startled, amused, or relieved not to have become his wife, especially when he informed me that his oldest daughter had been born in the middle of the Amazon rainforest. Our college friends may have envied his adventurous life, but it was clear to me that our marriage would have been a disaster.

Jerry and Zach began a lively discussion about foreign travel, and I moved away to chat with others. Some of us had become celebrities like the creator of a children's television show, the *Muppets*; a former network weather girl, who had called me from Hawaii to say she was coming but first wanted to have work done on her face; and a star of the TV cowboy series *Bonanza*. Charlie groused that we made too much fuss over the theatrical folk and not enough over outstanding authors who showed up. True enough. Later at the gala dinner, women fought to sit at the same table with the forever-handsome television actor instead of the dyspeptic journalist nominated for a Pulitzer. We were all heavier, more arthritic, unbecomingly wrinkled, and if not well behaved, at least more subdued. Neighbors did not have to phone the police this time.

Today I recall our No-Class Reunion with a tender smile. The dear and talented are no longer here; the brave World War II veterans and all those beautiful young coeds are now gone forever. But let the record show that long ago on a summer weekend in the late twentieth century, we became our younger selves one more time as we raised our glasses. I was proud of my friends, the greatest of the Greatest Generation and the noisiest of the Silent Generation. Throughout their lives, they remained creative, outspoken, still opinionated, still quirky misfits till the end.

The Swashbuckler's Sword

While I busied myself with the ghost of Columbus, Jerry received notice of an honor from UMIST, the University of Manchester Institute of Science and Technology. He begged me to accompany him on his trip to the UK for the ceremony, and I was tempted to escape the convoluted politics of winning support from the Christopher Columbus Quincentenary Jubilee Commission, over which a dark cloud hung. I couldn't fathom why the national chairman and others politely dodged me at every turn. Later the United States Congress conducted an oversight investigation of the commission and found evidence of fraud among certain persons associated with it. Although most of the commissioners were above board, they may have been reluctant to take me into the inner circle because I was a writer, a true believer in freedom of the press. Would I have spilled some beans? Yes, I would have.

Instead, I cast aside all worldly cares and flew to Heathrow with Jerry. In London we took the train from Euston Station to Manchester, 184 miles northwest. On the long ride, we ate cucumber sandwiches with a fellow traveler, Basil, an elderly gentleman who planned to marry a young Thai woman he had met while teaching deaf children in Asia. He described how, on her first visit to the United Kingdom, his girlfriend witnessed her first snowfall. "She became so excited she ran out into the street in her dressing gown," he said. "Shocking!" A good-hearted sort, Basil was on his way to visit his grandson. We were pleased that he seemed familiar with the same British soap operas we always watched on our public TV channel. In fact, he even resembled the butler in *Upstairs, Downstairs*, a precursor of *Downton Abbey*.

"Granada Studios are located in Manchester, you know," Basil said with a certain amount of pride. I didn't know that. We also learned from him that although Manchester is fifty-four miles from the open sea, its elongated harbor is fed by ship canals. Basil gave us a full history of the historic industrial city.

"Of course, you've heard of the *Guardian*," he said. "Manchester is a center of journalism second only to London." We hated to part with this sincere elderly gentleman, who had spent years doing humanitarian work in countries around the world. I still wonder if his May-December marriage ever took place and, if so, how it turned out.

Jerry's UMIST colleagues booked us into the Britannia Hotel, a gaudy Victorian palace, once a warehouse built in 1868 by a friend of Prince Albert. Decorated with heavy swathes of draped velvet, gilded mirrors, and lavender wall sconces, the venerable building was, according to a critic, "a luxurious Bordello out of a Fellini movie, all purple and gold." I thoroughly enjoyed the furry carpets, the dazzling chandeliers, and a grand staircase, all hinting of an earlier time when the sun would never dare to set on the British Empire.

Jerry's appearance at the Manchester university had been scheduled for the day after Yom Kippur, the most sacred holiday on the Jewish calendar. We arrived in the UK much earlier because we wanted to attend religious services, including Kol Nidre in the evening. Weeks before leaving Rockville, I found the name of a synagogue not far from our Manchester hotel, and wrote to let them know the Yanks were coming. In turn they airmailed us identity cards, which we showed to a security officer before he could let us enter the building. The *shamash* (beadle) informed us we could sit anywhere in the beautiful old sanctuary; the women were not separated from the men. His sparse congregation welcomed us, but it was obvious that these elderly folks were not accustomed to having Americans join them. Although the traditional service in Hebrew contained little English, the haunting Kol Nidre, played on an organ and sung by cantor and choir, did not differ from what we would have heard at home. Later, as we left for our hotel, the shamash heartily called to us, "Well over the fast!"

JOURNAL ENTRY: SEPTEMBER 19

> Yesterday, a unique Yom Kippur. Although the Britannia Hotel offered us breakfast, we didn't eat because we were fasting. Instead, a cab took us to a nearby suburb where we

> walked an additional block on a street lined with substantial brick houses, hedge rows, and the inevitable cabbage roses in every garden. The synagogue, a sprawling one-story brick building, surprised us with its sun-lit sanctuary, the wide glass windows revealing adjacent trees and greenery. It was not unlike our own place of worship back home.

The young rabbi, sporting a reddish Van Gogh beard, conducted the service with no cantor. His meager choir, eight women in their street clothes, sang familiar religious melodies, led by an organist. The sizable congregation read prayers in Hebrew and English from the British Reform Prayer Book, which contained snatches of traditional prayers, meditations, Hasidic wisdom, quotations from controversial philosopher Franz Rosenzweig, and even a Dorothy Parker poem about soldiers returning from war. The famed author of biting light verse and cynical short stories was the daughter of a Jewish father and a Scottish mother. I can't imagine what Parker's reaction would have been to see her verse included in a Jewish prayer book.

Although a friendly couple invited us to end our twenty-four-hour fast at their home, we left before *Neilah*, the final service of Yom Kippur. Back to the garish Victorian hotel we sped, where I unpacked tiny cans of grapefruit juice and tuna, those Old Faithful items I always toted with me on international trips. Hungrily, we gobbled everything down before dashing out to meet a UMIST colleague, who walked us to a surprise dinner in my husband's honor at a Chinese restaurant. "Weirdest breaking of the fast we ever had," Jerry commented later.

The entire evening spent with the Anglo-Saxon faculty professors from the University of Manchester Institute of Science and Technology underscored for me once more the cultural challenges and choppy social waters that Jews have navigated over the centuries. Instead of our familiar end-of-Yom Kippur cream cheese, bagels, and lox, we began our meal with a medium sherry and ate egg rolls washed down with Chinese beer, followed by sea bass, duck, fried rice, broccoli, green peppers, and pineapple sprinkled with walnut-like chips that tasted faintly like old-fashioned *taiglach*, a Jewish honeyed confection. Jerry turned a bit green when our lively hosts on their third bottle of wine ordered us a huge supply of strawberries, melon, and grapes, but my husband gamely filled his plate. After all, he had been flown across the Atlantic to be celebrated by his peers. Pepto Bismol chased away our blues before bedtime. "That yam-prawn dim sum was the worst," Jerry said.

JOURNAL ENTRY: SEPTEMBER 20

Today we attended the ceremony, where Jerry received a magnificent Wilkinson sword with the name Ulick R. Evans Award engraved on the blade. Evans, one of the guiding lights of his field, is known the world over as "father of the modern science of corrosion and protection of metals."

When Jerry accepted the sword, he bowed and said half under his breath, "How will they let me on the plane with this?" The audience of faculty and students laughed, and someone shouted, "We'll drop it in the mail for you!" Jerry proceeded to deliver his talk with panache. He elegantly flashed his sword like one of Victor Hugo's musketeers as he saluted the audience and then used the weapon to point to his slides projected on a screen.

Madeira Wine, Lisbon Fado

At the end of 1992 Jerry and I took a circuitous trip that began with snow, sleet, rain, and thunder in Maryland, followed by a delayed flight from Dulles to Kennedy Airport, where we were told our plane to Lisbon had been canceled because of mechanical problems. Taking a roundabout route via North Africa would allow Jerry to arrive in Funchal, the capital of Portugal's Madeira archipelago, in time for his talk scheduled for the first morning of a week-long corrosion conference.

JOURNAL ENTRY: SUNDAY, DECEMBER 13

Every traveler lives in fear of having luggage delivered to the wrong country somewhere on the opposite side of the world. Our flight to Casablanca has meant we'll probably lose track of our baggage, now checked through to Lisbon or so we're told.

The flight via TAP [Air Portugal] was laden with irate passengers kept awake all night by legions of screaming little Portuguese children under the age of three. When we appeared at the Royal Airlines Morocco reception desk, the unsmiling clerk seemed doubtful about our ever seeing our bags again because no one had issued us new baggage checks to show him. As time goes by, according to that song from the Bogart movie, the fundamental things apply. But slowly. In Casablanca we were quarantined in a cramped restricted area under the guard of armed soldiers, all with ominously black mustaches. We were promised lunch vouchers, denied lunch vouchers, and then had lunch reluctantly served to us. The agitated kiddies continued their shrieking until we felt like joining them.

The worrisome, endless layover caused me to tremble with fear even though Jerry with his usual sangfroid said, "Don't worry, their government has friendly relations with the U.S." I found little comfort in this while he continued to organize his slides and make final touches on his talk.

In Lisbon our lost baggage didn't materialize, and after a three-hour wait, we flew to Madeira, 360 sea miles off the African coast and 535 miles from Lisbon. On board the TAP plane Jerry greeted colleagues also headed for the meeting, including Herr Ludwig, a long-suffering German who resembled Albert Einstein. After we agreed with him to split cab fare to the Savoy Hotel, we landed at Funchal with the hardest bump I could remember. The screams of the little ones were enhanced by hysterical outcries from everyone else onboard.

Magically, our luggage did appear in Funchal although Herr Ludwig couldn't locate his. We felt obligated to wait for him at the gate and watched as all those noisy families debarked for the Christmas season. As they loaded tons of brown paper-wrapped packages into the arms of waiting relatives, we listened to the sounds of one last screeching toddler fade away into the distance. A mild-mannered Boston professor, also waiting to split taxi costs, muttered, "It makes you understand why some people commit murder." "With an axe," another scientific American said.

We lingered another half hour in the empty terminal until a desolate Herr Ludwig exited the gate with no suitcase in hand. Too tired to console him, we crowded into a cab to take us to the hotel, but first the driver felt his patriotic duty lay in showing us the welcome Madeira had in store for us tourists. He proudly drove us through the heart of downtown Funchal, past a glittering array of tiny white Christmas lights that outlined every single avenue, each tree, each streetlamp, each shop, and each telephone booth. It ended with two massive depictions of a man and a woman, at least eight stories high, all etched in miniature light bulbs. And just when our weary, reddened eyes could absorb no more, we approached a gargantuan fifteenth-century Portuguese galleon also formed by what looked like thousands and thousands of electric dots.

"It is somewhat exaggerated," Herr Ludwig muttered. The truth is we were all too dead tired to act properly awed, and our driver took our lack of enthusiasm as an insult. In the hotel elevator on the way up to our room, I spotted a sign that read, "Please do not feed the seagulls." After traveling on four different airplanes for two full days without sleep, neither of us intended to pander to those pesky creatures.

JOURNAL ENTRY: MONDAY, DECEMBER 14

It was raining when we woke up this morning, a lackadaisical sort of rain, oddly slanted with a sea breeze at its back. At noon today I'll eat at the Savoy restaurant with a very tired Jerry who is giving his paper this morning and speaking again later this afternoon. The weather is deceptive here. You expect it to be like summer, all warm and sunny, but it harbors the hidden chill of December. The shower has all but gone as I sit here on the hotel balcony facing the historic Bay of Funchal. The salty smell of the ocean drifts through the last of the raindrops.

I had no idea that my random voyages would ever carry me to a favorite harbor where Christopher Columbus dropped anchor five hundred years before. My thanks go to Björn Landström, the Finnish-born adventurer, researcher, and artist who wrote and illustrated *Columbus,* a comprehensive book on the man and his travels. That volume introduced me to the port city of Funchal and played an integral part during the three years it took me to write *Admiral of the Mosquitoes.* And now I am breathing the same sea air that invigorated Columbus. I am hearing the clu-cluck-cluck of perhaps twenty-five gluttonous seagulls circling the water in the same way as their winged ancestors swooped over the heads of Columbus and his crew. Having married a Madeira woman, he was always hospitably received in Funchal "for he was well-known there and had lived there for some time," according to Landström's quote from biographer Bartolomé de Las Casas. Columbus would have hooted at the idea of feeding a single crumb of his ships' larder to a flock of pesky seagulls.

JOURNAL ENTRY: TUESDAY, DECEMBER 15

This morning some women and I took a bus tour of Madeira, the largest volcanic island in this archipelago. We're situated on an island that's only about thirty-four miles long. The daunting peaks and deep ravines intrigue me, and the grand views of waves battering rocky shores remind me of Nova Scotia. Pico Ruivo de Santana is the highest point at 6,106 feet. In contrast to the foreboding basalt crags and boulders are the quiet tree-lined avenues of Funchal on the southern coast. A few miles out of town lie miles of vineyards where authentic Madeira is made from a blend of luscious black and white grapes. Also spellbinding for me are the whitewashed cottages and gardens filled with exotic tropical flora, unique species brought to the islands from Africa by sailors passing through this busy port of call. I suspect the plants were put into the rocky earth by deserted wives and abandoned sweethearts in memory of the seamen who dropped by for a few days of pleasure and then sailed away to other harbors and other women. As John Gay once wrote, *They'll tell thee sailors, when away / In every port a mistress find.* After weeks and months of abstinence at sea, those virile mariners must have left more than jungle flowers behind them.

I missed the early orientation program and had no chance to meet other spouses who had accompanied their scientist husbands. Alone and unattached in the hotel lobby, I discovered Marianne, a lively woman with a boyish haircut and a slight Scottish burr. We agreed on our good fortune in having missed the scheduled "wife trip" to a wicker basket factory, and instead we discussed linguistic differences and regional accents. An expert on language roots, this delightful octogenarian gave me a scholarly lecture, drawing connections among old English-, Germanic-, and French-based words. She told me she once lived in Versailles next door to Louis XIV's palace.

"I hate the French bureaucracy," she said casually, as if she were discussing a dislike of parsnips or head cheese. "If you send them a complaint, you must register the letter or they won't pay any attention to you." Her current job was helping university faculty wives become acclimated to life in Edinburgh. "I remind young Indian women always to wear warm clothing under their saris."

We chatted all morning about Shakespeare's comedies and tragedies as well as the poems of Robert Burns. From a hotel balcony, she and I watched boats of all shapes and sizes entering the port: tiny fishing boats pulling nets, mundane scows tooting away, the cruise ships bursting with tourists on holiday. "Aye, there's a gray mist on the sea's face," she whispered, quoting John Mansfield's "Sea Fever."

One of the saddest aspects of travel is having to say goodbye to rare people like Marianne. We enjoy our moments together, and then leave them behind forever. They become part of a frieze chiseled into time, and the setting can be neither retrieved nor duplicated. Even if we could gather up our Mariannes and bring them home as souvenirs, their storybook quality would fade. The magical blend of travel and memory elevates us; in foreign lands we become fictional characters, inviting others to suspend their disbelief in us just as we suspend ours in them.

Our week in Funchal ended; time to pack our bags for the next stop. We waved goodbye to the Se, a venerable cathedral built and rebuilt from 1485 to 1514, and I remember flying over a magnificent peak called Cabo Girão. In ninety minutes, losing an hour on the way, we landed in Lisbon, the westernmost city in Europe, from which Portuguese explorers once launched their caravels in search of gold and immortality.

At first the city struck me as a tired, worn-out place that had undergone too many invasions by Romans, Moors, Visigoths, Normans, and Castilians, to name a few. But when Jerry and I caught a three-hour city tour, I became enamored of the broad avenues, carved arches, gardens, parks, wooded areas, and the winding cobblestone streets of Alfama, the oldest part of town. We ate at a restaurant that served very salty cod and kid meat along with a fish soup. We drank Sagres, the national beer. My favorite spot was Queluz, an eighteenth-century palace designed by a French architect and built by a wealthy Portuguese. I hadn't expected to find such a mirrored, grandly appointed building in the heart of this Old World capital about which I had known nothing. The palace was almost a duplicate of the one that housed the French kings and queens at Versailles. And looking down from its highest points, I became convinced that Lisbon was indeed one of the most spectacular cities on the Continent. It throbbed with subtle colors and historic secrets.

That night in a cold, wintry downpour, we headed for our first introduction to Fado, the sad homespun music of the people. I was expecting something akin to the Enka compositions we heard in Japan—not the music itself, but the lyrics, conveying universal feelings of the poor and downtrodden. At the Fado restaurant, we located a table close to the stage area and ordered chicken in a pot for me and tasty whiting fish for Jerry. It was good but nothing like the superb freshly caught sardines for which the country is famous. Until that week, I had never eaten a good-sized sardine just pulled from the salt water of the bay. These tasty fish are in no way related to our supermarket variety, those brown flaky bits of cardboard found in flat cans that are impossible to open without a blowtorch.

The Fado show began with the appearance of string players, young men in their twenties, bored with playing music from an earlier time. In addition to their guitars and an instrument that resembled a ruptured mandolin, a parade of depressed singers materialized, including a heavy lady with red-dyed hair, who seemed to be the owner of the restaurant. She belted out her songs in a lusty contralto and didn't give a damn about whether her audience liked it or not. After her came a young tenor, who sang (what else?) "April in Portugal," which the older American tourists applauded because the song had once been popular in the States.

Mournful Fado songs were performed entirely in untranslated Portuguese, the tempo suggesting hopelessness and disappointment. A female singer doing a heartbreaking Edith Piaf–type number interrupted her agony to send murderous looks in the direction of three oblivious German businessmen loudly negotiating a deal at a nearby table.

In the finale, a debonair gentleman appeared in the spotlight to pour his passionate soul into several well-worn Fado dirges. He insisted on dramatically flinging a white silk scarf through the cigarette smoke to clear the air. I sensed the elderly singer had once been a popular Fado star in Portugal, a former matinee idol perhaps. Because the sparse audience was not impressed, Jerry and I applauded with extra enthusiasm, so much so that the singer hovered over our table and sang an extra series of gloomy melodies directly into our faces. We continued smiling and nodding our approval, but we couldn't fathom the lyrics. Portuguese is not Spanish, and the words sometimes end with a kind of mush-mouth syllable that surprises the listener. When the artist finished, he bowed to us, his eyes wet with grateful tears. "That's our good deed for the day," Jerry said afterward.

In Lisbon we stopped at a bookstore, Livraria Britânica, where I found an English translation of a book by one of Portugal's most renowned writers,

Fernando Pessoa. It was his journal, *The Book of Disquiet*, described by a critic as "the most beautiful diary of the century." Within its pages, I unearthed his cryptic observations of the human condition and the folly of traveling anywhere. I'll return to him later.

Rust, Glorious Rust

Our Lisbon trip had interrupted the sporadic promotion of *Admiral of the Mosquitoes*. On my own, I had tried to storm public radio and television with sardonic verse about the voyages of Columbus, all four of them, but the Washington area is awash with people who write excellent books; competition was brutal. On the other hand, Jerry, a professor of materials science at Johns Hopkins University, sailed calmly on metallurgical waters. With no effort on his part, free publicity always flowed his way. After an article ran about him in a campus publication, a Baltimore TV station invited him for an interview on an evening news program that included a segment about local figures engaged in uncommon pastimes.

"I never thought metallurgy was considered unusual," Jerry commented to me.

"Maybe they think anyone who spends his time watching how metals rust is a little nuts," I said, envious that this opportunity had fallen into his lap through no effort of his own while I struggled in vain to find any piddling outlet that would give Columbus his due.

Jerry's host on the TV program did not conduct the interview in the studio. He and Jerry met in a junkyard on the outskirts of the city. There on a drizzly day, lost in a dismal collection of the rustiest debris ever assembled in one spot, my husband delivered a mini-lecture on the reaction of water and salt on metals and the dollar-and-cents costs of corrosion to industry and government.

"And so," Jerry concluded, "rust can be caused by many things: direct oxidation, liquids, atmosphere, or electrochemistry. It can endanger anything from aircraft to ships to apartment buildings. Corrosion has been called the cancer of metals." He glanced at the hulks of deteriorating cars around him. "And I don't feel so good myself."

The camera faded out with a long shot of the two men, but not before the host bent over with laughter and could barely finish the show. He hadn't expected Jerry to ad-lib.

Over the years, a worrisome mass of unfinished manuscripts accumulated in my files. During those introspective, still-waters-run-deep years after spasmodic dysphonia ended my monologues and readings, I produced a pile of rejected work and reached a conclusion. No one takes light verse or funny essays seriously. A local paper, the *Gazette,* had run a couple of my prose pieces, true stories, one about a dog that followed me home and his ditzy owner who didn't want to take him back, and another inane piece about the importance of organizing underwear. But the *Washington Post* hadn't bought anything humorous from me in years.

All right, I thought, in a cynical moment. Enough of the bemused *luftmensch* approach. Let them receive from me something deliberately unfunny, as deep as Marcel Proust or as symbolic as James Joyce. It was only a matter of changing batteries. Why not resurrect a personal memory that would leave a hard-boiled editor blubbering in his/her Merlot? At the same time, the piece should deliver a fresh twist on an upcoming calendar date, some solemn day that challenged harried editors every year.

I decided to write about the 1930s and our elementary school observance of Armistice Day, now called Veterans Day. The article referred to my mother's immigrant brother, who enlisted in the U.S. Army during the Spanish-American War in 1898. Even my own eyes watered as I wrote about this forgotten tailor and his service in a conflict now barely remembered. The *Post* ran it under the heading "A Day Even for Uncle Frank." It was so sad that worried friends phoned to cheer me up.

That success inspired another bittersweet piece describing the World War II USO dances attended by my big sister Eleanor and me. "Last Dance on the Way to War" ran in the Sunday Outlook section of the *Washington Post* on Christmas Day 1994. I had reached an age when I enjoyed reminiscing even if it made me weep buckets. Maybe I should write an autobiography, a book about hard times in my hometown during the Depression and World War II? My brain stored that idea in an unvisited corner. Perhaps one day.

The more serious work gained ground and emboldened me. At the National League of American Pen Women convention in the early 1990s, the prestigious organization awarded prizes in letters, art, and music. Dozens of judges, male and female, practitioners in their fields, decided who would receive these coveted honors. I had never won anything in previous biennial competitions open to professional women from across the country. Casting inhibitions to the four winds, I swabbed the deck, tossed unpublished odds and ends into kraft envelopes, and shipped out a cargo of short stories, serious free verse, nonfiction articles, and even, the good Lord help us, Petrarchan sonnets, a mind-boggling form never attempted by me before. This would be my grand slam, my one and only effort to break into a national writing competition—and yet, a still, small voice within me whispered, "You have a Popsicle's chance in hell."

I was wrong this time. At the New York convention, the unsung, low-flying seabirds that had been caged in my file cabinet for the past ten years flapped their way into the sunlight. At the awards banquet, I was startled to hear officials announce my name in several categories; my winning entries included "Snowblind," a serious poem about the fickleness of memory, and two short stories: "Superfrog," centered around an earthly visit from the ghost of Emily Dickinson, and "I Never Met a Decade I Didn't Like," a tender tale of senior citizens. Also in the winner's circle were my published article "What Rhymes with 'Sincerely Yours'?" and, miraculously, two Petrarchan sonnets, "On Looking Back" and "Sonnet to a Line in the Book of Job." That evening a multitude of Pen Women, representing branches from all over the country, applauded politely but were not enthralled by my good fortune. In fact, everybody there hated me. The next year, NLAPW officials changed the rules; entries by one person would be limited to only two categories. I had scored in six of them, with first and second prizes as well as two honorable mentions. *Mea culpa.*

In the passing years, that same arts organization would hand me a Precepts and Advice Award for the light essay "Hello, Young Writers or Whatever You Are," and later they honored "Marcelle's Amulet of Bruxelles." I wrote the latter as a tribute to renowned Belgian sculptor Marcelle Pourbaix-Trojan, who after losing her sight could no longer create her magnificent works. She and husband Marcel Pourbaix, originator of the famed Pourbaix diagram (known to corrosion scientists throughout the world), were dear friends whom Jerry and I always visited on our European voyages. The poem, inspired by her sculpture *The Tree of Life,* was read at the annual banquet of an international corrosion symposium in Brussels. The verse celebrates a silver medallion she gave me, modeled after her larger sculpture, *L'arbre de Vie.* My poem ends with these lines:

> *Light captured by God's metal can deny*
> *the lonely fog that sullies branch and sky*
> *the Artist's dream sees farther than the eye.*

Lady Captains Courageous

One advantage of joining the Pen Women had been the opportunity to rub shoulders with not just writers, but also composers and artists. At meetings of our branch, I often displayed copies of *Yankee Shoes* and enlisted a fellow poet to read my work to the group. One of the members was Winifred Hyson, a published composer in search of American themes. Three poems about women in the Bicentennial book intrigued her.

"I liked 'Lemonade' Lucy Hayes, Eleanor Roosevelt, and Jacqueline Kennedy," she said. "Do some more First Ladies, and I'll set them to music."

Why not? It wasn't my first collaboration with musicians. In the 1970s, Elana Keller, a Massachusetts-based pianist/composer, discovered the book *Unholy Writ* and wrote more than a half dozen songs based on the poems. A music major at Wellesley College with graduate training at the University of Hartford, she played with the Hartford Symphony Orchestra and doubled as harpsichordist in their Chamber Music Orchestra. She joined forces with Victoria Morhaim, a mezzo-soprano from Boston who also concertized in New York. Together, they performed our songs with much success throughout New England.

Ten years later, Barney Bragin, a Brooklyn composer, asked permission to create melodies for poems he adapted from *More Unholy Writ*. Each time he introduced the work in New York and Miami, he phoned or sent glowing letters to describe how well audiences received those songs. I was indebted to Elana and Barney for bringing my verse to a widening band of readers. Sadly, he and I never met in person.

Wheels began grinding on the new project about presidents' wives. American history has always been my joy. Once more, I spent months of research at local libraries, read through stacks of biographies, and kept a file of newspaper clippings, random ideas, and snatches of verse that popped into my head at 3:00 a.m. The less heralded, unremembered first ladies fascinated me. I advanced as far as tragic Rachel Jackson, who had been wed once before but owned no official divorce papers when she married Old Hickory. His enemies had a field day about the impropriety of their relationship. The first two stanzas of my poem explained this sad situation. The following lines tell how the story ended:

Rachel D. and Andy J. were married one time more
But politics were dirtier than they had been before.
"That bigamist, adulteress," their enemies would say
Though Rachel knew her Bible and was holier than they.
Rachel D. and Andy Jackson rose above the mess
Andy bought his lady an Inauguration dress.
She wore it to her funeral instead on Christmas Eve
While rough and tumble Andy wiped his tears upon his sleeve.
Rachel D. and Andy Jackson took a carriage ride
Headed for the pearly gates of Heaven, Rachel sighed,
"I'd rather be a servant in the mansion of our God
Than mistress of that hell-hole on the foul Potomac sod."

As Winifred Hyson and I collaborated, we joked about becoming a female Rodgers and Hammerstein. It didn't take long to finish those poems about the White House and its female tenants. The opening verse, "North Portico: A Foreword," introduced the theme:

This is a look at our nation's addenda
Exhibit A: Presidents' wives
Matrons of money, or hard-scrabble sisters
Curated, catalogued lives.
These are our women, our own alter egos
Vulnerable live and dead
Of whom the majority wouldn't be noted
Except for the husbands they wed.
This is the song of the Marthas and Dolleys
Cast in a sisterly frieze
Lopsided hearts filled with love-hate initials
Carved on American trees.

Upstream, Downstream

Making its debut the following year, *Ladies First: Rhymes and Times of the Presidents' Wives and Other Female Fantasies* covered all the erstwhile chatelaines, ending with Hillary Clinton. Winifred Hyson selected six poems from a total of forty-three in the book. After I adjusted some of the lines to fit her melodic style, she produced a series of songs featuring lesser known ladies like Louisa Adams, Sarah Polk, Jane Pierce, Julia Grant, and Helen Taft.

"Except for Eleanor Roosevelt," she said, "we'll avoid the more recent ones. I'm not looking for trouble."

When finished, Winifred turned the music over to a professional mezzo-soprano and her accompanist, and the three of them created a concertized version, *The North Portico,* which was previewed by friends and local music groups. Meanwhile, I created a forty-five-minute script to include not only those songs but also readings of additional poems about Florence Harding, Grace Coolidge, Mamie Eisenhower, and Jacqueline Kennedy.

It turned out better than I expected. Here was a patriotic, entertaining program that appealed to women's organizations, civic and religious groups, government workers, and retirees. That earlier dream of mine, a musical based on the voyages of Columbus, might not have worked so well. Audiences identified more closely with American first ladies than with a power-hungry, egotistical foreigner who had been dead for five centuries.

"Looks like you have a hit on your hands," Jerry said after our first performance.

Although my vocal cords didn't permit me to read, I ached to tread the boards with the others in the show. "Audiences tend to ignore the playwright and composer," Jerry said. "It's the actors and singers who reap all the glory."

That's why I shamelessly wrote myself into the script as a mime/dancer, even spoofing Isadora Duncan's wild, interpretative style. In my mid-sixties, I returned, albeit voiceless and a little stiff in the joints, to the wicked stage. We called ourselves the First Lady Players, and bless us all, our ages ranged from sixty-three to seventy-nine.

Lee Bowdoin, a classically trained soprano and the youngest of the ensemble, introduced us to her longtime agent, who booked us into venues we might not have played had we marketed our production on our own. We set our modest fee high enough to split into five parts, including singer, pianist, composer, agent, and writer/mime. Our singer doubled as accountant, paymaster, and wardrobe mistress.

Pianist Mary Beth Beck, pushing eighty, arranged for her Baptist church to give us free rehearsal room and use of their piano. Keeping the performers to a high standard with frequent rehearsals, composer Hyson fine-tuned and rehearsed the musical content. I directed the spoken parts, which our singer delivered with occasional memory lapses that distorted rhyme schemes. All of us shopped thrift stores and pillaged our closets for authentic but inexpensive costumes. As mime/dancer, I bought my first black leotard, donned a pixie-cut Audrey Hepburn wig, and kept trim by taking brisk three-mile walks, chased by barking dogs.

Jerry insisted on repaying me for all the times I had put aside my dreams to bolster his career. He designed and built us a lightweight, easily portable stage set. Using a book of theatrical costumes, he helped me trace outlines of women in period dresses, and then we blackened these figures with India ink, photographed and enlarged them, and created six silhouettes twenty-five inches tall, mounted on white tagboard. My husband proceeded to build six collapsible wooden easels on which we could prop our illustrations of eighteenth-, nineteenth-, and twentieth-century fashions worn by first ladies. And it was also Jerry who loaded our car with all the paraphernalia that accompanied our traveling show, and he who drove me through sleet, hail, and record-breaking heat to venues throughout the Washington/Maryland/Virginia area.

Making More Waves

One engagement led to the next; *Ladies First*, the paperback, sold a goodly number of copies at each performance. Articles in the local press focused on the novelty of older women honoring the presidents' wives. We made the most of a book review from a national magazine, the *Small Press Review*. "In witty Ogden Nash–like nonsense," wrote critic Nick Dispoldo, "Kruger reflects the character and personality traits of our First Ladies. She pokes and prods like Dorothy Parker and her satire is always clean of cruelty . . . poetry with a girlish glow." A headline in the *Washington Post* read "Ladies First: No Longer Just Standing by Their Men." Other newspaper and magazine articles continued to appear with titles like "Troupe Puts First Ladies at Center Stage," "Ladies First—and Foremost," and an excellent national review by poet Marta Knobloch: "With her light touch and contagious humor, Kruger has given us an insightful lesson in American history. [Her] guided tour of the White House is a tour de force."

Those exhilarating years left little time for serious writing. We worked daytime, nighttime, weekdays, and weekends as our original cast soldiered on with the mission of bringing American history to the masses. We performed in unheated churches, store windows at shopping malls, apartment house lobbies, retirement community auditoriums, private homes, and a nursing facility where the public address system drowned us out with constant medical alerts. One hot August we even carted our home-style extravaganza to an old-fashioned wooden hall in a remote village, a former resort where late nineteenth- and early twentieth-century Chautauqua lectures and readings were held. It was here a summer lightning storm struck, knocking out the electricity. Until half of our neighborly audience ran home and returned with candles, I did my pantomime in the dark. There was an exciting historical authenticity in performing on a stage lit only by the miniature flames flickering all around us. Jerry, our faithful prompter in the wings, was less taken by the dramatic setting. "We're lucky they didn't burn the place down," he said.

The cast of *Ladies First* grew older. When our soprano retired to join her daughter on the West Coast, and when the elderly pianist married a childhood sweetheart in Mississippi and moved there, we felt ambivalent about continuing. Exhausted, I wondered at what point I could quit the show and return to writing full time. After my annual month-long bout of flu, we conducted auditions for a new cast. Earlier in the year, *Ladies First* had been invited to participate in "Jacqueline Kennedy's Washington," a citywide arts event. Would we meet this commitment? Could we be ready in time?

Luck saved us. A newspaper article about our show attracted the attention of a seasoned play director seeking a new project. Once on board, she infused our production with fresh ideas, and we attracted another classically trained singer, her accompanist, and a professional mime to replace me. The venerable Charles Sumner School Museum in Washington provided a unique setting. Established in 1872 for the education of African Americans in a building named for an abolitionist senator, our venue with its old-fashioned proscenium stage and velvety draped curtain offered the ambience of an earlier era. *Ladies First* had finally landed at a historic destination worthy of its theme.

By 2005 we had spent a decade performing at community colleges, residences for the elderly, civic organizations, and fundraisers for religious groups. It was time to put *Ladies First* in mothballs along with the lace mobcaps, fringed mourning shawls, rose-bedecked bonnets, and the ratty fox fur piece that our Eleanor Roosevelt wore. And then at last did I buckle down to finish my memoir or grind out the Great American Novel? No, I did not.

Recurrent rivulets swept me away in an opposite direction. During the previous decade, a new magazine, *Chesapeake*, was born in Maryland. The spunky regional Pen Women publication provided a showcase for unpublished material, including short stories I created during and after the Johns Hopkins writers conference. "Piano Blues," a minimalist quickie, was based on an episode in our marriage when we bought a bargain piano and found a mouse nest inside. Twenty years before I had sold another version of it as a humorous essay to the *Washington Post*. A second short story, "It's O.K. Really," involved a true account of a babysitter terrorized by an unexpected visitor in the basement. My favorite tale published by *Chesapeake* was "Amelia's Stone," which explored my childhood memory of an adult's nervous collapse. Regional magazines also ran free verse of mine, including "amerika" and "The Cats of Ahuza," as well as "Snowblind," a sonnet.

On the Shore Dimly Seen

Throughout the 1990s, markets for freelance journalism dried up and blew away. Thanks to the Internet, beloved American publications embarked on a farewell tour that continues to this day. Even the long-lived *Baltimore Evening Sun*, former bastion of Russell Baker and H. L. Mencken, appeared threatened.

During college, we budding journalists swooned over Mencken's journalistic output and tried to imitate his controversial style. I briefly dated a Baltimore youth whose parents lived on Hollins Street a few doors away from the Great Man himself. My friend interviewed Mencken for our campus magazine, noted his tenderness toward the neighborhood children, and questioned whether the old man was growing soft in his old age. We thought that was a daring evaluation for a twenty-year-old student to make about Baltimore's famed curmudgeon and author of *The American Language*.

Having moved to the Washington area, I deserted Mencken's newspaper with no qualms. Forty-five years later, in connection with *Admiral of the Mosquitoes*, a *Baltimore Sun* reporter arrived at our house to interview me about the book. The young man feared losing his job because of a pending merger with the morning edition of the *Sun*.

"Circulation of the evening paper is way down," he said. "Advertising has fallen off, subscriptions canceled. TV all-news programs and the Internet are taking their toll. I may go into computer programming."

Change seemed inevitable; the best and oldest publications of our time were disappearing fast all over the country, and they continue to vanish now in the twenty-first century. Even the mighty *Evening Sun* quietly folded in 1995. Nobody knew how saddened the demise left me, even though those skinflints never bought a single article from me. I went about the house singing the classic lyrics of a blues song by W. H. Handy: "I hate to see that *Evening Sun* go down."

"It's depressing," I told Jerry. "I remember composing the 1946 class prophecy for our high school yearbook. I presented it in the format of a newspaper with sections devoted to Sports, Comics, Women's Page, and Business, and that's how I predicted my classmates' future occupations, each one like a news item."

"And it all rhymed?" Jerry asked.

"Of course. And at the end I predicted that in ten years I'd be editor-in-chief of the *Evening Sun*."

"Pretty outrageous," Jerry said. "Back then, women didn't hold top jobs like that. You never told me you were an early-day feminist."

"I've never had the chutzpah to call myself a feminist. Just peg me a female writer born twenty years before her time."

I must have looked discouraged because my husband held out his arms to me. "Don't let the bastards wear you down, Molkalini," he said in a cheerful voice.

Under a Hot and Copper Sky

Mine is a touch-and-go vanity. It's hard to resist my self-indulgence. When a local women's club asked me to present a reading based on *Ladies First,* I agreed despite the spasmodic dysphonia that continued to harass me.

"This time I'll work around it," I promised Jerry. To circumvent any vocal difficulties, I prepared a program of selected First Lady poems to be read by talented members of the sponsoring group. We held a couple of rehearsals, which I conducted in semi-whispers. Although I couldn't read or sing my verse, I envied the women at center stage and decided there was one sure-fire way to outwit the devil. I would perform a musical solo unlike anything I had tackled before.

JOURNAL ENTRY: MARCH 1999

> The Old Me returns, rejuvenated, delighted to morph into Ulysses S. Grant's wife, Julia, complete with 1870s-style bonnet and shawl. Gesturing like Sarah Bernhardt and using an offstage audiotape made by our original mezzo-soprano, Lee Bowdoin, I managed to lip-sync her song from our show. I mugged shamelessly and even borrowed her triumphant exit, waving an American flag and shouting the suffragette's mantra, "Votes for Women! Votes for Women!" The audience appeared to like it. At least no one left early.

That minor success did wonders for my confidence. The time had come to vanquish the cruel disorder that had robbed me of a trustworthy voice.

"If speech fails me, dammit, I can still write," I often said to Jerry.

"And I can still corrode," Jerry said.

"You are the Marco Polo of Metals," I told him, "always opening up new vistas." It is necessary for me at this point of the narrative to record the distance my traveling partner covered in those final decades of the twentieth century. During his earlier years at the National Bureau of Standards, Jerry headed the Corrosion and Electrodeposition Section and experimented with the oxidation and passivation of copper, iron, and silver. Mired in what I considered "all this complicated stuff," he never lost his sense of humor. Once when he chaired a conference on the passivity of metals, he received applications from psychologists who thought the meeting dealt with a mental condition, not a metal one. "Maybe we should invite them for laughs," Jerry said.

Among a flock of other topics I couldn't begin to grasp, he continued to study pitting and stress corrosion, cracking, and the corrosion of metals used for nuclear waste containment. He was much concerned about the disposal of nuclear waste. "Even if it is encased in corrosion-resistant containers and buried deep in the ground," he said, "the metal will eventually fall apart, and one thousand years from now, people may find the containers and not realize what they are or what they're releasing into the atmosphere," he said. "That's worrisome."

Jerry also supplied the U.S. Congress with reports on the economic damage of metallic corrosion and its high cost to government and industry. Later in his career, he organized an international symposium for scientists, museum conservators, and archaeologists and taught courses to students planning careers in the preservation of metallic artworks. He and I once toured California museums for hours while he studied and marveled at the accumulating rust on notable works of sculpture. "Wow!" he said, genuinely excited. "Look at the patina on *that* nude!"

My husband always felt at home in museums; his preference lay with the French modernists like Cézanne and Braque. He defended the argument that science itself was an art, and within materials science there existed inherent beauty that most people didn't appreciate if they knew about it at all. He kept an enlargement of a single copper crystal on his office wall. The crystal, a yellow sphere, revealed three linked squares outlined in brown and might have passed for an expressionistic painting or a pale yellow basketball with accented tan seams. He and his co-workers developed a procedure for restoring and conserving the gilded bronze horses on the Memorial Bridge in Washington. He made a solo flight in a cherry picker that lifted him to the top of the statuary when the time came to inspect it. Dangerous living for a man who dreaded heights!

Jerry would publish his findings in six books and more than 160 scientific papers, all unfathomable to me, on such nifty topics as *Mechanisms and Applications of Nickel-Base Alloys, New Approaches to the Study of Localized Corrosion, Chemical Factors Important to the Environmentally Sensitive Fracture, The Nature of the Passive Film on Iron and Ferrous Alloys, Dynamic Imaging, Microellipsometry Imaging* (co-author), and *Nature of Passive Film on Iron: Does It Affect Breakdown?*

"I could have come up with some catchier titles," I once said, just to get a rise out of him.

He gave me a tolerant smile. "Not exactly my speed," he answered.

Our travels together multiplied as Jerry received more and more awards for his work. In addition to Chicago, New York, Denver, San Antonio, Houston, New Orleans, Los Angeles, Las Vegas, and San Francisco, we included assorted university towns in our itinerary. His career during those decades also took us overseas to destinations like Waterloo, Amsterdam, Cannes, Caesarea, Frankfurt, Bordeaux, and Düsseldorf. The Berlin Wall had come down, the Soviet Union ended, and we visited a German university in a village not far from the Harz Mountains. We were told that this part of East Germany inspired the Walpurgisnacht scenes in Goethe's *Faust*. It remains a gathering spot for witches from around the world, but I didn't stock up on any of the broomsticks offered in the souvenir shops.

In Germany I never felt fully at ease. Mine is a community of memory. I was born the same year as Anne Frank.

The Gordon Research Conferences in New Hampshire came and went, world without end. The conferences were a template for our marriage. We had been attending these week-long get-togethers each summer for forty-three years. In 1960 we had bought a new car, a Rambler, and treated ourselves to a grueling drive from Maryland to the Granite State with our two little ones, ages six months and three. That was ghastly, but as the children grew older, they played tag on the green campus of Colby-Sawyer College and took giant steps and baby steps in games of "Mother, May I?" Later we carted the boys to local concerts and musicals at nearby summer theaters. The New England conferences marked myriad life passages for us, even election-year political campaigns.

In the late sixties, after driving from New London to Cape Cod, our car was totaled in an accident, serious enough for the police to rush us to the nearby hospital. Although our boys in the back seat were not injured, I had a concussion and Jerry suffered injuries to his ribs. Afterward, both of us swathed in bandages, we watched the fractious 1968 Democratic National Convention televised from Chicago. Our sons, then eleven and nine, served us tuna salad for dinner at the Wellfleet cottage we had rented. After they grew older, became summer camp counselors, attended college, and worked at summer jobs, the boys started their own careers, attending meetings and conferences in their chosen fields. Jerry continued delivering his scientific papers and reports at the Gordon Conferences. I came along for the ride.

During the years of these summer conferences, I had learned who were the heroes and who were the villains. The scientists rarely went into much detail about the people they admired; a random sentence of praise would evoke nods of approval. Jerry was a hero, but there was one universal villain, who had published more papers than anyone else in the world, and whose name brought forth vitriolic statements even from the tolerant and good-natured. Call him Dr. Starfish, a living icon in the field of electrochemistry.

He had mentored legions of young PhDs, and not one of them had a good word to say about the man. Whenever his name entered the conversation, blood pressures soared. In the middle of casual chitchat, someone inevitably would mention Dr. Starfish, and a rocket exploded, igniting a multitude of pent-up passions, grudges, and humiliating experiences suffered at his hands. Men of science are as human as the rest of us.

Their invective amused me. Fighting boredom, I once jotted down, verbatim, overheard acidic evaluations of Dr. Starfish: "Impossible to work with." "Exploits his subordinates shamelessly." "Notorious for stealing credit from others." "Intensely contemptuous of anyone else's progress or success." "Insensitive, ill-mannered, overbearing, and deliberately obstructive." "Full of himself." "Married and divorced five times." The corrosion gentlemen appeared to enjoy dissecting him. I found a possible metallurgical reason in a quote from an ancient Greek named Antisthenes. He wrote, "As iron is eaten by rust, so are the envious consumed by envy."

A whole new generation of younger scientists now attended these venerable Gordon Research gatherings, some of them Jerry's former graduate students and post-docs from Johns Hopkins. In the late 1990s, as an active consultant following his retirement from the university, Jerry participated in a discussion titled "Corrosion Perspectives for the 21st Century." He predicted a rosy, rusty future. "I may not see all this happen," he concluded, facing the mixed audience of older colleagues and rising young stars of materials science, "but many of you will."

Afterward I watched a hesitant young man with Native American features. He lingered on the edge of the crowd as he waited nervously for a chance to speak to Jerry. I couldn't decipher the small print on his name tag. Just one word stood out: "Mexico." As we prepared to leave, he forced himself to come forward and said, "Dr. Kruger, your papers and your research will inspire us and live on through the next century." Jerry was deeply moved.

Later at bedtime I said, "That was a scene out of a 1930s film on Turner Classic Movies."

"Yeah," Jerry said dryly, *"Goodbye, Mr. Chips."*

Reversal of Flow

The Gordon Research Conferences in New Hampshire were often jumping-off points north to Maine, Nova Scotia, New Brunswick, and Prince Edward Island. Sometimes we detoured to Provincetown or Providence or Boston to sightsee on the Freedom Trail or to visit a place I had fantasized about, the Amherst home of the Dickinson family, where from her bedroom window, oddball Emily silently lowered baskets of goodies for neighborhood children. The building proved to be a conventional nineteenth-century brick house, not nearly so enigmatic as the mysterious, half-hidden residence next door, The Evergreens. This was the home of her scandalous brother Austin, a lawyer who engaged in an affair with one of Emily's close friends.

On one of our trips north into Canada, we discovered the magical Bay of Fundy and the diurnal phenomenon that occurs just before the St. John River flows into the bay. At that point, the river reverses and decides to move in the opposite direction. "That's the way I am," I said to Jerry. "I move along hell-bent in one route, and then at a critical point, I switch course and I'm off, going against the tide, headed away from where I'm supposed to be."

"It's called reversal of flow," Jerry said. "That river will eventually reach the place where it wants to go and so will you, kid."

In the final year of the twentieth century, we flew northwest to Alberta, where members of the Electrochemical Society met in May for a meeting on the passivity of metals. An early bus ride to Jasper Park took us on a ten-hour tour through the Canadian Rockies, past dazzling snowfields and massive glaciers we had not seen since our visit to Alaska in 1986. Moose and elk roamed everywhere, but we met no thousand-pound grizzlies. I was satisfied not to run into any of those hefty fellows or black bears even half that weight.

"Do you realize that this bus ride is taking longer than any of our plane trips to England or Belgium?" Jerry asked. I sat propped up by the portable back-support he designed especially for me. He constructed it by fastening together two large wooden squares with a black grosgrain ribbon, a simple device that went with me everywhere on our travels. It opened and closed like a book and dangled from a handbag strap encircling my wrist. This humble appliance rescued my disintegrating vertebrae from the tyranny of endless tours.

Our fellow tourists slumbered while the driver droned on about deciduous Canadian trees, ancient riverbeds, and curious rock formations.

"Just think," Jerry said in genuine wonder, "together we've seen the Alps, the Andes, Fuji in Japan, Sugar Loaf in Brazil, Mt. Hood, Mt. Rainier, the Harz Mountain chain, and now all this. Who ever dreamed we would reach such high places?"

"Do you remember, Jerry, once before we were married, I wanted to ride the Ferris wheel at a carnival, and you agreed. But when it stopped at the top and we rocked back and forth, you turned green and said you always detested heights."

He laughed. "High mountain peaks impress me but only from a distance," he said.

The thing I remember most about that Rockies trip was a conversation among scientists who ate dinner with us after another exhausting day of work for Jerry. It began for him at 7:00 a.m. with an executive board meeting, followed by another session of talks for which he served as chairman, and ending with a poster session which he had to review in late afternoon. We gathered for our evening meal in front of a window that looked out on Emerald Lake, a sparkling green jewel set against spectacular gray and white mountains. Around the table, seasoned corrosion people, all male, chatted, mourning how little the younger generation of scientists appreciated the early accomplishments of distinguished men like U. R. Evans and Marcel Pourbaix, two celebrated names in the materials science world.

"The young ones think they're doing new work that has already been done years ago by the founding fathers of materials science," said one weary-looking old-timer, a professor whom I had often met at these international meetings. Others agreed. Several men had already retired and two more planned to join them in another year. Personal glory in all fields of human endeavor eventually fades and dies; human corrosion takes its toll. I think my husband was aware of it that evening as he studied the familiar but aging faces around the table.

"The Twilight of the Gods," he commented later.

Throughout his career, Jerry traveled the country and the world, a remarkable accomplishment for a man with a disability that might have discouraged someone with less determination. A victim of polio at the age of five months, he soldiered through the years with a right leg shorter than the left and a malformed hip bone. Despite limitations that left him with a pronounced limp, Jerry was not a reluctant dragon like me when it came to travel. He enjoyed the wonderment of our voyages. "I was just a nice, quiet Jewish boy from Atlanta," he often said. "I never expected to be catching planes for London, Paris, Rome, Brussels, Rio, Tokyo, Sydney, Athens, and all over. It's amazing."

And so was he. Although manuscripts once again lay neglected on my desk, accompanying Jerry on his trips became essential. Increasingly, he tripped and fell, suffering bruises but not fractures. I wanted to be nearby whenever such accidents happened. Even so, he disliked any show of alarm or pity. He brushed away my concern with, "No big deal." Never did I know how often these accidents happened when he traveled alone. Neither of us wanted to admit that his mobility was ebbing with each swift year. And neither of us questioned when life itself would undergo stark change without our permission.

The Periodic Table of Elements does not include Time. We can't be sure of its properties, but I know from experience that Time is not corrosion resistant. Years do not hold up well, and at the end of each December, they disintegrate into memory if we're lucky. I felt the clock was running out. Would I ever meld together enough fragments of weeks and months to produce a novel? Or complete the Bel Air memoir on which I had already spent eight years? Or even gather enough snippets of verse to fill another slim poetry collection? To put it brutally, was I getting too old to become a late bloomer? "There's always a chance you can still catch the last boat out," Jerry said.

PART THREE

Ports of Recall

New Stars to Steer By

The millennium began with memories of my mother as a young immigrant girl who saw the nineteenth century slip away into the twentieth. To commemorate her struggle as an exploited eleven-year-old in a Baltimore sweatshop, I wrote "New Year's Eve: 1899 and 1999." It opens with these lines:

You, young girl who are to be my mother
you sit cross-legged, tailor style
half hidden by a mound of woolen sleeves
wrought by sweatshop immigrants
I watch you pull gray-white bastings
rip wicked threads
with a hooked silver needle
that bleeds your fingers
into the next century
You'll sleep tonight and will not hear
the bells of days to come . . .

The bells of days to come transformed themselves into emergency sirens. Early in the century, the September 11th terrorist attacks on United States territory stunned the entire world. My poet friends responded by attempting to capture the hurt on paper, but I couldn't manage words sad enough or significant enough to record this national tragedy. For me, the catastrophe needed generations to pass before any lasting monument of words could rise from the ashes. Our lives continued, shaken and humbled.

Although I never succumbed to Facebook or Instagram, I took classes in computer language (mostly jargon to me), Internet platforms, and other electronic bilge a writer must absorb to stay au courant. Most of it washed over me without sinking in. Having reached my golden years, I also wearied of playing cat-and-mouse with agents and publishers. "Why not revive our noble cottage industry?" Jerry asked. "Maryben Books will rise again."

Not a bad idea. Before this aging brain of mine could determine whether the Bel Air memoir would sink or swim, a phone call came from my friend, Doris Gold, at Biblio Press.

"It's fifteen years since we published *Daughters of Chutzpah*," she said. "How about a sequel for a whole new generation of feminists in the twenty-first century?"

The birth of two millennial grandchildren had already sidetracked me; I treasured the hours spent with them and hesitated to sign a contract with her. Ms. Gold insisted it wouldn't take much time or effort. "We'll include material from *Daughters of Chutzpah*," she said. "All you'd have to do is select and update some poems. As you know, Second Wave feminism has changed things since then."

That was news to me. I wasn't going to ask how it differed from the First Wave because Doris would take the next five hours to tell me. Although a staunch believer in women's rights, I never had bought a single copy of *Ms.* magazine or followed the steady drumbeat of Betty Friedan and Gloria Steinem. Still, the offer was tempting.

"That's all you need?" I said. "You'll go with the old stuff?"

"Oh, and you can just add twenty or so new poems to round things out."

There you have the trouble with topical light verse. People think a writer can dash it off while waiting for a taxi. It takes research, familiarizing yourself with the subject so that you can be knowledgeable enough to make a light or ironic statement about what you know. The treatment is funny, but you don't want to sound like a blithering fool. There are serious decisions about length, meter, and general attitude toward subject and reader. All this precedes tackling rhyme and vocabulary choices. It may not work for everyone, but it was the technique that kept me grinding out poetic newspaper columns each week for almost twenty years.

"Don't agonize," Jerry said that night when I weighed the pros and cons of tackling feminism once more. "Run with it."

The result in 2005 was an eclectic collection of verses contrasting biblical women and contemporary Jewish women, changes in Judaism, synagogue politics, female rabbis, and "Speaking in Tongues," an essay about my parents' difficulties with the English language. Ms. Gold thought we should call it *A Purse of Humorous Verse for the Jewish Woman*. It was a bland title, but Doris, like the rest of us, was getting on in years.

The "Purse" poems begged to be dramatized. They were better read aloud than ingested silently. Roping in two longtime friends in their seventies, I organized the Pocketbook Players, a troupe available to perform the verses, all blended together in a cohesive script, which we called simply "A Purse of Verse." We accepted gigs only for daytime performances because not one of us was keen on driving at night.

For ambience, we assembled a stage set loaded with contemporary and old-fashioned ladies' handbags, pouches, briefcases, fanny bags, change purses, backpacks, and duffle bags. After I wrote and distributed a brochure heralding the forty-minute program, we never lacked requests from women's groups. "I like what you're doing," publisher Doris Gold said, happy at last with the promotional efforts of her wayward author. Instead of the poems, our audiences seemed more fascinated by all the pocketbooks on display, but I didn't mind that. The women attending our show bought scores of books; we donated a percentage of sales to our sponsors. The Pocketbook Players lasted for two years until the cast wearied of too many pro bono readings, and I felt the need to spend more hours on my languishing memoir manuscript. "Seems I'm never going to finish that damned book," I complained to my sons and Jerry.

"You will," they said in unison, "you will."

Pounding Surf

They were whirlwind years. Our county historical society and local Comcast officials joined to create a new prize honoring achievement in promotion of the humanities. Certain anonymous powers named me the first recipient.

In an interview by Bernice August for the *Gazette* newspapers, I was still in shock over the September 11th attack. At my insistence, the journalist interviewed me via email and quoted me as saying, "I think it's more important than ever since the tragedy . . . that we look to the humanities for solace and inspiration. . . . We need languages, we need to study history, need to study great literatures. . . . Science and technology are terribly important, but unless we have a soul behind them . . . it's a pretty empty world. . . . It's through the humanities we learn how to react to adversity."

Ms. August asked for more, an evaluation of my life's work. In a giddy moment, I called myself "a loose cannon like the 20th century . . . my work reflects metamorphosis, molded by hard economic times, wars, prosperity, and the social commandments that have filtered through the smoke. The trick is not to become bogged down in self-pity and doubt. Neatness doesn't count; survival does." The reporter topped off her article with the heading "Mollee Kruger: Never at a loss for words." As someone with a disabled speaking voice, I took this as a major compliment.

No cash accompanied the prestigious award for "Achievement in the Humanities," according to the trophy, which consisted of a colorful glass ball the size of a California navel orange. The crystal sphere rested precariously on a black plastic base and, unattached, seemed ready to drop to the floor at any given moment. Handing the unwieldy trophy to me at a formal dinner held at a suburban country club, a young business executive delivered a list of reasons for the judges' choice. I don't remember what she said. My anxiety took over. That untethered glass ball was surely going to tumble to the floor, smash, or roll across the stage, and free-fall into the lap of a U.S. Congresswoman seated in the front row. I gave the shortest acceptance speech on record. The unexpected brevity appealed to the audience, a wildly applauding crowd of seven hundred souls in pricey evening gowns and obsolescent tuxedos, most of them affluent business owners, local politicians, patrons of arts organizations, lawyers, orthodontists, and corporate CEOs. They probably hadn't wanted to attend this expensive fundraiser in the first place, and now they could look forward to going home early.

Although the honor lacked the gravitas of a Pulitzer, or even a Miss America tiara, I deeply appreciated it, but in my heart burned the realization that these community activities, albeit worthwhile, had spirited me away from my writing desk for too long. The Bel Air memoir remained far from completion, and that Great American Novel had not yet been launched and would probably never be. I meant to buckle down, seriously and without distractions, until the ghost of Thomas Alva Edison led me astray.

Tom Edison and Crew

It was through Jerry that I became an unlikely flack for the prestigious Electrochemical Society, the worldwide professional association that supports the study of electrochemistry and solid-state science and technology. When this august group approached its centennial year, the top brass asked me to write a commemorative poem for the official celebration. It's not that I qualified for membership. For years I had attended their myriad conferences as Jerry's clueless sidekick, but a bachelor of arts degree didn't enable me to grasp what the hell these scientific geniuses were talking about.

"It's all beyond the ken of a lowly English major," I told Jerry.

"You're a generalist," he said. "You can do it, Molkalini."

Maybe. I thought back to my advertising days. In the late 1950s, while at home with a toddler and a baby on the way, I wrote freelance radio spots for a Baltimore company that sold hot dogs, ham, and bacon. They were marketing a mysterious product called a "picnic." As a Jewish woman who maintained a strictly kosher household, I felt stumped. How could I sell it if I didn't know what it was? My research ended with a Presbyterian neighbor, who said, "It's just a hunk of prepared smoked hog meat." The problem disappeared. In exquisite detail my radio commercials described the sheer ecstasy of consuming the unappetizing stuff, and no one was the wiser.

But it would be folly to try bluffing the Electrochemical Society, that international legion of brainy PhD scientists and no-nonsense engineers. In pursuit of scientific and technological knowledge, the group received financial support not only from their distinguished membership but also from corporations and universities, foreign and domestic. The primary ECS mission was to publish peer-reviewed research papers. Past members included the Wizard of Menlo Park, Thomas Edison himself, and other famed visionaries who advanced electrochemistry, which is a word defined in my dictionary as "the science of the interaction or interconversion of electric and chemical phenomena." That made sense to me.

"I can't fake it," I said, and struggled to find a way to handle this off-the-wall assignment. There are two kinds of advertising: product and institutional, and I wasn't selling processed meat this time. The situation called for institutional ad copy at its highest level. It had to be slanted toward highly trained professionals educated at the world's finest universities and colleges. With all that weight on my puny shoulders, it was impossible to begin without my own research, both basic and applied.

"I Sing the Body Electric" became my title, thanks to my good friend Walt Whitman. Bit by bit, this commemorative salute materialized into serious iambic pentameter lines praising the estimable organization for its accomplishments. Read by a past president at the centennial banquet, the work seemed to please the gathered scientific throng. At least it wasn't heckled by anybody. I felt honored when *Interface*, the ECS official magazine, asked permission to publish it. Herewith my Prologue:

Observe the world one century ago
A stage prepared by Volta, Faraday,
Galvani, who had made the current flow
Through legs of frogs . . . much to their green dismay.
This planet took what Edison had brought
But couldn't speculate or even guess
What Science and what Engineering wrought
When Philadelphia birthed the ECS.
That noble period when we were new
Empowered Industry and made it grow
Our bolt of progress lit the global view
And galvanized the future in its glow.

The Fallen Cherub

By this time, Jerry had left university life to become a consultant in his field. He retired twice, ending thirty-one years in the federal government, and then a decade at Johns Hopkins University. That included two years as chair of the Materials and Engineering Department. It was in one of the Hopkins classrooms that a beloved myth at the core of our marriage was forever shattered.

During his years as a professor, Jerry guided future PhD candidates and taught some undergraduate classes as well. Each year high school students interested in the scientific curriculum visited with faculty to learn more about courses offered. At the end of such a day, Jerry came home, exhausted but exuberant.

"The mystery of the ages is solved," he told me. "One of the young kids who came to my office today brought a transcript of her grades in chemistry and physics, and when I glanced at her last name at the top of the page, I couldn't believe it."

"What was it?"

"I wasn't a hundred percent sure, but I asked if her father had ever gone to Georgia Tech. She said yes. Turns out she was Herman's daughter!"

It couldn't be, not the Angel Herman, not that ethereal spirit sent by Providence to bring Jerry and me together back in the 1950s. But hadn't he ascended into the clouds, never to walk the earth again?

"Wait," Jerry said. "It gets better. She told me he was waiting outside, and would I like to see him? She ran out and came back with her father. I hardly recognized him after thirty-five years."

"Because it was another Herman."

"No, it was our Herman with the same Southern accent. And I mentioned you to him."

I didn't like where this was going.

"He remembered you, and then I apologized for stealing you away from him that night of the party at my apartment."

"You what?"

Jerry chuckled. "So Herman shrugged and said, 'That's okay. I never cared much for her anyway.'"

We never spoke highly of the Angel Herman again.

Old Boats Still Float

Early in the new century, I received a long-awaited dissertation from Susan, a graduate student in sociology at Buffalo State College, later part of New York University. Years before, she had sent a letter inviting me to contribute to her PhD dissertation, entitled "Creativity in the Older Woman." She described it as a scholarly examination of eleven mature creative women and the experiences that formed them. I had been the only person in her study who answered questions entirely by email. It was far easier than responding over the phone.

JOURNAL ENTRY: MARCH 2004

> I still don't know who Susan is or how she found me. We've never met in person. She assigned fictitious names for her case histories and asked if she could call me "Lesley" or "Ashley." Instead, I selected "Katie" because the "K" would stand for Kruger and, besides, how many Jewish women of my generation would ever sport a Waspy moniker like Lesley or Ashley?
>
> In her "Katie" chapter, Susan quoted directly from my answers. I weighed in heavily on the experiences of "us girls" at our male-dominated ad agency back in the day. I also described a dreadful appointment with an indifferent professor who discouraged me, at the age of twenty-one, from enrolling in graduate school and working for a master's and

PhD in English. Susan's interviews with other older women included similar instances of sexism in the '40s, '50s, and '60s.

I told her that creative females, old and young, can be found everywhere we look. They have existed since time began, and they will always be with us. With their inborn creativity, women protect and educate families, save nations, and sustain civilizations. I'm convinced that the unconscionable restrictions affecting women all over the world will be lifted one fine day. Stereotypes and prejudices will go. Creative women will produce a steady stream of new ideas, innovative ways to adapt to our changing planet and its changing people. If that sounds feminist, count me in.

Fairy Penguins Down Under

"I'm freezing," I said. "How long do we have to wait before these damned things decide to come home?"

My husband draped a cotton sweater around my head and tied the two sleeves together under my chin. The sharp wind on Phillip Island caught the flimsy material and whipped it in front of my face like the antennae of a frantic insect.

"We should have packed woolen hats," Jerry said, looking at his watch. "The penguins are scheduled to return ashore at dusk when it turns colder."

I huddled close to him in case he had any body heat to share. How could I know Australia would be this cold in November? I was swamped at home with final performances of *Ladies First* and hadn't found time beforehand to research the continent's weather and geography. I had expected bright and sunny skies everywhere. It would be warm like the Great Barrier Reef area around Cairns, where we had first landed on this tour, and where we had taken a ride on an old U.S. Army duck vehicle through a domesticated rainforest filled with labeled tropical plants and belligerent insects. I learned that the upcoming corrosion meeting would be in Melbourne, the capital of Victoria, along the northern shores of Port Phillip Bay. It was even hundreds of miles beyond Sydney, on the southern coast of this gigantic country about which I knew absolutely nothing.

"Here they come!" a fellow tourist yelled. "Hundreds of them!" a tall man near us cried. "Just look at those little buggers!" Six eager Japanese visitors pushed forward in front of us, blocking my view. Straining, I glimpsed a horde of tiny, wobbling bodies moving from the edge of the water to land. From our distant vantage point, it looked like a bolt of black and white tweed slowly unfolding over the sand.

"They call them fairy penguins," Jerry said, "mini-penguins. You can find this small size only in Australia."

Unfortunately, I am short, too, and couldn't catch much of the action. A swarm of aggressive onlookers jostled us to get a better view. I overheard an Australian father remark to the shivering little son in his arms, "You see, they get up early in the morning and swim in the cold water all day and then they come home just before dark. It's the only time we can see them."

"I'm cold," the child said.

The temperature dropped even lower as the sky darkened; the penetrating wind blinded us as we fought our way back to the heated tour bus.

"That was invigorating," Jerry said, his teeth still chattering. "Could you see anything?"

"No."

"Neither could I," my husband said, and we both laughed hysterically when one of the tourists asked the driver, "Hey, is our next stop the South Pole?"

We booked this packaged tour to fill in ten days before Jerry's conference was scheduled to begin. In our travels we rarely engaged in commercial trips of this kind, but how often did we have a chance to see Australia and New Zealand? We wanted to take in as much as possible. The first part of the journey took us from Washington, D.C. to Los Angeles, where a beautiful blonde tour guide ushered us onto a monster plane that carried us across the Pacific to the land down under.

I don't remember much about the Great Barrier Reef at Cairns. I'm sorry because at the time I write this, unchecked pollution is causing coral to disappear from the earth. My senses back then were dulled by exhaustion from a thirteen-hour transoceanic flight, not counting the preliminary jaunt from Virginia to California. What I do recall is flying two additional hours to a hotel in Cairns, called "Cans" in the 'strilian accent of the Aussies. When we discovered our rooms were not available until sunset, we bedraggled tourists were herded like lost lambs into a bus and taken to a free performance of native Aboriginal dancers, ferocious dark-skinned men, their faces, arms, and legs painted with intricate white patterns.

I felt uncomfortable watching these indigenous performers; I sensed their open hostility as they chanted native songs, probably about the white men who came to destroy their culture and landscape. Not so long ago, these were free-roaming Stone Age people and now, like circus creatures, they were forced to entertain us. I had experienced this same guilt at a Zulu presentation in South Africa and, more recently, on a tour through the mesa homes of sullen Native Americans on a New Mexico reservation. Although still numb with sleep deprivation, Jerry and I felt more at ease when the most threatening dancer of them all grabbed a microphone and greeted us with a cheery, "Good dye, mites!"

During the final days of the same tour, we flew south to visit the Museum of Sydney. Jerry was delighted with quotations on the walls describing the harbor, Port Jackson, especially the heartwarming line that alluded to "ships with smears of rust like the gum of eucalyptus trees." What interested me most was that Herman Melville and D. H. Lawrence had once docked at that beautiful port city. We were drawn to a display highlighting the first people of the continent, the Eora, and an excellent film, *Terra Nulius*, about the losing struggle of the bushmen against the colonizing English.

Australian billboards were outrageously candid—for instance, seven nude men hiding their private parts with a sign that read "Our largest organ." The bus driver passed that one at increased speed. "What are they selling?" I asked. Jerry remained silent. Along the route, another outrageous advertisement, this one for blue jeans, featured a reclining nude and a slogan underneath: "Covers every bum." That raised our eyebrows a bit, but my favorite Australian roadside sign read, "If you drink and drive, you're a bloody idiot."

Along with kangaroo meat, which I reluctantly sampled, the Aussies themselves are an acquired taste. They are candid and independent like Americans. The home folks we met especially enjoyed telling insulting jokes about New Zealanders. During the thirty-five years or so since our trip, the kangaroo herds dwindled for a while, but now, do we dare say, they have rebounded? To protect them from extinction, the government has issued multiple restrictions on scarfing down kangaroo steaks.

When eating out, my husband always explored the Gastric Unknown, often the least appetizing concoction on the menu. As he often reminded our children, "I like to experiment; I'm a scientist." At dinner that night in Cairns, Jerry said, "I was hoping for emu soup or poached platypus, but they don't offer it here." Australia imports much of its food. At one restaurant, when I ordered a simple turkey sandwich, the waiter answered cheerfully, "Only at Christmas, luv."

In Sydney we saw what every tourist sees: the magnificent Opera House on Bennelong Point; The Rocks, where convicts once labored, hacking away aboulders and stones; the sails and anchors of the little Maritime Museum at Cadman's Cottage; Harbour Bridge, Bondi Beach, Circular Quay. Then we waved goodbye to our chartered tour and traveled to Melbourne, busiest port on the Yarra River. From chatting with the locals, we learned about the stiff competition between their two major cities. Cultural Sydney thinks Melbourne is bland, and Melbourne shrugs off Sydney as shallow. It reminded me of municipal competition in Brazil, where a chemist informed us, "The serious citizens in São Paulo work hard so the people of Rio can play." The human animal thrives on rivalry.

Among international scientists at the Melbourne meeting was a lively Italian scientist we'll call Sophia, who felt compelled to destroy the cliché that all housewives in Italy are excellent cooks. "I must describe to you my mother's disgusting cooking," she said. "My husband warned me that if we continued to eat at Mama's house, he wanted a divorce." Sophia reminded me of Giulietta Masina, the pixilated star of Federico Fellini's film *La Strada*. Female scientists in general were a rarity at those conferences. I looked forward to seeing a young chemist from Poland who had given me a copy of *Bells in Winter*, a collection of translated poems by Nobel Laureate Czeslaw Milosz, but she was not invited.

At the inevitable Melbourne banquet following a week of scientific papers and discussions, Sean, one of Jerry's colleagues, stood to award prizes for his unique Contest of Detecting Errors. He followed it with the announcement that the moon was indeed made of green cheese and supported his thesis by analyzing the chemical properties of all elements found there. After imbibing cocktails and wine all evening, not one scientist challenged his results.

Jerry's impaired mobility worried me with each additional trip. When we first married, he walked with a pronounced limp, which didn't stop him from driving miles of superhighways by himself or hiking with our sons. In early middle age, he debonairly brandished a cane. Once when he sprained an ankle, he depended on crutches for a while and later relied on two canes. It didn't hinder him from hurrying to catch a cab in Paris or spanning an airport concourse in Atlanta. Now when he flew, he avoided walking the long distances between gates. He took to renting wheelchairs and tipping porters to whisk him away on shortcuts through isolated Kafkaesque passageways, leading to locked elevators off-limits to other passengers. Meanwhile, I maintained the speed of an Olympic runner to keep up with those fast-moving wheelchair pushers.

Apprehension about his footing never kept Jerry from work or trips to laboratories throughout the country and the world. "I have no fear of flying," he said, "but I do have a fear of flailing." At the time, I think we both were still unaware of a medical condition called post-polio syndrome. When we weren't looking, it sneaked into his life.

Frustrated with clumsy walkers and disdainful of wheelchairs, Jerry and his lemon-yellow scooter were inseparable. We outfitted our newly purchased SUV with a lift that enabled us to load the heavy vehicle into the back of the car. He enjoyed hot-rodding around the neighborhood on his trusty mechanized toy. If he encountered another elderly scooter driver on the street, he'd often stop and ask, deadpan, "Want to race?" Women would either ignore him or answer with indignation, "You know I can't race!" Men were more likely to answer, "Sure. Who's taking bets?"

The scooter allowed Jerry to shop with me at the supermarket and see movies at the neighborhood mall. We easily found accessible seating at plays and concerts. Those days his calendar was also filled with meetings at the National Institute of Standards and Technology, formerly NBS. He rarely missed a meeting, especially when he was elected president of the Standards Alumni Association. I drove him there and spent rare time on my memoir in the quiet museum/library of the Administration Building.

Back at home in our ranch-style house, he pushed a three-wheeled walker from room to room. This gave him easy access to the office we shared with its two desks, two computers, and printer. Early on, we installed a chairlift to carry him downstairs to the television set in our recreation room. "Can't we have a ride?" his two little grandchildren begged, and he tightly held them on his lap as they took exciting trips up and down, down and up.

A Victory Ship

In 2003 the Special Collections of the University of Maryland Libraries acquired ten full boxes of my papers, manuscripts, newspaper interviews, yellowing scrapbooks, and weekly letters describing my campus days. My mother, who died in 1969, had saved every girlish message sent to her from College Park. Dr. Beth Alvarez of the library staff and archivist Anne Turkos encouraged me to donate those letters. They would provide an informal history of campus life during the post–World War II years.

To mark the acquisition of those papers, Hornbake Library held an afternoon program honoring my life and work. Jerry played a key role in the celebration, which included a catered tea and readings from a staged script, "A Garage Sale of the Mind." The event was presented with much fanfare at the newly opened Clarice Smith Performing Arts Center. Perhaps the donated letters and papers were my legacy to empower future immigrants and their children, who, like me, may be the first in their families to attend college. The celebration was also a tribute to my own crew. They had cheered me on throughout a choppy writing career. I wanted them all on stage with me—sons, daughters-in-law, and grandchildren, ages eight and ten.

Jerry found his niche that afternoon. Instead of appearing in the dramatic presentation, he supervised sound and lighting for the entire show in the control room high above the action. At one point, his voice boomed down from the heights, greeting the overflow audience and letting them know that, as always, he was on the job, technologically speaking.

Dry Dock

"I'm not driving anymore at night," Jerry said a few months later. "It's hard for me to judge depth and distance around me." During the day, however, he insisted on hauling us to the supermarket, which supplied indoor scooters for shoppers like him. We tore our grocery list in half, and he selected items from the lower-lying shelves while I reached for the higher ones. When additional eye strain plagued him, the doctor ordered cataract operations. That's when I assumed all driving chores, which multiplied day by day.

Despite the speedily passing years, I still wanted to produce a memoir of those bygone days of the Great Depression and the 1940s war years. The manuscript title changed from "Bel Air Vignettes" to "Bunion Acres" to "Who's Minding the Store?" An editor at a regional historical society seemed interested in publishing the book, but he warned that their funding had been slashed. "It's still worth a try," Jerry said.

JOURNAL ENTRY: FEBRUARY 2004

> Today, aided by my in-house scientific genius vis-à-vis our unreliable computer, I mailed three requested chapters and a synopsis of the Bel Air memoir to the historical society previously mentioned. Will they go for it?

JOURNAL ENTRY: MARCH 1, 2004

> The society's publications committee has spoken. Their editor liked it, but again he cited budget problems. Nothing there.

Fragmented hours and weeks spent on the Bel Air memoir continued. Two helpful books were *Main Street* by Sinclair Lewis and *Middletown in Transition*, left over from a college sociology course. They provided a less emotional, more objective way of looking at my own hometown.

"How much longer will it take to finish?" Jerry asked. I couldn't predict. I worked in dribs and drabs, fits and starts.

Driving our formidable new SUV didn't bring pleasure into my life either. I was five feet tall and shrinking fast. My legs strained to reach the gas and brake pedals; severe backaches resulted from overstretching. The job of full-time chauffeur became more daunting. One rainy night after dinner out with friends, we headed home on busy Interstate 495. I trembled with panic, not daring to pass anyone. Two monster trucks walled me in. In the darkness, I couldn't see cars behind me because the lift and the scooter blocked the rearview window.

"You'll have to change lanes soon," Jerry said, "or we'll wind up in Baltimore."

"But I can't see on my left. I'm driving with blinders through a coal mine."

"Take it easy. Use your side-view mirror."

"That never helps me even in the daytime."

"Do the best you can," Jerry said in a cheerful voice. "You'll get through it, Molkalini."

When we arrived home that night, I vowed, "No more night driving for either of us." But even in broad daylight, backing that behemoth of a car out of our driveway was a tour de force. As Jerry's health continued to decline, an additional roster of specialists filled our days with appointments. "This is costing a fortune," Jerry said when we took expensive cab rides from the suburbs to physicians' offices in the city. A friend, also suffering from post-polio syndrome, recommended a health-care company that provided medically trained drivers and dependable transportation to and from visits to doctors.

"At least you'll have a couple of hours to yourself," Jerry said. "Now you don't have to come along each time." I still drove him to physical therapy sessions a couple of times a week.

His consultation business behind him, he decided to donate all his slides and papers to the Materials Science and Engineering Department at the

University of Virginia, where several colleagues and a couple of his former graduate students worked. As he systematically reviewed his life's work, he came upon a book published in Italy by a professor of "Corrosion and Protection of Metallic Materials."

"It's a copy of *Colors on Titanium* by my friend Pietro Pedeferri," Jerry said, excitedly turning the pages. "It was hidden under all this stuff. Didn't know where I put it." He stared down at a colorful illustration. "Look! You'll appreciate this, Moll!" he said.

He flipped some more pages, and at first all I could see were puzzling line drawings and sprinklings of electrochemical formulae. "You know full well it's all beyond me," I said, "especially the part in Italian." He was insistent. "No, no, just look at these incredible titanium colors."

What he showed me were colors and designs that no abstract impressionist artist could ever achieve. Azure blues and rich gold in curved lines like the feathers of tropical birds, rich purple saber-like stabs of horizontal color, fine royal purple lines like the staff drawn on sheet music, all directions of rolling stripes, vertical streaks resembling ancient columns, a swipe of blue horizon against white shreds of clouds, rising waves of browns and greens exploding on what looked like nubby red sand, a hidden universe of shapes and textures coaxed from titanium.

"Read Pedeferri's introduction. It's done by oxidation of titanium with a brush or by immersion or spraying," Jerry said.

"You've lost me. I don't even know what titanium is."

"It's the metal most resistant to corrosion," Jerry said. "But you don't have to know anything about electrochemistry to enjoy these spectacular colors. This is not just science. This is poetry. This is art."

On many a long, drab day, Jerry enriched my hours with his vitality and imagination. I had sensed these qualities in him the first time we met. I had not been wrong.

A Sea Change

One afternoon in 2007, Dr. A, our primary care physician, made a startling suggestion. "You ought to get rid of your house," he said. "Consider moving to a retirement community, a place with on-site health services and with no lawn to tend."

We tried to laugh that off. For years, we had been paying a grumpy old alcoholic to cut our grass and trim bushes. To keep the homestead tidy, I turned to an agency that offered a troop of young Latinas who swooped in and cleaned the entire house in one speedy hour. But faucets dripped and sinks kept clogging up, the carpets cried out for intensive care, shingles abandoned their hold on the roof, and the raccoons returned to the attic. For me, chores seemed harder to handle, although we continued to scoff at the idea of giving up our home. "We'll get by," Jerry said. "We always do."

Although Herman Melville wasn't a metallurgist, he once wrote, "Faith and philosophy are air, but events are brass." Indeed, the passing months grew harder and harder. My plans to complete the memoir dissolved into the mist. A sobering incident decided the future for us. After leaving a nearby eatery one night, Jerry's legs gave out; he sank to the ground and couldn't stand. Four men came running from the restaurant to carry him to the car; we had to face the inevitable.

Change couldn't happen overnight. I found a professional planner to help us clear our basement of all the dear things that can collect over a half century of marriage, everything from our sons' crayoned drawings of lopsided trees to faded report cards from twelve years of public school to ancient albums of 78-rpm vinyl records of Fred Waring and His Pennsylvanians singing "Her Beaux Are Only Rainbows." These had originally belonged to a long-dead aunt who also left me a dusty collection of Moran and Mack vaudeville dialogues and a recording of a tinny-sounding tenor rendering "Vienna Remains Vienna" in German.

Even in its prime, our basement junk room never looked orderly with its rickety wooden worktable and tool chests heavy with broken hammers and rusty pliers and all imaginable sizes of nails left over from Jerry's woodworking days. Even so, it hurt to give up the ship. For years that windowless, cinderblock downstairs storage room, the "hold," if you will, of our listing ship, boasted a useless cargo of broken dining room chairs that Jerry never got around to fixing. And cartons of Maryben books still waiting to be sold. And moldy dark green sleeping bags from camp. And an old steamer trunk jammed full of theatrical costumes: blue chiffon sashes, yellowed lace scarves, battered straw hats, a blue and white calico bonnet, a hand-embroidered tablecloth that once doubled as a peasant skirt in a TV show, a faded brunette ponytail I wore during the 1960s.

And an entire wall of warped wooden shelves bearing federal and state tax papers dating back to the start of the Ice Age. And a disabled Candyland game board, assorted green, white, and black marbles from a Chinese checkers set, and isolated Lego pieces. And a badly dented wrought-iron bookcase half-filled with stray volumes of the *World Book Encyclopedia*. And a kayoed Rock 'Em, Sock 'Em Robot toy. And deflated basketballs. And a smashed Wiffle ball. And a stack of old *Commentary* magazines. And scattered endless cardboard cartons tied with raveling hemp rope. And fifty or sixty black skullcaps, once the inspiration for my immortal poem that opened with the line, *There's a yarmulke in my teapot*.

Our professional planner deemed what was valuable to keep, and then mercilessly hauled the hoarded memories of our existence to the county landfill. She took care of everything, which resulted in spare time for me to send three chapters of my neglected Bel Air memoir to a local book publisher, a literary type, who after reading it suggested, "Try to tap more into your meta-conscious."

"My what?" I asked Jerry. He didn't know either.

At the Captain's Table

In the 1990s we had celebrated forty years of marriage with an ocean cruise to the United Kingdom on the elegant *Queen Elizabeth II*. On board, we struck up a friendship with a suave British couple who, I was convinced, were international jewel thieves. Although I sported only my copper necklace and copper earrings, gifts brought to me over the years by my metallurgist husband, I warned Jerry, "Don't give them our home address or phone number."

"If they were what you think they are," Jerry said, "they wouldn't waste their time on us."

A much different trip occurred a decade later with our children and grandchildren on a cruise to Bermuda. This time Jerry boarded the ship in his motorized scooter. At dinner, he piloted his mechanical chariot to our table, parked, and shifted to a chair. The dining room serving staff fought for the thrill of zooming away on his scooter to a hidden corner, and after dessert, steering the vehicle back to the table, where Jerry would reclaim his hot rod and ride away into the sunset. The young Asian waiters found Jerry's vehicle a welcome diversion from the monotony of exhausting days on the water. "I'm happy to bring a little excitement into your lives," my husband told them.

Jerry's whimsical sense of humor led him into mischief that often surprised but never hurt anyone. Admittedly the world's worst violinist, he enlisted me in the following scenario when we entertained dinner guests:

(The scene is set in a typical suburban living room. After a home-cooked meal, Jerry seats everyone in the living room and nods in my direction.)

Me *(in casual wifely manner)*: Did you know that Jerry plays the violin?

First Guest *(politely)*: Oh, really?

Second Guest *(excitedly)*: How about playing something for us, Jerry?

Him *(pretending to be embarrassed)*: No. *(looking shyly down at floor)* You don't want to hear me.

Third Guest: Don't be so modest, Jerry. *(Others agree, murmuring encouragement.)*

First Guest: We'd love it.

Others *(still pleading)*: Come on. Don't hide your light under a bushel. Let's hear it for Jerry! *(Everyone applauds enthusiastically. After a bit more coaxing, he reaches into a nearby closet for the violin case, removes the violin, raises it with quiet confidence to his chin.)* Any requests?

Me: Do you know that Irish song, "I Will Take You Home, Kathleen"?

Him: Certainly. *(He pauses, closes his eyes for inspiration, and then plays the most screechy, off-key melody ever to insult the human ear. His audience doesn't know whether to laugh or to cry.)*

First Guest: You do a very good comic violin. Now play something serious.

Him: That's the best I can play.

Second Guest: Oh sure. Come on. Play something classical.

Me: How about "March Slav"?

Him: Certainly. *(As formal introduction, he beats his bow against the strings in a dramatic fashion and then scratches out a godawful version of "March Slav." He finishes with a flourish, and tucks the violin back into its case.)* Well, that's enough of that.

Most of his American listeners caught on. He never tried it with European or Asian colleagues, except for one Englishman who, after hearing Jerry play, responded, "Bloody hell!"

—•◆•—

The Bel Air memoir deteriorated into wishful thinking and even that faded. My frustrations grew each day like ugly toadstools. At odd hours of the day and night, I scribbled on the backs of envelopes and pillaged my schoolgirl diaries for ideas. A voice inside said, Baby, you're running out of time. Don't waste a minute more. Just write *Finis* on a page and be done with it.

The years were capsizing the boat. At the start of the 2008 recession, we sold our house after thirty-eight years of ownership and moved to a retirement facility that offered a fitness room for my daily treadmill ordeal and an in-house health center to take care of Jerry's growing physical therapy needs. Once settled in our new residence, I found time to perform artificial resuscitation on the memoir and even renamed it *The Cobbler's Last*. That title seemed more apropos for a homespun tale about my shoemaker father, his wife, and his six children, including me, the baby of the family.

Hammering away at shoes on his steel last, my father never had much to say to me. Perhaps by the time I arrived, he was all talked out. There were certainly generational and cultural seawalls between a man born in a Lithuanian log cabin in 1877 and his youngest daughter, the product of a rural Maryland town during Franklin D. Roosevelt's New Deal. To escape being forced into the army of tyrannical Czar Nicholas II, my dad came to Baltimore in the late nineteenth century. Struggling to make his way, he led an immigrant's precarious life that included the birth of two boys, the death of his wife in 1919, and his remarriage to her younger sister, my mother. Six months before my birth, I became an aunt to a baby nephew, my lifelong contemporary.

I had never known my father as a young man. During his long life, he had witnessed the dawn of the twentieth century, the coming of the horseless carriage, the airplane, moving pictures, radio, television, two world wars, and the atomic bomb. Once when he was well past eighty, I asked him what he considered the most remarkable thing he had lived to see. Not hesitating, he answered, "John Glenn flying around the moon."

At the age of eighty-eight, when our cobbler lost his right leg to diabetes, he insisted that he be outfitted with a prosthesis. "Why should I spend the rest of my life in a wheelchair?" he asked. Although never ready to run the Boston Marathon, he learned to walk with an artificial leg until his death at ninety. I think his determination still speaks to me in a way that words can't. Cherish life, keep moving, he seemed to say, because if we will it, each one of us has the power to circle the moon. Or at least the block.

Musical Waves

The memoir took longer than I expected; interruptions and distractions did not end. Our new life at the retirement community had its distractions. Even so, the change of address did offer unforeseen blessings. In our new apartment, space was at a premium; no longer did we feel obligated to house and feed overnight visitors. "The end of an era," Jerry called it, but for once, he was wrong.

A decade earlier when the offspring of our music-making relatives went away to college, their tumultuous family visits had already tapered off. Jerry's brother and wife retired from the Columbus Symphony Orchestra. The seasons passed, and in our final years as homeowners, we entertained few sleepover guests until a startling thing happened. A second generation of musicians entered the picture.

The lively offspring of our musical kin from Georgia never forgot us. Two daughters had grown up to become professional musicians like their parents, and now we heard from their oldest, a violinist with a master's degree in music from the University of Indiana. She sometimes passed through town on her way to auditions for jobs and later brought along her husband-to-be, another classically trained violinist. Her sister, a viola player educated at the same school, also chose music as her career. One afternoon a couple of years before we moved from our house, we were surprised, and, I confess, pleased, to receive The Call from the New Jersey Turnpike. "May we crash at your pad tonight?" our young niece asked over the phone.

Later that evening a secondhand van, called the Larkmobile, lumbered into our driveway, the doorbell sounded, and there stood our niece, Anna, and three other beautiful young women. They belonged to the gifted Lark Quartet of which Anna was a founder. Bustling with energy, the vivacious four entered, bearing denim backpacks, suitcases, a first violin, a second violin, a viola, and a cello that barely made it through the front door. Down the steps Anna led them to our world-famous recreation room and international hostel.

"At least they didn't bring any cats with them," Jerry said.

The Lark Quartet was becoming an international favorite, playing at concert halls all over the globe. We were honored to host such marvelous players, who would practice at our house before their appearance at venues like the Kennedy Center or Constitution Hall. Each young musician would head into a separate room of our house to rehearse in private before performances. As the magnificent notes filled our halls, I remembered a sonnet by Edna St. Vincent Millay, written on listening to a Beethoven symphony:

> *Sweet sounds, oh, beautiful music, do not cease! . . .*
> *This moment is the best the world can give:*
> *The tranquil blossom on the tortured stem.*

In quiet, reflective moments I still close my eyes and hear those sweet sounds of the Lark Quartet, and I remember how exhilarating it was to have Beethoven, Mozart, and Dvořák spend the night at our house. And we didn't have to feed them.

Our most treasured payback was yet to come when Anna's sister Becky, first violinist with the Cincinnati Symphony Orchestra, arrived at our retirement home with her fourteen-year-old son, our grandnephew. He had brought his cello on the plane all the way from Ohio to give a concert exclusively for us and our fellow residents. The third generation of family musicians, he later became a Juilliard graduate. Jerry and I were repaid a thousand times for those hectic early years when babies, toddlers, and a traumatized feline descended upon us full blast.

A Maelstrom of Memories

The Cobbler's Last took twenty-four additional months to finish, a total of eleven years in progress. At eighty-one, I held the memoir in my hands and wept at what time had brought. Hey, World, I whispered, whether you care or not, here is my two-cents' worth. In 2010 the book made its debut at a staged reading sponsored by the retirement community where we lived. We were aided by the professional staff in promoting the event. Talented residents and longtime friends assisted with the reading. Our sons and their wives helped with props, costumes, and set. Our young grandchildren stood at the door to distribute programs. The event attracted a massive audience from the entire Washington area.

My neighbors at the retirement residence surprised me with their reaction to the memoir. Because they were mostly urban New Yorkers or hailed from other cities like Philadelphia, Pittsburgh, Boston, and Cleveland, I feared they would find nothing in common with the stories of a country lass like me. Instead, strangers came forward, excited over how much they identified with the life of the author. Almost all of them were either the American-born children or grandchildren of immigrants. Their personal stories easily could have filled a sequel to *The Cobbler's Last*.

One gentleman lived over his parents' candy shop in Brooklyn. "The neighborhood kids used to crowd into our store to splurge on penny candy," he said. An eighty-five-year-old grandmother recalled her family grocery. "My father would leave at four o'clock every morning to pick up fresh fruit and vegetables at the city market," she told me. A friend recalled an incident in her papa's Baltimore haberdashery. "Your chapter about watching suspected shoplifters?" she said. "It reminded me of the time when I was five. I saw a thief in the act and told my dad that the man was trying to hide a new shirt under his old one. My father quietly removed the stolen shirt and asked, 'Do you need a tie for this?' Then he sold him the shirt, a tie, and a pair of pants!"

"Remembrance of Things Past Offers Clues to the Present" was the headline of a local review by Brooke Kenny. *The Cobbler's Last*, she wrote, "reminds elder readers of simpler times and offers younger readers perspective on surviving tough economic times." The book appeared in 2010, two years after Wall Street plumbed the depths and the U.S. real estate market collapsed. I suppose that by this time the public was ready for a strong dose of nostalgia. In recalling old songs and movies, the wartime sacrifices of Americans, and the lives of 1940s teenagers, I hoped readers of all backgrounds would find common ground. A review in a local county publication swept me away:

> *The Cobbler's Last* is an engrossing tale of life in a rural county, the immigrant experience in America, and the drama of childhood's heights and depths. . . . [T]he book provides the opportunity to revisit the kinder, simpler times when farms bordered Bel Air and everybody came to Town on a Saturday night. . . . Many of [her] adventures will make you laugh. . . . For everyone, this trip through [her] eyes will be nostalgic and enjoyable.

After the memoir appeared, I heard from my only surviving sibling. A ninety-one-year-old World War II veteran, my brother Harold had served four years in the Army and after his discharge found a job with the American Oil Company. Later, my brother switched careers and worked in human relations for the Maryland state government. After retirement he moved to be near his son and grandchildren in South Carolina. For years, we communicated with an occasional phone call or birthday card. *The Cobbler's Last* changed everything. In a seven-page letter, Harold wrote:

> I never knew I would be able to re-live that part of my life. I "teared up" and kept hearing the voices of Mom and Pop speaking the dialogue in the book. I was intrigued by the descriptions of your lives during the war. I was away all that time and didn't know much about how the people of my hometown reacted back then.

The Cobbler's Last brought my big brother back to me. Eleanor had passed away earlier and brother Stanley as well. Our two half-brothers had died many years before. Only Harold was left to identify fully with the memories. Ten years older than I, he could even add details that I had been too young to remember. Although I was never to see him again, we corresponded frequently for the next two years until his death.

Rocking the Boat

One worry kept me awake nights. How would the folks of Bel Air and surrounding Harford County react to this book? Remembering the admonitions of Thomas Wolfe, I imagined angry protests on Main Street and even burnings in effigy. It would be best to avoid going back, wouldn't it?

I did mail a few copies to Jewish friends who had run businesses in the town, people with whom I hadn't communicated in fifty years. One of them, Dave, retired from his men's clothing store on Main Street, showed *The Cobbler's Last* to his neighbor, the owner of a popular drugstore mentioned in the book. Their two shops were almost next door to each other, and for years Dave stopped by each morning for coffee with his pharmacist neighbor and his wife, Mary. Not a native of the area, she was deeply interested in books about the town and county. She read the memoir and immediately ordered four copies to see if she could stir the pot among her customers. "I'm sure they would all love to see you again," she said. I doubted it.

My parents and their offspring lived in Bel Air for twenty-five years. We were not the most popular family in town. We children of struggling immigrants attended the local schools, stayed home from classes on Jewish holidays, and ate kosher food at home. Even if they had been invited (and they hadn't), my parents never participated in civic or cultural activities. They struggled to make a living and kept to themselves. An outlier growing up, I became an observer on the sidelines, a teenaged maverick, clashing with teachers and the high school principal over outspoken ideas, especially those expressed in my county newspaper column.

I had no desire to return. Jerry couldn't fathom why I took this stand. His memories of his youth in Atlanta were much more benign. "Look," he said, "you've been away from that place for more than a half century." He added, "Most teenagers feel alienated one way or the other. You're a big girl now and can handle it."

"I'm an old girl now, and even more sensitive," I said.

Promotion of the book continued to occupy my time. Washington-area newspapers asked for interviews; photographers arrived at our apartment to take pictures. A community center requested a reading, which with the help of my performing family, morphed into a program called "The Making of a Memoir." People wanted advice on how to write their life stories. My spasmodic dysphonia had worsened, but a good microphone helped. I kept my responses short and found that if I notified the audience immediately about the voice disorder, they kept still and listened harder.

Meanwhile, back in Bel Air, that Main Street pharmacy sold all four copies and ordered twelve more. "Your book is taking on a life of its own," Mary, the druggist's wife, said. She asked for another dozen, but we had only ten left. We went into a third printing. I had no idea who was buying all those books. Mail orders rolled in from other parts of the country too.

"I need extras," Mary said, "for your high school graduating class." She also told me of plans to create a window display of the book to coincide with the Memorial Day parade. "The crowds will be congregating all up and down Main Street," she said. "I want everyone to see your books."

A fourth and fifth printing soon followed. Mary called again in a panic. "We've sold our last copy," she said. "Please send whatever you have left."

Rivers Wide and Deep

JOURNAL ENTRY: DECEMBER 2011

I'm exhausted. This memoir has been much more labor intensive than any earlier books. I just mailed eight copies to Mary and left three for any special requests from friends. A sixth printing isn't a good idea right now.

JOURNAL ENTRY: FEBRUARY 2012

I almost forgot the journal because these days I'm not doing any writing or accomplishing much. I've been swallowed up by taking care of Jerry; a litany of unlovely details plays out here daily. Every day it seems I'm driving him to one doctor or another, the urologist, the cardiologist, the dermatologist, the internist, the podiatrist, the dentist. The worst part happens when we go to a movie or a restaurant, and I must steel myself to push the wheelchair into the Men's Room. I always pray no male will enter while we're there. They look startled when they see me and often flee before taking any action.

Jerry's health continued to go downhill. We hired an aide to help him dress in the morning and another person in the evening to get him ready for bed.

Our children shopped for us and handled paperwork. A newly purchased maroon recliner chair now sat in our living room, where Jerry could nap or watch television. Eventually, we found a reliable transport service to drive him to doctors' offices in Washington. He continued to visit an endless list of specialists, each one prescribing pills that multiplied like of spores of mold. They didn't work.

JOURNAL ENTRY: MARCH 2012

> I'm producing zilch right now. Will try to find energy for compiling an anthology of my poetry, working title: "The Incomplete Works of M. Kruger." Went through clips of old "Unholy Writ" columns, sorted out poems not included in any previous books. Trying to figure out how to present specific poems about travels, some of them culled from earlier work and those from later columns written in the 1980s. Also want to include serious free verse. My energy is at a low ebb; insomnia every night. The less I do as far as this collection goes, the less I want to. I did check out anthologies of Paul Laurence Dunbar and Robert Frost to see how their editors organized their poetry in the table of contents. It's harder to do it all by myself.

JOURNAL ENTRY: APRIL 2012

> The malaise continued until the very end of the month when we had lunch with Madeleine, at the Chinese restaurant just across the street from our residence. There is still no traffic light to help us cross. Cars stop, or they're supposed to. Jerry in his faithful scooter, with me at his side, edge slowly over the pedestrian crosswalk. Using my improvised "red flag" technique, I signal to drivers by flapping at them with my scarlet woolen muffler. I don't care if the moth holes show or not. I also try to stare down all drivers as if to say, "Hey, we're crossing here! Show some respect for your elders, and don't run us down." It gives me a sense of power, which I sorely need these days. . . .
>
> We're having an insane spring, high pollen levels, more insects, summer heat. I was hoping that a lunch with dear

friend Madeleine would sweep me back into action after a December–April five-month hiatus. When I complained about how overwhelming the task of keyboarding those anthology poems is . . . especially on my uncooperative laptop . . . Madeleine offered to do it. She often flies overseas in her job. "I rarely close my eyes on the plane," she said. "This will help me pass the time on sleepless nights." She insisted, and I guess it's the only way to finish the book. She'll copy the poems on a flash drive. I really don't understand how all these electronic doodads work. So now things are looking up although I'm still very much occupied with seeing to Jerry's needs all day and all evening. I've had to call 911 several times when he fell. I couldn't lift him.

JOURNAL ENTRY: MAY 2012

The doctor says, "Get away to do things for yourself." I've been leaving Jerry in the care of aides and going on occasional bus trips sponsored by the retirement home . . . to the Martin Luther King memorial and to a guided tour of a quilter's studio. I surprised myself by speaking out to our group of old folks, telling them I had worked with that quilter, a fellow Pen Woman, on a nationally sponsored Peace Quilt, and a short anti-war poem of mine was duplicated on cloth and sewed into the center of the quilt. It went on display in Denver and later traveled the country. Raspy voice or not, at least I spoke out.

Toward the end of that month, after summoning rescuers to help Jerry, who had slid out of bed again at 3:00 a.m. and needed someone strong to put him back, I realized that he needed more competent care than I was able to give. It was difficult to face. In the past nine months he had grown weaker in his upper body and could no longer switch from chair to scooter without substantial help. I was unhappy and so was he. Something had to change, perhaps more aides? Physical therapy did nothing for him. A medication prescribed by his urologist wreaked irreparable damage on Jerry's brain. This brilliant, caring man to whom I had been married for almost fifty-eight years, changed into a person unknown to me.

The next month, Madeleine reported progress on keyboarding *Kosher Salt*, the anthology. She described how each poem brought a new smile to her face, and she felt uplifted. "Your creativity and joy, not to mention your juxtaposition of very funny and unusual things, is amazing," she emailed. "I miss our time together. And I feel for you."

The month melted into a blur. I worked two more times on organizing the remainder of the anthology and typed copies of poems rewritten or lost. It was left unfinished.

Jerry needed more from me, full-time. I made inroads on hiring better home aides and engaged a registered nurse to monitor his illness each week. This would be an interim approach until we could move to an assisted care facility. What lay ahead I had no idea.

As matters worsened, Jerry was taken to the hospital in an enormous former fire truck now used by the county as an emergency rescue vehicle. I rode up front with the driver and thought if Jerry and I were children on a class field trip, this would have been great fun, hurtling through the sluggish Washington traffic, siren wailing. If we were forty years younger, how Jerry and I would laugh at the thought of such a bizarre journey. Imagine, the two of us in a fire truck dashing through lines of cars that scattered as we approached. We should have been wearing blazing red helmets. I glanced over my shoulder at him lying in pain on the ambulance gurney. Now, as two elderly people, we had embarked on still one more journey, but I could have done without the siren.

Hospital tests showed a tumor. "We can't remove the kidney because of his age," the doctors said.

"What d'you mean?" Jerry said, pretending to be insulted, but his voice sounded weak. "I'm still a young buck of eighty-five." The hospital doctors laughed. Throughout his life, my husband could establish instant rapport with physicians. He considered himself their equal and engaged in lengthy discussions with them on all aspects of scientific progress. Even a simple phone call to the doctor's office from Jerry brought forth a quick callback and a cozy chat about his problem, accompanied by male banter. I felt more at ease with women doctors.

When all else failed at the hospital, a nephrostomy followed. There is no point in further details. This book is not a medical treatise. Besides, Jerry never made a fuss over any of the obstacles that befell him—the unsuccessful leg operations, the injuries from falls throughout childhood and adult years, the crutches and, later, the canes, the walkers, the transport chairs, the wheelchairs, and his scooters.

Shortly after his operation, Jerry spent a month in rehab and when the Medicare coverage expired, transferred to a palliative care ward, where I visited and ate lunch or dinner with him every day. The entire dismal floor held the frailest elderly, the very sick and dying.

"Get me the hell out of here," he said to me. "I don't want to hit the end of the trail in this place!"

Manifest Destiny

Although at first our children disagreed, arguing that it would be too hard for me if he came home, I insisted. Almost in triumph, Jerry returned to our sunny apartment at the retirement community where we had lived for the past four years. To remain there, he needed aides around the clock, daytime, night, weekends, but at least we could see him whenever we wished. The children converted our home office into a quiet, uncluttered room where Jerry could sleep uninterrupted by the coming and going of interns, technicians, nurses, housekeepers, and other noisy medical personnel.

In his newly rented hospital bed, the next day he whispered to me through the fog of his illness, "You're my best friend." He paused to catch his breath and then repeated a line from an old song. "Crazy 'bout you, Baby," he whispered. Where he learned that, I'll never know.

Jerry's home health aides specialized in being cheerful. One lively middle-aged woman, Margaret from Trinidad, tried including him in a memory game. Evenings when she arrived for her all-night shift, she playfully asked him, "What's my name?"

He didn't answer. Jerry was cognizant of everything going on around him, and he didn't like the condescending tone of her voice. As she adjusted sheets and blankets around him, she repeated her question.

"What's my name?" she asked. Jerry didn't want to give her the satisfaction of an answer. He remained silent.

She became insistent. "Come on, come on, what's my name?"

Jerry half-opened his eyes. "You ought to know what your name is by now," he said.

Margaret passed his answer on to the other helpers, and he became a legend in his own time among the community of home health care aides, amazed at how sharp he remained despite great odds. "We never had anybody last this long in hospice and keep joking," the ladies said.

Everything else remained in the realm of suspended animation. I did no writing. Earlier in September, I finished reading an English translation of Stefan Zweig's *Marie Antoinette: The Portrait of an Average Woman*, written by the Austrian author in 1932. It was relaxing to lose myself in the intrigue of eighteenth-century politics during the French monarchy. Zweig and his wife left Austria before the Holocaust, lived in New York, and moved to Brazil, where in 1944 the two desperate souls committed suicide together. I was moved by their story. When reality seems overwhelming, sometimes it helps to escape into the troubles of others. Reading novels and biographies did much to carry me through that heartbreaking winter.

At times when I sat beside Jerry's bed and he dozed off, my mind would return to our travels. If I closed my eyes and pretended to count sheep, I could imagine New Zealand and the snowy flocks covering the hillsides. From the windows of our tour bus, we passed them, mile after mile, sometimes causing us to stop and wait until every single sheep crossed the road. We both became so bored on this endless ride that we escaped into one of our classic silly moods. Throughout our marriage we often fell back on creating our own songs, and this one was a parody on an old show tune, "Makin' Whoopee." In honor of the sheep, we called it "Makin' Wooley." Our immortal words still make me smile:

Another ram, Another ewe,
Another gift shop, Another loo,
Another kiwi, Another pee-pee . . .
We're making wooley.

Then we went completely berserk.

"Favorite actor?" Jerry demanded.

"Monty Wooley."

"How about Wooley Allen?" Jerry said.

"How about Norma Shearer?"

We were beyond saving at this point, helplessly giggling so hard we hurt. The other tourists on the bus cast worried looks in our direction, fearful that they were missing some marvelous entertainment to which they were entitled.

"Okay," Jerry said. He took a deep breath. "No more wool-gathering."

"There's no wool like an old wool," I said, and that touched us off again.

Looking back as I sat in his darkened sickroom, I shook my head, remembering how deliciously absurd that bus ride had been.

JOURNAL ENTRY: DECEMBER 2012

> I've started reading *Nightwood* by Djuna Barnes. It's not a barrel of laughs. Her papers are held at the University of Maryland library in the Literary Authors Collection shared by the likes of Katherine Anne Porter. I think they placed my letters and manuscripts in the Special Collections next to Spiro Agnew's. That's okay, I'll take what I can get. This so-called writing career of mine has come to a discouraging halt. I prepared an outline for another book, a novel about societal leftovers, eighty-year-olds adapting to life in a retirement community. (Wonder where I got that idea.) Couldn't do much else this month.
>
> Sad news. Lee Bowdoin, our original mezzo-soprano in the *Ladies First* musical show, has died on the West Coast. When Mary Beth Beck, her accompanist, held a memorial service nearby at her Maryland farm, I brought my scrapbook. The singer's grown children loved those rare photos taken during dress rehearsals. I'm glad to have been able to show them their mother performing onstage in costume as Martha Washington and Eleanor Roosevelt. I also included an audiotape of her with Mary Beth at the piano. An appreciative audience in the old farmhouse that afternoon almost made me feel like myself again. I think it lessened everyone's pain a bit, mine most of all.

Just when the flood of reality threatened to drown me, rising wave after wave each week, some tiny word or act provided relief. Jerry had been sleeping almost all day. He wouldn't even bother to open his eyes. By evening, he became aware of his surroundings. As the on-duty aide heated a cup of chicken broth for him, I leaned over his bed only to find his eyes closed again.

One evening the sight of his pale, emotionless face moved me, and I burst out with, "I love you, Jerry. Oh, I love you so much." He opened his steady gray eyes and answered in a normal voice, "Don't get carried away."

He was so like the witty man I had married that I started to laugh. A phantom smile crept across his lips. He looked pleased to have gotten off a good one-liner.

Alone in our bedroom, I would lie awake, mentally listing the wonders of the world we had seen together. In a sleepless spell, I revisited Stonehenge on the Salisbury Plain, where tourists like us still passed in awe between mysterious blue-gray stones. I remembered Cairo and the pyramids of Giza and the shattered face of the Sphinx, and the golden glow of Jerusalem still casting light over the centuries. For a moment, I dipped my toes into the mucous-like wetness of the Dead Sea and wondered how many people over the ages had done the same. I rekindled the glory of a lost civilization at Machu Picchu built on a site more than eleven thousand feet high in the Andes. I saw the Acropolis elevated in nighttime splendor above Athens and envisioned the Coliseum in Rome and the tiny park where we were surrounded by thieves who stole our plane tickets. I wandered once more through the ruins of Pompeii and observed a wide-eyed nun there, fascinated by ancient pornography on the walls, and I wearily climbed stairs of the opera house at La Scala and shuddered at the death mask of Verdi openly on display like a Hallowe'en disguise for schoolchildren.

I could hear the roar of the crowd at a football match in Quito when Ecuadoran soldiers ringed the playing field and aimed their machine guns at spectators to prevent them from rioting. And I had visions of the *couchette* on an overnight Amsterdam-to-Paris train, a compartment shared with two young Asians, whom a Border Control agent awakened past midnight to search for smuggled drugs, and I could hear my voice afterward whining, "But maybe they hid the stuff in our luggage while we slept," and Jerry's reply, "Right. I can see the headlines: 'U.S. Scientist and Wife Arrested in French Drug Bust.' Come on, I have a meeting in the morning."

Night after night, memories kept me company. On another trip, we arrived in Paris the morning after Princess Diana was killed in an automobile crash and later watched her funeral on TV. On a South American jaunt, I could see my husband struggling with borderline acrophobia as he kept his eyes tightly shut during our cable car ride to the top of Corcovado in Rio. I delighted once again at the sight of the glittering Grand Place in Brussels, and at a nearby restaurant tasting *waterzoie* for the first time. Sometimes when the clock hands refused to budge, I could imagine in the distance a line of elephants strung together like enormous gray beads against a South African sunset. Meanwhile, my anxiety swirled across the ceiling overhead like the *khamsin* blowing all the way from the lonely sweep of the Negev.

JOURNAL ENTRY: JANUARY 2013

> Unrelenting sadness. In random moments Jerry speaks loudly enough for me to hear him and makes good sense. At other times he becomes a sick old man I can't recognize as the same person who traveled the world with me, the loving husband who never found anything too difficult to do for me or for his sons.
>
> I sit with him each evening; together we watch old Hollywood films, Greer Garson, Humphrey Bogart, Errol Flynn, Bette Davis. Our boys have set up a television set he can view from his bed. I'm not sure that any of the action on screen even registers with him now. In the old days when we would see a movie or TV documentary about some foreign place we had once visited, either he or I would announce with a touch of triumph in our voices, "WE were there!" Now I say it for both of us, "We were there, Jerry, remember?" But most of the time he stares ahead and rarely answers.

Jerry died of kidney disease in the spring of 2013. I held his hand as the breath went out of him.

Life Jackets

Were there weeks and months that followed? I don't remember. I lost myself in the deadening paperwork that bedevils every widow. That lonely voyage comes with heartaches no woman expects no matter how much she has planned. Daily exercise on the treadmill kept me in motion and gave my day structure and strength. I remembered reading in some self-help book long ago, "If you do it, you will have the power. If you don't do it, you will not have the power." Such books ought to be banned for their smug self-righteousness.

JOURNAL ENTRY: JUNE 2013

> On today's agenda, bank accounts to close and a new will at the lawyer's office. Despite all, I plan to start writing again. I'll let the "Kosher Salt" manuscript rest in a file drawer and get to it later. Strategy for my new opus: forge together the tidbits I've jotted down to describe life in a retirement home and its inhabitants. It won't be a series of essays. That's too easy. How about a novel, tentatively called "Ring Out Wild Belles"? Although Tennyson's poem describes bells ringing in the New Year, my title refers to the elderly belles who eat with me every morning. I'm borrowing the breakfast table format of Oliver Wendell Holmes, who liked the idea so much he used it in three books. He effectively described and analyzed

his odd assortment of characters eating together in their New England boardinghouse. If it worked so well for him in the nineteenth century, maybe it can do the same for me in the twenty-first.

These days practically everyone in the world wants to take me out to lunch. ("Let's cheer up the old lady!") Took a couple of bus trips, one to the National Gallery of Art for an exhibit of Edvard Munch's depressing stuff. And another to the National Botanical Gardens, where in a secluded nook of exotic Asian plants was posted a Chinese blessing, "May your rice never burn." Did it refer to the scorched earth policy in wartime? Or was it a mysterious message left for my eyes alone? Twice this month I cooked brown rice and couldn't rescue the pot before smoke filled the entire apartment. It even briefly touched off the in-house fire alarm. May my rice never burn again, but it probably will. Kismet.

JOURNAL ENTRY: AUGUST 2013

This month, the earnest pursuit of two goals: (1) finish editing "Kosher Salt," (2) develop more fully characters in "Ring Out Wild Belles." The dialogue comes easily, based on authentic conversations with fellow residents and odd incidents recorded here each day and evening. On sleepless nights an obsolescent phrase like "put that in your pipe and smoke it" will pop into my head, and I scribble it down before I forget, which occurs too often when a woman reaches eighty-four. Sometimes, however, such world-shaking thoughts are better off ignored.

In August something unexpected happened, a twist of plot from a 1930s Frank Capra movie. After a sixty-year absence from my hometown of Bel Air, I received a call from an official with a request that jolted me. The gentleman identified himself as a representative of the county historical society. He had read and liked *The Cobbler's Last* and wondered if I would be available to appear in October for a "meet and greet." The event would be held at the society's headquarters on North Main Street, only two blocks away from the place of my birth. In fact, when I lived in this tiny rural town, everything in Bel Air seemed to be only two blocks away from the place of my birth.

"What's your organization's address again?" I asked, stalling for time, thinking, no, it's too soon to start doing this kind of thing again. Jerry was gone, and I hadn't finished mourning. This stranger obviously hadn't heard about my loss.

"The headquarters now was once the post office," the man said. For the first time in years, I pictured the building, a solid gray and white structure, built in 1937 as a New Deal project. During the war, it was a place my sister and I visited once a week to mail Tollhouse cookies and V-mail letters overseas for our brothers in the Army. From clerks who knew me by name, I bought penny postal cards and books of three-cent stamps for First Class Mail. In my most productive trip to that postal facility, I mailed a piece of light verse to the *Woman's Home Companion*, which responded by sending me a check for $15. They published the poem, my first to appear in a national magazine, heady stuff for a girl of seventeen. And now, my caller said, this beloved federal outpost on Main Street had moved to a new location without consulting me. How could I return to my birthplace and not even know where to find the post office?

An octogenarian does not like drastic changes. More important, my high school classmates once saw me as an outsider, a Jewish misfit among all those farmers in the dell. I was not one of the pack. At that time, I considered myself an advocate of equality for all. "In the future there will be a woman president," I said, shocking our Problems of Democracy class. My ideas often overstepped the bounds of what teenagers of the time were supposed to think. Teachers never knew quite what to do with me. "Get off your soapbox," one of them said.

And yet and yet. Who was left after all those years? Why would they invite me if they didn't want me there? Not only the post office had changed. I took a deep breath. It would make my family ghosts proud, especially Mom, and I could hear Jerry saying, "Nice going, Molkalini."

Throughout the year he died, I grasped at anything to keep me moving. Now if Fate included a return to the old homestead, so be it. That attitude would also explain how professional baseball entered my life for the first time. All summer long I watched every televised Washington Nationals game, much to the amazement of my sons, longtime fans. The season wasn't our team's finest, but the energy of those young athletes carried me through that first summer without Jerry.

JOURNAL ENTRY: OCTOBER 2013

> The historical society director called yesterday with further details about the upcoming Bel Air program. She has only twelve copies of *The Cobbler's Last* in their gift shop and advised me to bring more for the October 26th event. The script I'm working on includes readings and discussion of the memoir. Not much time now for working on the novel. By now there are twenty-two thousand words, hard to come by in the face of many distractions.
>
> I've already forgotten the best way to shut down the new laptop. I click it on and off too much. Last night it suffered a meltdown and registered a blank screen accompanied by a rushing wave of static that wouldn't stop no matter how much I yelled at it. Sweating like a stevedore, I disconnected the whole damned thing and left it in the center of the kitchen floor, far away from anything flammable, isolated in disgrace, sentenced to solitary confinement lest it explode or cause a fire. That punishment worked. The next morning the feckless gizmo reconsidered its bad behavior and cooperated until my printer ran out of ink.
>
> Consequently, the "Cobbler" script for the Bel Air presentation suffered. With the computer on the fritz, I did a hasty revision of scripts written for other gigs. The result was bloated with changes; the white labels pasted over deleted passages kept peeling off. Didn't use smelly Wite-Out to hide corrections because at 110 pounds, I haven't enough strength left to force open the apartment windows for ventilation. Jerry used to do that.

Our stalwart crew of sons and daughters-in-law, who had been drafted to perform as readers, saved me once again. Son Joe and daughter-in-law Dina stayed up late to retype the whole mess the night before. They volunteered because they found my mutilated draft too unsightly to use in public. I had slaved over the thing for two weeks, up to the last minute, and didn't have any heart left to battle that demonic computer one more time.

The night before the trip back to my hometown, I dreamed a mob of angry citizens marched through the streets. They carried torches and stormed the old post office. An irate farmer armed with a pitchfork shouted to me, "My father bought a pair of shoes at your store and they gave him hammertoes. I've waited all these years for my revenge!" He thrust his weapon into a copy of *The Cobbler's Last*, and I woke up whispering, "Wait, let me autograph it for you!"

On the big day, my sons and their wives accompanied me to Bel Air. We parked the car in the lot behind the historical society's headquarters and walked on Main Street to the block where my father had repaired old shoes and sold inexpensive new ones. It was hard to pinpoint exactly where that store had once sat. I didn't recognize any landmarks. This wasn't my rural village, the place where farm families congregated on a Saturday night to shop for Easter clothes. Where was the Rexall drugstore on the corner? Where was Henry, the gravedigger for the vanished funeral parlor? What had become of our beloved un-air-conditioned movie theater with Wrigley's gum stuck to the bottom of the seats?

We looked for a place to eat and found a Chinese restaurant on Main Street (imagine that!) and real Asian people working inside! I think the exotic eatery served its wontons in the same historic location where our shoe store once stood.

"It was here," I told my children over an egg roll, "that your grandmother, in a drafty upstairs apartment, gave birth to me. Herbert Hoover was still president although I didn't know it at the time."

Later inside the old post office, I wondered if we were in the right place. What happened to the posters selling defense stamps and war bonds? Whither the bulletin board with those grainy FBI "Wanted" mug shots? Where was the New Deal mural painted by a hungry artist for the Works Projects Administration, the WPA?

With disbelieving eyes, I stood staring at linen-covered tables set for tea in the social hall of the county historical society, which now owned the place. A great rush of people filled the room. Who were they and where did they come from? Certainly not from my past. They were too young to have been my classmates during the war years of the 1940s. I couldn't identify anyone, no one who even resembled the town fathers and mothers of bygone days nor the rigid starchy teachers I once endured nor the jitterbugging dancers of my callow youth.

Good grief, I thought, *these are the children and grandchildren of my deceased high school classmates!* Here from wall to wall, from sea to shining sea, stood the generation of rock-and-rollers, the Baby Boomers, bless them, assembled in homage to a time that they were not old enough to remember. Once instructed, "Never trust anyone over thirty," they now were spending a Sunday afternoon with the likes of me, a living, breathing relic, a reminder of parents and grandparents during hard times that transformed this country in the first half of the twentieth century.

The readings and discussion, presented by my children, proceeded without a hitch, our best shot ever. The audience laughed at the funny excerpts, and some may have wept for a way of life that no longer existed. A sit-down reception awaited: tables set with fresh garden flowers, gleaming sterling silver teapots, cloth napkins, and fragile saucers and teacups. Not an inch of plastic, the real McCoy, as we used to say.

After our program ended, well-wishers and book buyers stood in a line that snaked around the room. An older gentleman handed me a gift, a copy of the original deed and right-of-way town documents for my parents' store. An official of the historical society supplied a gratis copy of *An Architectural History of Harford County*. Turning the pages, I felt tears sting my eyes, blurring the photos of town buildings and old farmhouses no longer standing.

I hoped but really did not expect to see my favorite editor of the county paper, the person who encouraged me to write a weekly column for teenagers. A loyal friend, he had defended me when criticism arose from adults upset by my view of their conventional world. I felt indebted to him for his journalistic guidance. For a surprise at Christmas, he gave me a copy of *This Is My Best*, an anthology of stories, essays, and poems self-chosen for publication by ninety-three of America's greatest authors still alive in the 1940s.

In that book, an adolescent girl who longed to become a writer first discovered Theodore Dreiser, Ernest Hemingway, John Steinbeck, Willa Cather, Upton Sinclair, Stephen Vincent Benét, and scores of others. Today, seventy-five years later, I still reach for that book to treat myself to essays by Robert Benchley, James Thurber, Stephen Leacock, Ogden Nash, Irvin S. Cobb, S. J. Perelman, and Ludwig Bemelmans. Their wit restores me; my sense of humor returns, the aging mind sharpens. I am once more bouncing with energy in my bobby sox.

But my favorite editor did not appear that Sunday in Bel Air. Instead, three of his grown children identified themselves. I recalled only one, an infant the last time I saw him. Another son presented me with a gift that touched me deeply. It was an actual cobbler's last, an antique copper treasure the size of a child's foot. *I am the cobbler's last,* I had written in the book, *the youngest of my father's six children.* Today, I cherish those souvenirs. They take me back to an afternoon in a former post office full of memories waiting for Special Delivery. Thomas Wolfe, about never being able again to go home? You got it all wrong.

Safe Harbors

This event ended the mourning period and left me ready to tackle that elusive novel, the tale of resilient elderly souls living in a retirement community. Each morning I woke up at five o'clock and wrote for a couple of hours until breakfast. By 2015 I had the novel in my hands. No longer did it bear the title *Ring Out Wild Belles* or *Who's Minding the Store?* Borrowing from the poet/essayist Oliver Wendell Holmes, I called the book *The Swift Seasons,* a tale of love and renewal. The title came from his fine poem, "The Chambered Nautilus."

At eighty-six I no longer felt wildly energetic, running a one-woman operation, handling promotion and distribution of another book. The Internet played a greater role in my life. Now published by Amazon, *Cobbler* still attracted readers, and I enlisted the company's publishing facilities for *The Swift Seasons.* Of this I was certain: I had reached a new era. No more direct mail brochures for me to grind out, no more flyers to be duplicated at print shops, no tiresome hours of soliciting independent bookstores, no addressing of labels, and no more labor-intensive trips to the post office with piles of paperbacks stuffed into padded mailing envelopes.

"I'm shutting down my Shipping Department," I told my sons, both of whom had been key figures in advising, editing, formatting, and running interference between publishing house and me. The exhausting legwork of my younger days was over. I said goodbye to all that and forced myself to embrace fully the dreaded Electronic Age. Come what may, what the hell.

With the assistance of family and friends, we launched *The Swift Seasons* at the retirement community where I live. In constructing the narrative, I had camouflaged the characters of the book as much as possible to avoid the wrath of my fellow octogenarians, who could be cranky if aroused. Above all, I wanted to prevent lawsuits from them or their irate kinfolk. After the staged reading to a full house, the most valued comment came from a resident who had read the book beforehand. "I didn't recognize a single person," she said in a disappointed voice.

"That's what I had in mind," I said to my sons.

The best part of all was finding unsolicited five-star reviews online from readers, some of them professional writers of myriad genres. An author of young adult books wrote: "The depth of the characters, their stories, and the accessible compelling way they are rendered reminds me of Pulitzer Prize winner Tracy Kidder's books. . . . This book is fiction, but it delivers truth as well."

A distinguished writer whose work includes a book entitled *Playing God: Human and Divine in the Age of Biotechnology,* wrote: "I realized . . . how little is written about the lives . . . of people in their seventies and eighties and beyond. . . . [T]he book moved me as few novels had . . . and allowed me to understand the deeply human experience of creating new bonds at a time in one's life when so many important old bonds have been severed. . . . [A] wonderful and profound book."

Another critic, a teacher and historian, had this to say: "Elderly persons, and those with older friends and relatives, will appreciate its very human, poignant, and at times profound depiction of the problems of growing old in a youth-oriented society. . . . [It] is surprisingly funny, filled with [her] wry sense of humor and keen observations. [She] is a master of clever dialogue and the use of irony that students of writing will especially appreciate. And although *The Swift Seasons* plays out in a Jewish community, persons of all backgrounds will enjoy Kruger's take on the universality of her topic."

Having completed my first and only novel, my own Great American Novel, I turned to the long-delayed poetry collection, *Kosher Salt,* which friend Madeleine had keyboarded five years before. It included travel poems and sardonic meditations on writers and writing. I referred to this mountain of eclectic Judaic verse as contemporary Jewish folk poetry, written in the vernacular of the present but often describing the glories of the past.

A writer never can predict if or when rebirth will strike. In 1995 *Ladies First* was published, and in 2018, the musical program based on *Ladies First* was revived after fifteen dormant years. A professional young cellist, who worked at our retirement community as its music director, discovered the music and lyrics for the first time. To celebrate Women's History Month we presented a staged recital based on the popular musical show that ran ten years, ending in 2005. Our original soprano and pianist, both now dead, would have loved hearing the gifted young women who provided the music. Closing my eyes, I could feel the presence of Lee Bowdoin and Mary Beth Beck as they lingered in the wings together with Jerry holding the book, still prompting when necessary. I neither mimed nor danced in this revival. It was enough to supervise, work backstage once more on costumes and props, and take a bow as playwright. I couldn't make a curtain speech, but this unexpected revival of *Ladies First* said everything that stirred in my heart.

Tacking and Veering

I have no idea what those words mean, but they blend in well with the fake nautical similes and metaphors throughout this book. The words do appear in Samuel Taylor Coleridge's narrative classic *The Rime of the Ancient Mariner,* created around 1797. I recently found his masterpiece in a coverless paperback of English poetry and instead of laboring away on my memoir, I procrastinated and read his entire poem for the first time in seven decades. Imagine, an uncut seaworthy version, twenty pages containing almost one hundred fifty verses divided into seven grisly parts. He may have been hitting the opium pipe with this one. Although Mr. Coleridge was beset by his narcotic demons, at least he didn't have to face my diabolical computer every day. In reading his work, I noted that he often referred to the elderly mariner's "glittering eye." It's a strong image. My unpoetic ophthalmologist calls it a blocked tear duct.

JOURNAL ENTRY: JULY 2019

> Today I found on the shelf a reminder of how much Eleanor influenced me as a writer. For my tenth birthday, my big sister bought me *A Book of Famous Poems: For Older Boys and Girls,* compiled by Marjorie Barrows and published in 1931. As I turn those yellowed, crumbling pages, I remember that it was preceded by an earlier gift from my big sister, *One Hundred Best Poems for Boys and Girls.* That little volume introduced me

> to whimsical verse by Florence Page Jaques about a puffin in the shape of a muffin and Edward Lear's "Table and Chair" in which the two pieces of articulate furniture chatted with each other and even took a walk together. These were the first books I ever owned outright. It was here that I succumbed to the irresistible dance of rhyme and rhythm.

For me, however, creating prose fiction came before poetry. In second grade our teacher asked us to write a description of a pet dog or cat. The homework assignment threw me into a panic. Because we lived in a cramped apartment over a shoe store, my mother never allowed animals underfoot. "I'm not taking in any more boarders," she said. To avoid a failing grade, I invented an endearing kitten named Blackie, who drank milk from the saucer laid down before her each day. Neither teacher nor classmates ever learned of my magnificent deception, and I was amazed at how easy it was to grow ideas in my mind and communicate random fancies simply by putting words down on paper.

At Arbor Day the next year, we pupils were commanded to write an entire poem about a favorite tree. Living on Main Street, I was surrounded only by storefronts and concrete sidewalks. A favorite tree? The only tree I knew intimately was a stunted crab apple tree adjacent to the school; I climbed it once but didn't feel any emotional attachment to it. I did, however, enjoy munching on ripe apples purchased from a nearby orchard.

The next afternoon Miss Kelly posted on our class bulletin board a piece of unsentimental doggerel that read as follows:

We are apple blossoms
With petals pink and white
And people who pick us
Are not at all right.
For we shall soon be apples
All juicy and red
But if you pick us
We will all be dead.
And you will have no apples
So crispy and sweet
To buy a basket of us
And eat and eat and eat.

Frankly, I didn't know what an apple blossom looked like and never saw anybody pick one, but who knew that except me, the writer? Imagination to the rescue; I was hooked for life.

Nowadays solicitous friends inquire, "Are you still writing?" Answer: I'm not done yet. The process of sorting out thoughts and words has slowed a bit, but there are still a few leftovers in the freezer, and it would be wasteful to toss them out. Only recently have I become acquainted with the phrase "serial memoirist." Perhaps I, too, am someone who needs more than one shot to explain her life. A December scribe like me, however, is expected to dish out some enduring wisdom even if it's warmed over from other how-to books. I can't do that. I can't say, "You, too, will live the same life that I have lived if only you follow these rules." For heaven's sake, discover how to live the hard way from experience. Don't bother me with it.

In my nine decades, here is some residue. Young people often undervalue the kindness of others. At twenty-two I never fully appreciated Mr. Kamenetz and his advertising brigade. Out of generosity or sheer pity, he created a niche for me. Seasoned copywriters taught me how helpful or how deceiving words can be. From commercial artists I acquired appreciation of graphic skill and the awareness that these were gifted artists, some of whom once hoped to become Rembrandt but settled for less. I sensed a kinship with them.

I didn't realize at the time that everything happening to me would somehow be useful later. In middle age, I became an independent publisher who summoned enough chutzpah to conceive, design, and publish books. Unfettered, I created and ran my own business; thousands of people bought and read my work. Today in the twenty-first century, the Internet and social media have opened that door for everyone, attracting both good and evil.

I owe much to astute, professional editors. Because of their assignments and their guidance, I was privileged to meet Vice President Hubert Humphrey at a charity ball and to interview an Academy Award nominee in addition to painters and historians, dancers and singers, professors and janitors. And meanwhile, my topical poems covered everything from air pollution to Vietnamese refugees to gun control to John Kennedy's grave at Arlington Cemetery. All this, thanks to the support of thoughtful enablers along the way.

The use of "enabler" as a noun carries a pejorative tinge these days. My three well-worn dictionaries yield only definitions of a verb, "to enable, to supply the means, knowledge, or opportunity to be or do something." The word "enabler" can be positive or negative. I'm proud to admit that I was my husband's enabler, and Jerry was mine. We were Equal Opportunity Enablers. That defines marriage for me; others may see it differently. Let them.

My mother tops the list of all who empowered me even though we disagreed about the longitude and latitude of my journey. In Mom's American Dream, educators represented the highest rung of achievement. Teaching implied dignity, communal respect, prestige, and lifelong security. Although she made sacrifices to send me to college and lived for the proud moment when her youngest child would become a schoolteacher, I insisted on steering my own course. Was mine the better choice? I think it was. At any rate, tension between us disappeared with my marriage to Jerry and the arrival of two impressive grandsons. Although she died when they were twelve and ten, she gloried in their accomplishments, and she would have been proud of their achievements as adults.

Throughout her life, Mom harbored a negative view of Travel. No sane person, she argued, would wish to leave America for the Old World, which in her mind represented only a poverty-stricken *shtetl* and brutal pogroms. "What's so wonderful about going to Europe?" Mom countered whenever my talk turned to college dorm mates and their romantic ideas about heading for London and Paris after graduation. "Young girls wandering around alone? Nobody knows them, nobody cares about them. It's so foolish, don't even talk about it."

Travel won't change your personality, she reasoned, or your inborn family traits, your nature, your blood. Mom was shaped by her own sad childhood. Lithuanian born, at the age of ten she crossed the Atlantic in the company of strangers. Her impoverished mother, a widow, remained behind to care for an older daughter with tuberculosis. Mom remembered Europe only as a hellish place from which people escaped as soon as possible. According to her, sightseeing in foreign places didn't make a *mensch* out of anyone or create character when there was no raw material to begin with. In a way, my mother's attitude reflected the philosophy of Lisbon poet Fernando Pessoa, who wrote, "To travel you simply need to exist." Any road, he said, will take us to the end of the world, but once we've circled it, the beginning and the end are simply what we think it is. According to Pessoa, "It is only within us that landscapes become landscapes."

Perhaps. No matter how far we travel, do we remain the same vulnerable human being lodged inside ourselves? The Portuguese author thought so. He wrote, "The traveler is the journey. What we see is not what we see but who we are."

Very well then, what defines me? Pretentious questions like that remind me of a childhood riddle: "I'm not my sister. I'm not my brother. Yet I am the child of my father and mother. Who am I?" Neither a registered feminist nor a compulsive homemaker, I believe with a perfect faith in advancing the equality of women and men all over the world. I believe in the innate resilience and kindness and creativity of my fellow human beings. I am certain we shall clear the oceans of the earth, purify the air, and restore the wastelands. And I believe that humanity must knock the chip off its shoulder. As for me, the following essay, circa 1993, washes ashore the inscrutable flotsam and jetsam of my meta-conscious . . . whatever that means:

SOMETHING FROM THE OVEN

In a supermarket tabloid one day, you may be startled to read a headline that screams "Unhinged Dinosaur Terrorizes Senior Citizens!" Don't panic. It's only our 1965 Model RCA Whirlpool Blanket of Flame, an eccentric gas oven, literally fit to be tied. Even as I write this, the turquoise oven door is tightly bound up with a strip of blue seam binding. Nowadays, roasting or baking, I set the temperature, unhitch the door, insert pans, close, and then tether the door handle to a hitching post of sorts. When not in use, the appliance remains strapped down, harnessed to protect the innocent.

The first time I unleashed the oven, my son eyed the seam binding and spoke two sarcastic words: High Tech. Like many of his generation, he couldn't understand why I didn't chuck the relic and replace it with a microwave, which I consider a transitory gadget doomed to early extinction. What's more, loyalty is important to me. My noble appliance has lived through six presidents in the White House as well as an unrelenting parade of skinless chicken breasts. Some things are sacred.

The oven first showed signs of decay last year when I was cleaning it and leaned too hard on the open door. It refused to close. My husband said it could use a new hinge because the old one had corroded. But he found that they don't make hinges that size anymore. Then he said all it really needed on one side was a new spring, and he bought one at the hardware store. Although he kept taking the heavy oven door off and putting it back on, muttering darkly to himself, no spring of any size would fit into the hard-to-see slots hidden by primordial grease. When he reattached the door, it listed dangerously to the left.

Affected by this invasive surgery, the oven door went psycho, a painful experience to watch. It would fall open unannounced, sometimes whacking friends in the derriere, bruising outraged in-laws, and almost causing an international incident with a French guest. Once in exasperation, I gave the door a good thrashing with a pair of pliers. A sliver of turquoise enamel came off, leaving an unsightly black scar on the front. After that, the oven door behaved for a full day, and then swooped down, knocking a bowl of instant oatmeal out of my hands. Clearly, it was becoming a violent appliance.

I experimented with a wide adhesive bandage, but it came loose right away. Fuzzy brown twine looked too tacky even for me. For a while I found the best thing was pink seam binding, hooking the door handle to the knob of a non-working electric clock just above the oven door. It didn't look half bad if I tied the ribbon in a butterfly bow. Later I replaced it with a length of first-aid gauze, securely tied to keep the oven from being a further menace to society. Unfortunately, last July 4 an unkind relative hooted at my bandaged oven and compared it to *The Spirit of '76*, the historic painting by Archibald Willard. "All it needs is a fife and drum," she said.

I know I'll have to put the oven down one of these days, but please, as humanely as possible. And now other aging kitchen appliances are also demanding equal time. I must engage in mortal combat with glib salespeople, wrestle with floor plans, and trade nostalgia for sleek robots. They bring with them indifferent digital numbers and tiny red lights that will burn without warmth into my uncomprehending twentieth-century soul.

If the author of this memoir is blasted for barely skimming the surface, so be it. Let critics complain, "I wish she had probed deeper into her superficiality."

And interviewers may demand of the writer, "At what age did you become superficial and why?" Or literary busybodies will inquire, "Have you ever met any celebrities who influenced your superficiality?" At the age of ninety-plus, I needn't answer to anybody. One person's depth is another's triviality.

For famous parting words, turn to the final paragraph of *Sybil, or The Two Nations,* Benjamin Disraeli's novel published in 1845. If we substitute the words "the United States" for "England" and replace "Monarchy" with "Republic," it fits our own situation nicely. Disraeli wrote:

> That we may live to see England once more possess a free Monarchy and . . . a prosperous People, is my prayer; that these great consequences can only be brought about by the energy and devotion of our Youth is my persuasion. We live in an age when to be young and to be indifferent can be no longer synonymous. We must prepare for the coming hour. The claims of the Future are represented by suffering millions; the Youth of a Nation are the trustees of Posterity.

Rendered herewith then, sincerely and less than perfect, have been the occasional voyages of Mrs. Corrosion and the metallurgist who was smitten with her, and she, with him. Of these two let it be proclaimed unto the generations:

For joy they lusted
In rust they trusted.

Rockville, Maryland, 2019

About the Author

In her ninety-plus years, Mollee Kruger has done just about every kind of writing except skywriting, which, for carbon footprint reasons, she avoids. Born in Bel Air, Maryland, six months before the start of the Great Depression, the veteran author has labored at her craft ever since. When she was twelve, her first poem was published in a county newspaper. At seventeen her work appeared in a national women's magazine, and at college she edited campus publications and wrote a prize-winning essay for *Mademoiselle*.

Since then, Kruger has received numerous national and regional awards for serious, humorous, and inspirational poetry, essays, and short stories. She wrote a weekly syndicated newspaper column of light verse for twenty years and collaborated with composers and choreographers who set her poetry to music and dance. At the beginning of the twenty-first century, she received an award for achievement in the humanities, and in 2003 the University of Maryland, her alma mater, included her papers in its holdings of literary manuscripts and letters. Her novel, *The Swift Seasons,* was published in 2016.

Married for fifty-eight years to the late internationally recognized scientist Jerome Kruger, she has two sons, two daughters-in-law, and two grandchildren. She has lived in Rockville, Maryland, for the past half century and plans at least two more books. The author agrees with the French novelist Stendhal, who wrote in his memoir, "Without work, the vessel of life has no ballast."

Made in the USA
Middletown, DE
24 January 2020

83608092R00159